DAY BY DAY
WITH JOHN CALVIN

DAY BY DAY
WITH JOHN CALVIN

Compiled by
Mark Fackler, Philip Christman,
Donald Dumbacher, Paul Stob

Hendrickson Publishers, Peabody MA

Day by Day with John Calvin
Copyright © 2002 by Hendrickson Publishers, Inc.
P.O. Box 3473
Peabody, Massachusetts, 01961-3473

Printed in the United States of America

ISBN 1-56563-653-8

First printing—October 2002

All Scripture references in this book are taken from the *Holy Bible: King James Version.*

Cover design by Richmond & Williams, Nashville, Tennessee
Interior design by Design Corps, Batavia, Illinois
Developed and produced exclusively for Hendrickson Publishers by The Livingstone Corporation (www.LivingstoneCorp.com), Carol Stream, Illinois
Compiled and edited by Dr. Mark Fackler, Philip Christman, Donald Dumbacher, Paul Stob, Christopher D. Hudson

Library of Congress Cataloging-in-Publication Data

Day by Day with John Calvin / Christopher D. Hudson, editor;
   Mark Fackler, editor
         ISBN 1-56563-653-8 (cloth)
      1. Devotional calendars.   I. Mark Fackler
   BV4810.D345   2002
   242′ .2-dc21

                                                      99-29485
                                                      CIP

Introduction

ew people in all of church history have been as influential as John Calvin, yet his works continue to be under-read by Christians in today's church.

The gift of critical thinking and theology that Calvin (1509–1564) gave to the church has benefited Christians for hundreds of years, and his teaching continues to have an almost all denominational lines.impact on churches across While perhaps best loved (and perhaps hated) for his doctrine of predestination, Calvin's influence in the church is far greater than this one concept. Calvin's firm commitment to the authority of Scripture, as well as his rejection of the abuses and errors of the Roman Church, solidified the Protestant Reformation a generation after Martin Luther.

While he studied law and theology as a young man, Calvin was never ordained in the Catholic Church. Instead, he devoted his life to the cause of the Protestant Reformation. By age twenty-six, he completed the first edition of the *Institutes of the Christian Religion* and spent the next decades writing more than 2,200 sermons and thousands of letters and expanding the *Institutes*.

While few Christians today aspire to read the thousands of pages written by Calvin, his material is too important to be neglected. This book contains 365 short readings intended to introduce new readers to his writings and to reinforce the breadth of his teaching to those already familiar with his work.

JESUS IN THE FLESH

And the Word was made flesh, and dwelt among us, (and we beheld his glory, the glory as of the only begotten of the Father,) full of grace and truth.—John 1:14

he Evangelist shows what was that coming of Christ which he had mentioned; namely, that having been clothed with our flesh, he showed himself openly to the world. Although the Evangelist touches briefly the unutterable mystery that the Son of God was clothed with human nature, yet this brevity is wonderfully perspicuous. The word "flesh" expresses the meaning of the Evangelist more forcibly than if he had said that he was made man. He intended to show to what a mean and despicable condition the Son of God, on our account, descended from the height of his heavenly glory. When Scripture speaks of man contemptuously, it calls him flesh.

Now, though there be so wide a distance between the spiritual glory of the Speech of God and the abominable filth of our flesh, yet the Son of God

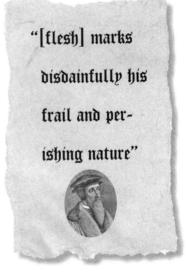

"[flesh] marks disdainfully his frail and perishing nature"

stooped so low as to take upon himself that flesh, subject to so many miseries. The word "flesh" is not taken here for corrupt nature (as it is often used by Paul) but for mortal man, though it marks disdainfully his frail and perishing nature, as in these and similar passages; for he remembered that they were flesh (Ps. 78:39) and that all flesh is grass (Isa. 40:6).

1

TRUE ABUNDANCE

And of his fulness have all we received, and grace for grace.
—John 1:16

h e begins now to preach about the office of Christ—that it contains within itself an abundance of all blessings—so that no part of salvation must be sought anywhere else. True, indeed, the fountain of life, righteousness, virtue, and wisdom is with God; but to us it is a hidden and inaccessible fountain. But an abundance of those things is exhibited to us in Christ, so we may be permitted to have recourse to him; for he is ready to flow to us, provided that we open up a channel by faith.

He declares in general that out of Christ we ought not to seek anything good, though this sentence consists of several clauses. First, he shows that we are all utterly destitute and empty of spiritual blessings; for the abundance which exists in Christ is intended to supply our deficiency, to relieve our poverty, to satisfy our hunger and thirst. Secondly, he warns us that, as soon as we have departed from Christ, it is ill vain for us to seek a single drop of happiness, because God hath determined that whatever is good shall reside in him alone. Accordingly, we shall find angels and men to be dry, heaven to be empty, the earth to be unproductive, and, in short, all things to be of no value if we wish to be partakers of the gifts of God in any other way than through Christ. Thirdly, he assures us that we shall have no reason to fear the want of anything, provided that we draw from the fullness of Christ, which is in every respect so complete that we shall experience it to be a truly inexhaustible fountain. And John classes himself with the rest, not for the sake of modesty, but to make it more evident that no man whatever is excepted.

THE LIVELY IMAGE OF GOD

No man hath seen God at any time; the only begotten Son, which is in the bosom of the Father, he hath declared him.—John 1:18

Certainly when Christ is called the lively image of God (Heb. 1:3) this refers to the peculiar privilege of the New Testament. In like manner, the Evangelist describes something new and uncommon when he says that the only-begotten Son, who was in the bosom of the Father, has made known to us what was formerly concealed. He therefore magnifies the manifestation of God which has been brought to us by the Gospel, in which he distinguishes us from the fathers and shows that we are superior to them (as also Paul explains more fully in the third and fourth chapters of the Second Epistle to the Corinthians). For he maintains that there is now no longer any veil, such as existed under the Law, but that God is openly beheld in the face of Christ.

That vision which Moses obtained on the mountain was remarkable and more excellent than almost all the rest. And yet God expressly declares, "Thou shall not be able to see my face, only thou shall see my back" (Ex. 33:23); by this metaphor he shows that the time for a full and clear revelation had not yet come. It must also be observed that when the fathers wished to behold God they always turned their eyes towards Christ. I do not only mean that they beheld God in his eternal Speech, but also that they attended with their whole mind and with their whole heart to the promised manifestation of Christ. For this reason we shall find that Christ afterwards said, "Abraham saw my day" (John 8:56); and that which is subordinate is not contradictory.

It is therefore a fixed principle that God, who was formerly invisible, has now made himself visible in Christ. When he says that the Son was in the bosom of the Father, the metaphor is borrowed from men, who are said to receive into their bosom those to whom they communicate all their secrets. The breast is the seat of counsel. He therefore shows that the Son was acquainted with the most hidden secrets of his Father, in order to inform us that we have the breast of God laid open to us in the Gospel.

3

LETTING GO OF YOUR "RIGHTS"

*Settle matters quickly with your adversary who is taking you to court.
Do it while you are still with him on the way, or he may hand you over
to the judge, and the judge may hand you over to the officer, and you
may be thrown into prison. —Matthew 5:25, NIV*

Christ appears to go farther, and to exhort to reconciliation not only those who have injured their siblings, but those also who are unjustly treated. But I interpret the words as having been spoken with another view: to take away occasion for hatred and resentment, and to point out the way to cherish good-will.

For where do all injuries come from, but from this—that each person is too tenacious of her or his own rights, that is, each is too ready to consult his or her own convenience to the disadvantage of others? Almost all are so blinded by a wicked love of themselves that, even in the worst causes, they flatter themselves that they are in the right. To meet all hatred, hostility, fighting, and injustice, Christ rebukes that stubbornness which is the source of these evils and enjoins his own people to cultivate moderation and justice, and to stop short of pressing an argument as far as they could, so that by such an act of justice they may get for themselves peace and friendship.

It were to be wished, indeed, that no controversy of any kind should ever arise among Christians—and undoubtedly people would never break out into abuse or quarrelling if they possessed a due share of meekness. But, as it is scarcely possible that differences won't sometimes happen, Christ points out the remedy by which they may be immediately settled: to put a restraint on our desires, and rather to act to our own disadvantage, than follow up our rights with unflinching rigor.

GOD'S DELAYS

Now Jesus loved Martha, and her sister, and Lazarus.
—John 11:5

These two things appear to be inconsistent with each other, that Christ remains two days beyond Jordan, as if he did not care about the life of Lazarus, and yet the Evangelist says that Christ loved him and his sisters; for, since love produces anxiety, he ought to have hastened immediately. As Christ is the only mirror of the grace of God, we are taught by this delay on his part that we ought not to judge of the love of God from the condition which we see before our eyes. When we have prayed to him, he often delays his assistance, either that he may increase still more our ardor in prayer, or that he may exercise our patience and, at the same time, accustom us to obedience.

Let believers then implore the assistance of God, but let them also learn to suspend their desires if he does not stretch out his hand for their assistance as soon as they may think that necessity requires. For whatever may be his delay, he never sleeps, and never forgets his people. Yet let us also be fully assured that he wishes all whom he loves to be saved.

> "we ought not to judge of the love of God from the condition which we see"

YOUR LIFE, JESUS' GIFT

All that the Father giveth me shall come to me; and him that cometh to me I will not cast out. —John 6:37

esus is not the guardian of our salvation for a single day, or for a few days, but that he will take care of it to the end—so that he will conduct us, as it were, from the commencement to the termination of our course. Therefore, he mentions the last resurrection. This promise is highly necessary for us, who miserably groan under so great weakness of the flesh, of which every one of us is sufficiently aware. At every moment, indeed, the salvation of the whole world might be ruined, were it not that believers, supported by the hand of Christ, advance boldly to the day of resurrection. Let this, therefore, be fixed in our minds: that Christ has stretched out his hand to us, that he may not desert us in the midst of the course, but that, relying on his goodness, we may boldly raise our eyes to the last day.

There is also another reason why he mentions the resurrection. It is because, so long as our life is hidden (Col. 3:3), we are like dead men. For in what respect do believers differ from wicked men, but that, overwhelmed with afflictions and like sheep destined for the slaughter (Rom. 8:36), they have always one foot in the grave and, indeed, are not far from being continually swallowed up by death? Thus there remains no other support of our faith and patience but this: that we keep out of view the condition of the present life, and apply our minds and our senses to the last day, and pass through the obstructions of the world—until the fruit of our faith at length appear.

THE IMPORTANCE OF MERCY

[Then Joseph's brothers] said to one another, "Surely we are being punished because of our brother. We saw how distressed he was when he pleaded with us for his life, but we would not listen; that's why this distress has come upon us." —Genesis 42:21, NIV

Joseph's brothers acknowledge that it is by the just judgment of God that they obtained nothing from Joseph, now ruling in Egypt by their begging, because they themselves had acted so cruelly towards their brother in the past. Christ had not yet uttered the sentence, "With the measure you use, it will be measured to you" (Matt. 7:2), but it is a dictate of nature that they who have been cruel to others are unworthy of sympathy. We ought to be more careful that we do not prove deaf to the many threats of Scripture on this matter. Dreadful is that condemnation that "if a man shuts his ears to the cry of the poor, he too will cry out and not be answered" (Prov. 21:13).

Therefore, while we have time, let us learn to exercise humanity, to sympathize with the miserable, and to stretch out our hand to give assistance. But if at any time it happens that we are treated roughly by others and our cries for pity are proudly rejected by them, then, at least, let us ask whether we ourselves have in anything acted unkindly towards others. For although it is best to be wise beforehand, it is, nevertheless, of some advantage to us to reflect whether, when others proudly despise us, those with whom we have to deal have not experienced similar hardships from us. Moreover, their cruelty was hateful to God because—since his goodness is dispersed through heaven and earth, and his beneficence is extended not only to people, but even to brute animals—nothing is more contrary to his nature than that we should cruelly reject those who implore our protection.

Standing Against Temptation

Heal me, O LORD, and I will be healed; save me and I will be saved, for you are the one I praise. —Jeremiah 17:14, NIV

We are taught by these words that whenever stumbling-blocks come in our way, we ought to call on God with increasing passion and earnestness. For we all know our weakness; even when we don't have to fight, our weakness does not allow us to stand uncorrupted. How then will we do when Satan assails our faith with his most cunning devices? Thus, while we now see all things in the world in a corrupted state, so that we are seduced by a thousand things from the true worship of God, let us learn by the example of the Prophet to hide ourselves under the wings of God and to pray that he may heal us; for we shall not only be apparently vicious, but many corruptions will immediately devour us, unless God himself brings us help. Hence the worse the world is, and the greater the licentiousness of sin, the more necessity there is for praying to God to keep us by his wonderful power, as if we were in the very regions of hell.

A general truth may be also gathered from this passage: that it is not in us to stand or to keep ourselves safe, so as to be preserved, but that this is the peculiar kindness of God. For if we had any power to preserve ourselves, to continue pure and unpolluted in the midst of corruption, no doubt Jeremiah would have been given such a gift. But he confesses that there is no hope of healing and of salvation, except through the special favor of God. For what else is healing but purity of life? It is as if Jeremiah had said, "O Lord, it is not in me to preserve that integrity that you require," and hence he says, "Heal me, and I shall be healed." And then, when he speaks of salvation, he no doubt means that it is not enough for the Lord to help us once or for a short time, unless the Lord continues to help us to the end. Therefore the beginning, as well as the whole progress of salvation, is here ascribed by Jeremiah to God.

Grant, Almighty God, that we may learn, whether in need or in abundance, to submit ourselves to you, so that it will be our only and perfect happiness to depend on you and to rest in that salvation (the experience of which you have already given us) until we shall reach that eternal rest where we shall enjoy it in all its fullness—having been made partakers of that glory which has been procured for us by the blood of your only-begotten Son. Amen.

GOING BY DAY

Are there not twelve hours in the day?
—John 11:9a

hrist borrows a comparison from Day and Night. For if any man perform a journey in the dark, we need not wonder if he frequently stumble, or go astray, or fall; but the light of the sun by day points out the road, so that there is no danger. Now the calling of God is like the light of day, which does not allow us to mistake our road or to stumble. Whoever, then, obeys the word of God and undertakes nothing but according to his command, always has God to guide and direct him from heaven, and with this confidence he may safely and boldly pursue his journey. For, as we are informed, whosoever walks in his ways has angels to guard him, and, under their direction, is safe, so that he cannot strike his foot against a stone (Ps. 91:11).

And this knowledge is highly necessary to us; for believers can scarcely move a foot to follow him, but Satan shall immediately interpose a thousand obstructions, hold out a variety of dangers on

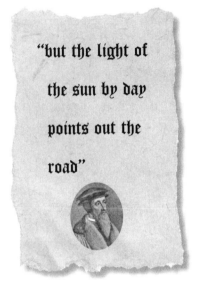

"but the light of the sun by day points out the road"

every side, and contrive, in every possible way, to oppose their progress. But when the Lord invites us to go forward, by holding out, as it were, his lamp to us, we ought to go forward courageously, though many deaths besiege our path; for he never commands us to advance without at the same time adding a promise to encourage us, so that we may be fully convinced that whatever we undertake agreeably to his command will have a good and prosperous issue.

MIRROR OF UNRIGHTEOUSNESS

Moreover the law entered, that the offence might abound. But where sin abounded, grace did much more abound: That as sin hath reigned unto death, even so might grace reign through righteousness unto eternal life by Jesus Christ our Lord. —Romans 5:20–21

The Law is a kind of mirror. As in a mirror we discover any stains upon our face, so in the Law we behold, our impotence; then, in consequence of it, our iniquity; and, finally, the curse, as the consequence of both. He who has no power of following righteousness is necessarily plunged in the oppression of iniquity, and this iniquity is immediately followed by the curse.

Accordingly, the greater the transgression of which the Law convicts us, the severer the judgment to which we are exposed. To this effect is the Apostle's declaration that "by the law is the knowledge of sin" (Rom. 3:20). By these words he only points out the first office of the Law as experienced by sinners not yet regenerated. In conformity to this, it is said "the law entered that the offence might abound," and, accordingly, that it is "the ministration of death," that it "works wrath" and kills (Rom. 5:20; 2 Cor. 3:7; Rom. 4:15).

For there cannot be a doubt that the clearer the consciousness of guilt, the greater the increase of sin—because to transgression a rebellious feeling against the Lawgiver is added. All that remains for the Law is to arm the wrath of God for the destruction of the sinner, for by itself it can do nothing but accuse, condemn, and destroy him.

Assuredly, if our whole will were formed and disposed to obedience, the mere knowledge of the law would be sufficient for salvation. But since our carnal and corrupt nature is contradictory and opposed to the divine Law (and is in no degree amended by its discipline) the consequence is that the Law which, if it had been properly attended to, would have given life becomes the occasion of sin and death. When all are convicted of transgression, the more it declares the righteousness of God, the more it discloses our iniquity; the more certainly it assures us that life and salvation are treasured up as the reward of righteousness, the more certainly it assures us that the unrighteous will perish.

THE ONLY HAVEN OF SAFETY

And for this cause he is the mediator of the new testament, that by means of death, for the redemption of the transgressions that were under the first testament, they which are called might receive the promise of eternal inheritance. —Hebrews 9:15

It is now easy to understand the doctrine of the law: God, as our Creator, is entitled to be regarded as a Father and Master and should, accordingly, receive fear, love, reverence, and glory. For indeed, we are not our own, to follow whatever course passion dictates, but are bound to obey him implicitly and to comply entirely in his good pleasure. Again, the Law teaches that justice and rectitude are a delight, injustice an abomination to him, and therefore, as we would not with impious ingratitude revolt from our Maker our whole life must be spent in the cultivation of righteousness. We cannot be permitted to measure the glory of God by our ability. Whatever we may be, he ever remains like himself—the friend of righteousness—the enemy of unrighteousness, and whatever his demands from us may be, as he can only require what is right, we are necessarily under a natural obligation to obey. Our inability to do so is our own fault.

Contrasting our conduct with the righteousness of the Law, we see how very far it is from being in accordance with the will of God, and, therefore, how unworthy we are of holding our place among his creatures, far less of being accounted his sons. Moreover, taking a survey of our powers, we see that they are not only unequal to fulfill the Law, but are altogether null. The necessary consequence must be to produce distrust of our own ability, and also anxiety and trepidation of mind. Conscience cannot feel the burden of its guilt, without beforehand turning to the judgment of God, while the view of this judgment cannot fail to excite a dread of death. In like manner, the proofs of our utter powerlessness must instantly cause despair of our own strength. Both feelings are productive of humility and embarrassment, and hence the sinner, terrified at the prospect of eternal death (which he sees justly impending over him for his iniquities), turns to the mercy of God as the only haven of safety.

A PROFITABLE ABSENCE

Then said Jesus unto them plainly, Lazarus is dead. And I am glad for your sakes that I was not there, to the intent ye may believe; nevertheless let us go unto him. —John 11:14–15

The goodness of Christ was astonishing, in being able to bear with such gross ignorance in the disciples. And indeed the reason why he delayed, for a time, to bestow upon them the grace of the Spirit in larger measure was that the miracle of renewing them in a moment might be the greater. He means that his absence was profitable to them, because his power would have been less illustriously displayed if he had instantly given assistance to Lazarus. For the more nearly the works of God approach to the ordinary course of nature, the less highly are they valued, and the less illustriously is their glory displayed. This is what we experience daily; for if God immediately stretches out his hand, we do not perceive his assistance. That the resurrection of Lazarus, therefore, might be acknowledged by the disciples to be truly a divine work, it must be delayed, that it might be very widely removed from a human remedy.

We ought to remember, however, what I formerly observed that the fatherly kindness of God towards us is here represented in the person of Christ. When God permits us to be overwhelmed with distresses, and to languish long under them, let us know that, in this manner, he promotes our salvation. At such a time, no doubt, we groan and are perplexed and sorrowful, but the Lord rejoices on account of our benefit, and gives a twofold display of his kindness to us in this respect. That he not only pardons our sins, but gladly finds means of correcting them.

WHAT GOD MAKES CLEAN

About noon the following day as they were on their journey and approaching the city, Peter went up on the roof to pray. He became hungry and wanted something to eat, and while the meal was being prepared, he fell into a trance. He saw heaven opened and something like a large sheet being let down to earth by its four corners. It contained all kinds of four-footed animals, as well as reptiles of the earth and birds of the air. Then a voice told him, "Get up, Peter. Kill and eat." "Surely not, Lord!" Peter replied. "I have never eaten anything impure or unclean." The voice spoke to him a second time, "Do not call anything impure that God has made clean."
—Acts 10:9–15, NIV

When he says, "Do not call anything impure that God has made clean," he speaks of meat, but this sentence must be extended unto all parts of life. The sense is that it is not for us to allow or condemn anything, but as we stand and fall by the judgment of God alone, so is he judge of all things (Rom. 14:4). On the subject of meat: After the abrogating of the Law, God pronounces that they are all pure and clean. If, on the other side, a mortal stands up, making a new difference, forbidding certain things, that person takes unto him or herself the authority and power of God by a sacrilegious boldness.

But let us trust to the heavenly oracle, and freely despise inhibitions. We must always ask the mouth of the Lord, that we may thereby be sure what we may lawfully do—so it was not lawful even for Peter to make something profane which was lawful by the Word of God. Furthermore, this is a place of great importance to beat down on the backwardness of people, which they make too many perverse judgments. There is almost no one who does not grant liberty to herself or himself to judge other people's doings. Now, as we are churlish and malicious, we lean more toward the worse part, so that we take from God that right to judge which is his. This message alone ought to suffice to correct such boldness: that it is not lawful for us to make this or that unclean, but that this power belongs to God alone.

PERPETUAL LIFE

And whosoever liveth, and believeth in me shall never die.
—John 11:26

This is the exposition of the second clause, how Christ is the life; and he is so, because he never permits the life which he has once bestowed to be lost, but preserves it to the end. For since flesh is so frail, what would become of men if, after having once obtained life, they were afterwards left to themselves? The perpetuity of the life must, therefore, be founded on the power of Christ himself, that he may complete what he has begun.

The reason why it is said that believers never die is that their souls, being born again of incorruptible seed (1 Peter 1:23), have Christ dwelling in them, from whom they derive perpetual vigor. For though the body be subject to death on account of sin, yet the spirit is life on account of righteousness (Rom. 8:10). That the out-

> "The perpetuity of the life must . . . be founded on the power of Christ himself"

ward man daily decays in them is so far from taking anything away from their true life, that it aids the progress of it, because the inward man is renewed from day to day (2 Cor. 4:16). What is still more, death itself is a sort of emancipation from the bondage of death.

RESPONDING TO FEAR

Before the spies lay down for the night, she went up on the roof and said to them, "I know that the LORD has given this land to you and that a great fear of you has fallen on us, so that all who live in this country are melting in fear because of you." —Joshua 2:8–9, NIV

rahab recognizes that it's the work of a divine hand that has struck fear into the people of the nations of Canaan, which, in a way, causes them to pronounce their own doom upon themselves in anticipation. Rahab infers that the terror which the children of Israel have inspired in the Canaanites is a token of the Israelites' victory, because the Israelites fight under God as their Leader. In the fact that, while the courage of Canaan had melted away, the Canaanites prepared to resist the Israelites anyway—with the obstinacy of despair—we see that when the wicked are broken and crushed by the hand of God, they are not so subdued as to receive God's yoke, but in their terror and anxiety become incapable of being tamed.

Here, too, we have to observe how, when afflicted by the same fear, believers differ from unbelievers, and how the faith of Rahab displays itself. She herself was afraid, just like every other one of the Canaanite

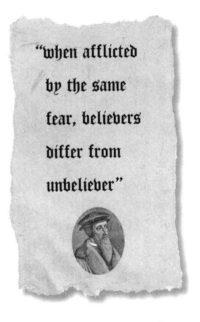

"when afflicted by the same fear, believers differ from unbeliever"

people; but when she reflects that she has to deal with God one way or the other, she concludes that her only remedy is to avoid evil by yielding humbly and placidly, since resistance would be altogether useless. But what is the course taken by all the wretched inhabitants of Canaan? Although terror-struck, so far is their sin from being overcome that they stimulate each other to the conflict.

GOD NEARER TO US

In him was life; and the life was the light of men.
—John 1:4

e speaks here, in my opinion, of that part of life in which men excel other animals; and he informs us that the life which was bestowed on men was not of an ordinary description, but was united to the light of understanding. He separates man from the rank of other creatures, because we perceive more readily the power of God by feeling it in us than by beholding it at a distance.

Thus Paul charges us not to seek God at a distance, because he makes himself to be felt within us (Acts 17:27). After having presented a general exhibition of the kindness of Christ, in order to induce men to take a nearer view of it, he points out what has been bestowed peculiarly on themselves; namely, that they were not created like the beasts, but having been endued with reason, they had obtained a higher rank.

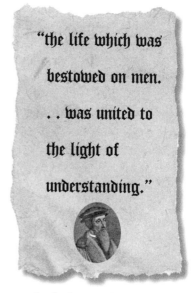

"the life which was bestowed on men. . . was united to the light of understanding."

As it is not in vain that God imparts his light to their minds, it follows that the purpose for which they were created was that they might acknowledge him who is the Author of so excellent a blessing. And since this light has been conveyed from him to us, it ought to serve as a mirror, in which we may clearly behold the divine power of the Speech.

FAITH AND OUR RENEWAL

But as many as received him, to them gave he power to become the sons of God, even to them that believe on his name: Which were born, not of blood, nor of the will of the flesh, nor of the will of man, but of God. —John 1:12–13

he Evangelist affirms that no man can believe unless he be begotten of God, and therefore faith is a heavenly gift. It follows, secondly, that faith is not bare or cold knowledge, since no man can believe who has not been renewed by the Spirit of God. It may be thought that the Evangelist reverses the natural order by making regeneration to precede faith; whereas, on the contrary, it is an effect of faith, and therefore ought to be placed later. I reply that both statements perfectly agree—because by faith we receive the incorruptible seed (1 Peter 1:23), by which we are born again to a new and divine life. And yet faith itself is a work of the Holy Spirit, who dwells in none but the children of God. So then, in various respects, faith is a part of our regeneration, and an entrance into the kingdom of God that he may reckon us among his children. The illumination of our minds by the Holy Spirit belongs to our renewal, and thus faith flows from regeneration as from its source; but since it is by the same faith that we receive Christ, who sanctifies us by his Spirit, on that account it is said to be the beginning of our adoption.

Another solution, still more plain and easy, may be offered; for when the Lord breathes faith into us, he regenerates us by some method that is hidden and unknown to us. But after we have received faith, we perceive, by a lively feeling of conscience, not only the grace of adoption but also newness of life and the other gifts of the Holy Spirit. For since faith, as we have said, receives Christ, it puts us in possession, so to speak, of all his blessings. Thus so far as respects our sense, it is only after having believed that we begin to be the sons of God. But if the inheritance of eternal life is the fruit of adoption, we see how the Evangelist ascribes the whole of our salvation to the grace of Christ alone; and, indeed, how closely men examine themselves, they will find nothing that is worthy of the children of God, except what Christ has bestowed on them.

A BOLD SPIRIT

And now, O Lord GOD, thou art that God, and thy words be true, and thou hast promised this goodness unto thy servant.
—2 Samuel 7:28

Our prayers depend on no merit of our own, but all their worth and hope of success are founded and depend on the promises of God, so that they need no other support and require not to look up and down on this hand and on that. It must therefore be fixed in our minds that though we equal not the glorified sanctity of patriarchs, prophets, and apostles, the command to pray is common to us as well as them; and faith is common, so if we lean on the Word of God, we are in respect of this privilege their associates.

For God's declaring, that he will listen and be favorable to all encourages the most wretched to hope that they shall obtain what they ask. Accordingly, we should attend to the general forms of expression, which exclude none from first to last: only let there be sincerity of heart, self-dissatisfaction, humility, and faith, that we may not, by the hypocrisy of a deceitful prayer, profane the name of God. Our most merciful Father will not reject those whom he not only encourages to come but also urges in every possible way. Hence David's prayer: "And now, O Lord GOD, thou art that God, and thy words be true, and thou hast promised this goodness unto thy servant, that it may continue forever before thee." Also, in another passage, "Let, I pray thee, thy merciful kindness be for my comfort, according to thy word unto thy servant" (Ps. 119:76).

Whatever be the pretexts which unbelievers employ, when they do not flee to God as often as necessity urges, nor seek after him, nor implore his aid, they defraud him of his due honor just as much as if they were fabricating to themselves new gods and idols, since in this way they deny that God is the author of all their blessings. On the contrary, nothing more effectually frees pious minds from every doubt than to be armed with the thought that no obstacle should impede them while they are obeying the command of God, who declares that nothing is more grateful to him than obedience. A bold spirit in prayer well accords with fear, reverence, and anxiety.

THE GIFT OF PERSEVERANCE

His lord said unto him, Well done, thou good and faithful servant:
thou hast been faithful over a few things, I will make thee ruler over
many things: enter thou into the joy of thy lord. —Matthew 25:21

As to perseverance, it would undoubtedly have been regarded as the gratuitous gift of God had not the very destructive error prevailed: that it is bestowed in proportion to human merit, according to the reception which each individual gives to the first grace. This having given rise to the idea that it was entirely in our own power to receive or reject the offered grace of God, that idea is no sooner exploded than the error founded on it must fall.

The error, indeed, is twofold. For, not only does it teach that our gratitude for the first grace and our legitimate use of it is rewarded by subsequent supplies of grace, but it also teaches that grace does not operate alone, saying it co-operates with ourselves. As to the former, we must hold that the Lord, while he daily enriches his servants and loads them with new gifts of his grace (because he approves of and takes pleasure in the work

which he has begun), finds that in them which he may follow up with larger measures of grace. To this effect are the sentences, "To him that has shall be given," (Luke 19:26) and, "Well done, good and faithful servant: thou hast been faithful over a few things, I will make thee ruler over many things," (Matt. 25:21, 23, 29).

But here two precautions are necessary: It must not be said that the legitimate use of the first grace is rewarded by subsequent measures of grace, as if man rendered the grace of God effectual by his own industry. Nor must it be thought that there is any such reward, as it ceases to be the grace of God. I admit, then, that believers may expect as a blessing from God that the better the use they make of previous, the larger the supplies they will receive of future grace. But I say even this use is of the Lord, and this remuneration is bestowed freely of mere good will.

SUBJECT TO SATAN

And you hath he quickened, who were dead in trespasses and sins;
Wherein in time past ye walked according to the course of this world,
according to the prince of the power of the air, the spirit that now wor-
keth in the children of disobedience. —Ephesians 2:1–2

that man is so enslaved by the yoke of sin, that he cannot of his own nature aim at good either in wish or actual pursuit, has, I think, been sufficiently proved. Moreover, a distinction has been drawn between compulsion and necessity, making it clear that man—though he sins necessarily—nevertheless sins voluntarily.

But from his being brought into bondage to the devil, it would seem that he is actuated more by the devil's will than his own. Augustine (in Pss. 31 and 33) compares the human will to a horse preparing to start, and God and the devil to riders: "If God mounts, he, like a temperate and skilful rider, guides it calmly, urges it when too slow, reins it in when too fast, curbs its forwardness and over-action, checks its bad temper, and keeps it on the proper course; but if the devil has seized the saddle, like an ignorant and rash rider, he hurries it over broken ground, drives it into ditches, dashes it over precipices, spurs it into obstinacy or fury."

With this simile, since a better does not occur, we shall for the present be contented. When it is said that the will of the nat-ural man is subject to the power of the devil and is actuated by him, the meaning is not that the will, while reluctant and resisting, is forced to submit (as masters oblige unwilling slaves to execute their orders), but that, fascinated by the impostures of Satan, it necessarily yields to his guidance and does him homage. Those whom the Lord favors not with the direction of his Spirit, he, by a righteous judgment, consigns to the agency of Satan.

Wherefore, the Apostle says, that "the god of this world has blinded the minds of them which believe not, lest the light of the glorious Gospel of Christ, who is the image of God, should shine into them." And, in another passage, he describes the devil as "the spirit that now works in the children of disobedience" (Eph. 2:2). The blinding of the wicked and all the iniquities consequent upon it are called the works of Satan—works the cause of which is not to be sought in anything external to the will of man, in which the root of the evil lies, and in which the foundation of Satan's kingdom (in other words) sin is fixed.

DIVINE PROVIDENCE

But he took note of their distress when he heard their cry; for their sake
he remembered his covenant and out of his great love he relented. He
caused them to be pitied by all who held them captive.
—Psalm 106:44-46, NIV

n those actions, which in themselves are neither good nor bad and concern the corporeal rather than the spiritual life, the liberty which man possesses has not yet been explained. Some have conceded a free choice to man in such actions.

While I admit that those who hold that man has no ability in himself to do righteousness hold what is most necessary to be known for salvation, I think it ought not to be overlooked that we owe it to the special grace of God whenever, on the one hand, we choose what is for our advantage and our will inclines in that direction; and whenever, on the other, with heart and soul we shun what would otherwise do us harm.

And the interference of Divine Providence goes to the extent not only of making events turn out as was foreseen to be appropriate, but of giving the wills of men the same direction. If we look at the administration of human affairs with the eye of sense, we will have no doubt that, so far, they are placed at man's disposal. But if we lend an ear to the many passages of Scripture which proclaim that even in these matters the minds of men are ruled by God, they will compel us to place human choice in subordination to his special influence.

Who gave the Israelites such favor in the eyes of the Egyptians, that they lent them all their most valuable commodities (Ex. 11:3)? They never would have been so inclined of their own accord. Their inclinations, therefore, were more overruled by God than regulated by themselves. And surely, had not Jacob been persuaded that God inspires men with diverse affections as seems to him good, he would not have said of his son Joseph (whom he thought to be some heathen Egyptian), "God Almighty give you mercy before the man" (Gen. 43:14). When the Lord was pleased to pity his people, he made them also to be pitied of all them that carried them captives (Ps. 106:46).

TURNED BY GOD'S HAND

The king's heart is in the hand of the LORD, as the rivers of water: he turneth it whithersoever he will. —Proverbs 21:1

henever God is pleased to make way for his providence, even in external matters he turns and bends the wills of men. Whatever the freedom of their choice may be, it is still subject to the disposal of God. Daily experience teaches that your mind depends more on the agency of God than the freedom of your own choice. Your judgment often fails, and in matters of no great difficulty your courage flags. At other times, in matters of the greatest obscurity, the mode of explaining them at once suggests itself, while in matters of moment and danger, your mind rises superior to every difficulty. In this way, I interpret the words of Solomon, "The hearing ear, and the seeing eye, the LORD has made even both of them" (Prov. 20:12). For they seem to me to refer not to their creation, but to peculiar grace in the use of them. When he says, "The king's heart is in the hand of the LORD as the rivers of water; he turneth it whithersoever place he will" (Prov. 21:1), he comprehends the whole race under one particular class.

If any will is free from subjection, it must be that of one possessing magnificent power, and in a manner exercising dominion over other wills. But if it is under the hand of God, our will surely cannot be exempt from it. On this subject there is an admirable sentiment of Augustine, "Scripture, if it be carefully examined, will show not only that the good wills of men are made good by God out of evil, and when so made, are directed to good acts, even to eternal life, but those which retain the elements of the world are in the power of God, to turn them to what place he pleases, and when he pleases, either to perform acts of kindness, or by a hidden, yet indeed, most just judgment to inflict punishment."

A SMELLY DISTRACTION

Lord, he already stinketh. —John 11:39

There being nothing more inconsistent with life than putrefaction and offensive smell, Martha infers that no remedy can be found. Thus, when our minds are preoccupied by foolish thoughts, we banish God from us, if we may be allowed the expression, so that he cannot accomplish in us his own work. Certainly, it was not owing to Martha that her brother did not lie continually in the tomb, for she cuts off the expectation of life for him and, at the same time, endeavors to hinder Christ from raising him; and yet nothing was farther from her intention. This arises from the weakness of faith. Distracted in various ways, we fight with ourselves, and while we stretch out the one hand to ask assistance from God, we repel, with the other hand, that very assistance, as soon as it is offered. True,

Martha did not speak falsely, when she said, "I know that whatsoever thou shalt ask from God he will give thee"; but a confused faith is of little advantage, unless it be put in operation, when we come to a practical case.

We may also perceive in Martha how various are the effects of faith, even in the most excellent persons. She was the first that came to meet Christ— this was no ordinary proof of her piety—and yet she does not cease to throw difficulties in his way. That the grace of God may have access to us, let us learn to ascribe to it far greater power than our senses can comprehend; and, if the first and single promise of God has not sufficient weight with us, let us, at least, follow the example of Martha by giving our acquiescence when he confirms us a second and third time.

INCONVENIENCES

If we let him thus alone, all men will believe on him: and the Romans shall come and take away both our place and nation. —John 11:48

ow it is wicked to consult about guarding against dangers, which we cannot avoid, unless we choose to depart from the right path. Our first inquiry ought to be, What does God command and choose to be done? By this we ought to abide, whatever may be the consequence to ourselves.

Those men, on the other hand, resolve that Christ shall be removed from the midst of them, that no inconvenience may arise by allowing him to proceed as he has begun. But what if he has been sent by God? Shall they banish a prophet of God from among them, to purchase peace with the Romans? Such are the schemes of those who do not truly and sincerely fear God. What is right and lawful gives them no concern, for their whole attention is directed to the consequences.

But the only way to deliberate in a proper and holy manner is this: First, we ought to inquire what is the will of God. Next, we ought to follow

"First, we ought to inquire what is the will of God."

boldly whatever he enjoins, and not to be discouraged by any fear, though we were besieged by a thousand deaths; for our actions must not be moved by any gust of wind, but must be constantly regulated by the will of God alone. He who boldly despises dangers—or, at least, rising above the fear of them sincerely obeys God—will at length have a prosperous result. For, contrary to the expectation of all, God blesses that firmness which is founded on obedience to his word.

GOSPEL GATHERING

And this spake he not of himself: but being high priest that year, he prophesied that Jesus should die for that nation; And not for that nation only, but that also he should gather together in one the children of God that were scattered abroad. —John 11:51–52

by saying that Jesus would die, the Evangelist first shows that the whole of our salvation consists in that Christ should assemble us into one; for in this way he reconciles us to the Father, in whom is the fountain of life (Ps. 36:9). Hence, also, we infer, that the human race is scattered and estranged from God, until the children of God are assembled under Christ their Head.

Thus, the communion of saints is a preparation for eternal life, because all whom Christ does not gather to the Father remain in death, as we shall see again under the seventeenth chapter of John. For the same reason, Paul also teaches that Christ was sent, in order that he might gather together all things which are in heaven and in earth (Eph. 1:10).

Wherefore, that we may enjoy the salvation brought by Christ, discord must be removed, and we must be made one with God and with angels, and among ourselves. The cause and pledge of this unity was the death of Christ, by which he drew all things to himself; but we are daily gathered by the Gospel into the fold of Christ.

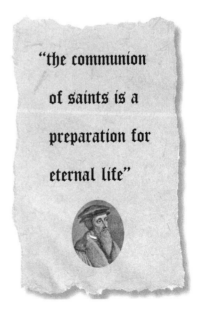

"the communion of saints is a preparation for eternal life"

COURAGEOUS PRAYER

Thy kingdom come. Thy will be done in earth, as it is in heaven.
—Matthew 6:10

e ought to derive from these verses a profitable admonition. For if we are members of the Church, the Lord calls upon us to cherish the same desire which he wished believers to cherish under the Law; that is, that we should wish with our whole heart that the kingdom of Christ should flourish and prosper, and that we should also demonstrate this by our prayers.

In order to give us greater courage in prayer, we ought to observe that he prescribes to us the words. Woe then to our slothfulness, if we extinguish by our coldness, or quench by indifference, that ardor which God excites. Yet let us know that the prayers which we offer by the direction and authority of God will not be in vain. Provided that we be not indolent or grow weary in praying,

he will be a faithful guardian of his kingdom, to defend it by his invincible power and protection.

True, indeed, though we remain drowsy and inactive, the majesty of his kingdom will be firm and sure. But when, as is frequently the case, it is less prosperous than it ought to be or rather falls into decay, as we perceive it to be at the present day, fearfully scattered and wasted this unquestionably arises through our fault. And when but a small restoration, or almost none, is to be seen, or when at least it advances slowly, let us ascribe it to our indifference. We daily ask from God "that his kingdom may come" (Matt. 6:10), but scarcely one man in a hundred earnestly desires it. Justly, therefore, are we deprived of the blessing of God, which we are weary of asking.

ORIGINAL SIN

Therefore, just as sin entered the world through one man, and death through sin, and in this way death came to all men, because all sinned.
—*Romans 5:12, NIV*

Original sin may be defined as a hereditary corruption and depravity of our nature, extending to all the parts of the soul, which first makes us obnoxious to the wrath of God, and then produces in us works which in Scripture are termed works of the flesh. This corruption is repeatedly designated by Paul by the term "sin" (Gal. 5:19). The works which proceed from it—such as adultery, fornication, theft, hatred, murder, reviling—he terms, in the same way, the fruits of sin, though in various passages of Scripture, and even by Paul himself, they are also termed sins.

The two things, therefore, are to be distinctly observed: that being thus perverted and corrupted in all the parts of our nature, we are, merely on account of such corruption, deservedly condemned by God, to whom nothing is acceptable but righteousness, innocence, and purity. This is not liability for another's fault. For when it is said that the sin of Adam has made us obnoxious to the justice of God, the meaning is not that we, who are in ourselves innocent and blameless, are bearing his guilt, but that since by his transgression we are all placed under the curse, he is said to have brought us under obligation. Through him, however, not only has punishment been derived, but pollution instilled, for which punishment is justly due.

Next comes the other point: that this perversity in us never ceases, but constantly produces new fruits, in other words, those works of the flesh which we formerly described— just as a lighted furnace sends forth sparks and flames, or a fountain without ceasing pours out water. Our nature is not only utterly devoid of goodness, but so prolific in all kinds of evil, that it can never be idle.

NATURALLY VICIOUS

This only have I found: God made mankind upright, but men have gone in search of many schemes. —Ecclesiastes 7:29, NIV

Let us have done with those who dare to inscribe the name of God on their vices, because we say that men are born vicious. The divine workmanship, which they ought to look for in the nature of Adam, when still entire and uncorrupted, they absurdly expect to find in their depravity. The blame of our ruin rests with our own carnality, not with God, its only cause being our degeneracy from our original condition. And let no one here claim that God might have provided better for our safety by preventing Adam's fall. This objection, which, from the daring presumption implied in it, is odious to every pious mind, relates to the mystery of predestination, which will afterwards be considered in its own place. Meanwhile let us remember that our ruin is attributable to our own depravity, that we may not insinuate a charge against God himself, the Author of nature. It is true that nature has received a mortal wound, but there is a great difference between a wound inflicted from without and one inherent in our first condition. It is plain that this wound was inflicted by sin; therefore, we have no ground of complaint except against ourselves.

We say, then, that man is corrupted by a natural viciousness, but not by one which proceeded from nature. In saying that it proceeded not from nature, we mean that it was rather an outside event which befell man, than an inherent property assigned to him from the beginning. We, however, call it natural to prevent any one from supposing that each individual contracts it by depraved habit, whereas all receive it by a hereditary law. And we have authority for so calling it. For on the same grounds, the Apostle says that we are "by nature the children of wrath" (Eph. 2:3). How could God, who takes pleasure in the meanest of his works, be offended with the noblest of them all? The offence is not with the work itself, but the corruption of the work. Wherefore, if it is not improper to say that, in consequence of the corruption of human nature, man is naturally hateful to God, it is not improper to say that he is naturally and inherently vicious and depraved.

EXPECTANT PRAYER

In the morning, O LORD, you hear my voice; in the morning I lay my requests before you and wait in expectation. —Psalm 5:3, NIV

In praying, we must truly feel our wants and—seriously considering that we need all the things which we ask—accompany the prayer with a sincere, nay, ardent desire of obtaining them. Many repeat prayers in a perfunctory manner from a set form, as if they were performing a task to God. And though they confess that this is a necessary remedy for the evils of their condition—because it were fatal to be left without the divine aid which they implore, it still appears that they perform the duty from custom, because their minds are meanwhile cold and they ponder not what they ask. A general and confused feeling of their necessity leads them to pray, but it does not make them solicitous as in a matter of present consequence, that they may obtain the supply of their need. Moreover, can we suppose anything more hateful to God than this fiction of asking the pardon of sins, while he who asks at the very time either thinks that he is not a sinner—or, at least, is not thinking that he is a sinner; in other words, a fiction by which God is plainly held in derision? But mankind is full of depravity, so that in the way of perfunctory service they often ask many things of God which they think come to them without his beneficence, or from some other quarter, or are already certainly in their possession.

There is another fault which seems less heinous, but is not to be tolerated. Some murmur out prayers without meditation, their only principle being that God is to be propitiated by prayer. Believers ought to be specially on their guard never to appear in the presence of God with the intention of presenting a request unless they are under some serious impression and are, at the same time, desirous to obtain it. Nay, although in these things which we ask only for the glory of God, we seem not at first sight to consult for our necessity, yet we ought not to ask with less fervor and vehemence of desire. For instance, when we pray that his name be hallowed, that hallowing must be earnestly hungered and thirsted after.

NO TIME WITHOUT PRAYER

And pray in the Spirit on all occasions with all kinds of prayers and requests. With this in mind, be alert and always keep on praying for all the saints. —Ephesians 6:18, NIV

I f it is objected that the necessity which urges us to pray is not always equal, I admit it. James properly taught us this distinction: "Is any among you afflicted? Let him pray. Is any merry? Let him sing psalms" (James 5:13).

Therefore, common sense itself dictates that as we are too sluggish, we must be stimulated by God to pray earnestly whenever the occasion requires. Thus David calls a time when God "may be found" a seasonable time; because, as he declares in several other passages, the more heavily grievances, annoyances, fears, and other kinds of trial press us, the freer is our access to God, as if he were inviting us to himself. Still not less true is the injunction of Paul to pray "always" (Eph. 6:18); because, however prosperously, according to our view, things proceed, and however we may be surrounded on all sides with grounds of joy, there is not an instant of time during which our want does not exhort us to prayer. A man abounds in wheat and wine; but as he cannot enjoy a morsel of bread, unless by the continual bounty of God, his granaries or cellars will not prevent him from asking for daily bread. Then, if we consider how many dangers impend every moment, fear itself will teach us that no time ought to be without prayer.

This, however, may be better known in spiritual matters. For when will the many sins of which we are conscious allow us to sit secure without asking for freedom from guilt and punishment? When will temptation give us a truce, making it unnecessary to hasten for help? Moreover, zeal for the kingdom and glory of God ought not to seize us by starts, but urge us without intermission, so that every time should appear seasonable. God promises that he will be near to those who call upon him in truth, and declares that those who seek him with their whole heart will find him. Those, therefore, who delight in their own pollution cannot surely aspire to him.

REPENTANT PRAYER

And when ye spread forth your hands, I will hide mine eyes from you: yea, when ye make many prayers, I will not hear: your hands are full of blood. —Isaiah 1:15

One of the requisites of legitimate prayer is repentance. Hence the common declaration of Scripture: God does not listen to the wicked; their prayers, as well as their sacrifices, are an abomination to him. For it is right that those who seal up their hearts should find the ears of God closed against them, that those who, by their hardheartedness, provoke his severity should find him inflexible. In Isaiah he thus threatens, "When you make many prayers, I will not hear: your hands are full of blood" (Isa. 1:15). In like manner, in Jeremiah he says, "Though they shall cry unto me, I will not hearken unto them" (Jer. 11:7–8, 11); because he regards it as the highest insult for the wicked to boast of his covenant while profaning his sacred name by their whole lives. Hence he complains in Isaiah, "This people draw near to me with their mouth, and with their lips do honor me; but

have removed their heart far from me" (Isa. 29:13).

Indeed, he does not confine this to prayers alone, but declares that he abominates pretense in every part of his service. Hence the words of James, "You ask and receive not, because you ask amiss, that you may consume it upon your lusts" (James 4:3). It is true, indeed (as we shall again see in a little), that the pious, in the prayers which they utter, trust not to their own worth. Still the admonition of John is not superfluous, "Whatsoever we ask, we receive of him, because we keep his commandments" (1 John 3:22); an evil conscience shuts the door against us. Hence it follows, that none but the sincere worshippers of God pray aright, or are listened to. Let everyone, therefore, who prepares to pray feel dissatisfied with what is wrong in his condition, and assume, which he cannot do without repentance, the character and feelings of a poor beggar.

CONFIDENCE RISING

Fear not, daughter of Sion: behold, thy King cometh, sitting on an ass's colt. —John 12:15

In these words of the Prophet, as the Evangelist quotes them, we ought to observe first that never is tranquility restored to our minds, or fear and trembling banished from them, except by knowing that Christ reigns among us. The words of the Prophet, indeed, are different; for he exhorts believers to gladness and rejoicing. But the Evangelist has here described the manner in which our hearts exult with true joy: It is when that fear is removed, with which all must be tormented until being reconciled to God that they obtain that peace which springs from faith (Rom. 5:1).

This benefit, therefore, comes to us through Christ—that freed from the tyranny of Satan, the yoke of sin being broken, guilt canceled, and death abolished—we freely boast, relying on the protection of our King, since they who are placed under his guardianship ought not to fear any danger. Not that we are free from fear, so long as we live in the world, but because confidence, founded on Christ, rises superior to all.

Though Christ was still at a distance, yet the Prophet exhorted the godly men of that age to be glad and joyful, because Christ was to come. "Behold," said he, "thy King will come; therefore fear not." Now that he is come, in order that we may enjoy his presence, we ought more vigorously to contend with fear, that, freed from our enemies, we may peacefully and joyfully honor our King.

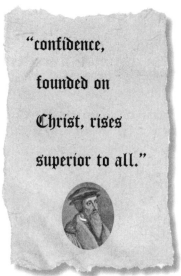

"confidence, founded on Christ, rises superior to all."

GRADUAL LEARNING

These things understood not his disciples at the first: but when Jesus was glorified, then remembered they that these things were written of him, and that they had done these things unto him. —John 12:16

When it is said that they at length remembered that these things had been written concerning him, the Evangelist points out the cause of such gross ignorance, by which their knowledge was preceded. It was because they had not the Scripture at that time as their guide and instructor to direct their minds to just and accurate views. For we are blind unless the word of God go before our steps and it is not even enough that the Word of God shine on us, if the Spirit do not also enlighten our eyes, which otherwise would be blind amid the clearest light. This grace Christ bestowed on his disciples after his resurrection, because the full time, when the Spirit should bestow his riches in great abundance, was not come until he was received into the heavenly glory, as we have seen under John 7:39.

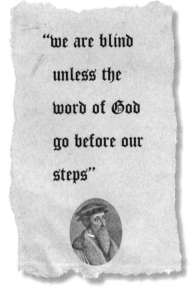

"we are blind unless the word of God go before our steps"

Taught by this example, let us learn to form our judgment of every thing that relates to Christ, not by our own carnal feelings, but by the Scripture. Besides, let us remember that it is a special favor of the Holy Spirit to instruct us in a gradual manner, that we may not be stupid in considering the works of God.

33

THE FIRST COMMANDMENT:
NO OTHER GODS

And God spoke all these words: "I am the Lord your God, who brought you out of Egypt, out of the land of slavery. You shall have no other gods before me."—Exodus 20:1–3, NIV
When you enter the land the Lord your God is giving you, do not learn to imitate the detestable ways of the nations there.
—Deuteronomy 18:9, NIV

It is too well-known from experience how eagerly the human race lays hold of bad examples, and how prone we are to imitate them. Especially those who come into a foreign land readily adapt themselves to its manners and customs. This is the reason why God expressly commands the Israelites to beware that when they come into the land of Canaan, they should catch any infection from its inhabitants. Moreover, Moses explains clearly in this passage what it is to have other gods: to mix up the worship of God with profane things, since its purity is only maintained by banishing from it all uncongenial superstitions. In general, God wished to deter his worshippers from the fallacies with which, from the beginning, Satan has deluded and fascinated miserable humanity.

Since humans have a natural desire for knowledge, even in superstitious peoples this desire has always proceeded from a good principle, inasmuch as God has implanted it in the minds of all, when he would distinguish our race from the lower animals. Neither in this was there anything to be blamed, that humans, being conscious of their own ignorance, thought that they were to obtain knowledge in no other way than by consulting God. Now this was the only purpose of the Gentiles when they inquired of magicians and sorcerers: to seek from heaven that knowledge of which they saw themselves to be destitute. By doing so, they undoubtedly confessed themselves to be overwhelmed with darkness, and that the light of understanding was the special gift of God.

But since by his wiles the devil perverts what is right in itself, these principles implanted in us by nature, have been corrupted by two errors: for both an inappropriate desire of knowing more than is lawful has crept into our minds, and we have had recourse to forbidden means of knowledge. From these sources, foolish curiosity and unrestrained cheekiness, all the superstitions and errors have flowed by which the world has been assailed.

GOD'S JEALOUSY

You shall not make for yourself an idol in the form of anything in heaven above or on the earth beneath or in the waters below. You shall not bow down to them or worship them; for I, the LORD your God, am a jealous God, punishing the children for the sin of the fathers to the third and fourth generation of those who hate me, but showing love to a thousand generations of those who love me and keep my commandments. —Exodus 20:4–6, NIV

As in the first commandment, the Lord declares that he is one, and that besides him no gods must be either worshipped or imagined. He also more plainly declares what his nature is, and with what kind of worship with which he is to be honored, in order that we may not presume to form any carnal idea of him.

The purpose of the commandment, therefore, is that he will not have his legitimate worship profaned by superstitious rites. In general, he calls us entirely away from the carnal frivolous observances which our stupid minds are inclined to devise after forming some gross idea of the divine nature. At the same time, he instructs us in the worship which is legitimate, namely, spiritual worship of his own appointment.

The grossest vice here prohibited is external idolatry. To induce us to this, he proclaims his authority which he will not permit to be impaired or despised with impunity. He calls himself jealous because he cannot bear a partner. He declares that he will vindicate his majesty and glory—if any transfer it either to the creatures or to graven images—and that not by a simple punishment of brief duration, but by one extending to the third and fourth generation of such as imitate the impiety of their progenitors. In like manner, he declares his constant mercy and kindness to the remote posterity of those who love him and keep his Law.

THE SECOND COMMANDMENT:

NO GRAVEN IMAGES

You shall not make for yourself an idol in the form of anything in heaven above or on the earth beneath or in the waters below. You shall not bow down to them or worship them; for I, the LORD your God, am a jealous God, punishing the children for the sin of the fathers to the third and fourth generation of those who hate me, but showing love to a thousand generations of those who love me and keep my commandments. —Exodus 20:4–6, NIV

he object and sum of the Second Commandment is that God is insulted when He is clothed in a bodily image. Moreover, the name of God is transferred to idols, according to common speech and the corrupt opinion of the heathen—not that unbelievers thought that the Deity was included in the corruptible material, but because they imagined that their god was nearer to them if some earthly symbol of its presence were standing before their eyes. In this sense, they called the images of the gods their gods, because they thought they could not ascend to the heights in which the Deity dwelt, unless they mounted by these earthly aids. For Moses' point is to restrain the rashness of people, lest they should travesty God's glory by their imaginations; for another clause is immediately added, "I am the LORD your God," in which God reminds them that he is despoiled of his due honor whenever humans devise anything earthly or carnal representing him. No other statues are here condemned, except those which are erected as representations of God.

Moses teaches the human race that as soon as they imagine anything gross or terrestrial in the Deity, they altogether depart from the true God. It is plain that the false representations, which travesty God, are so called to mark them with disgrace and shame. Whatsoever withdraws us from his spiritual service, or whatsoever humans introduce alien from his nature, is repudiated by him.

GIVING GOD ALL THE GLORY

You shall have no other gods before me. —Exodus 20:3

The purpose of this commandment is that the Lord will have himself alone to be exalted in his people, and claims the entire possession of them as his own. He orders us to abstain from ungodliness and superstition of every kind, by which the glory of his divinity is diminished or obscured and he requires us to worship and adore him with truly pious zeal. It is not enough to refrain from other gods. We must, at the same time, devote ourselves wholly to him, not acting like certain impious despisers who regard it as the shortest method to hold all religious observance in contempt. But here precedence must be given to true religion, which will direct our minds to the living God. When duly imbued with the knowledge of him, the whole aim of our lives will be to revere, fear, and worship his majesty, to enjoy a share in his blessings, to have recourse to him in every difficulty, to acknowledge, laud, and celebrate the magnificence of his works, to make him, as it were, the sole aim of all our actions.

Further, we must beware of superstition, by which our minds are turned aside from the true God and carried to and fro after a multiplicity of gods. Therefore, if we are contented with one God, let us call to mind what was formerly observed: All fictitious gods are to be driven far away, and the worship which he claims for himself is not to be mutilated. Not a particle of his glory is to be withheld; everything belonging to him must be reserved to him entirely.

Therefore, having by his present power and grace declared that he had respect to the people whom he had chosen, God now (in order to deter them from the wickedness of revolt) warns them that they cannot adopt strange gods without his being witness and spectator of the sacrilege. Therefore, our conscience must keep aloof from the most distant thought of revolt, if we would have our worship approved by the Lord. The glory of his Godhead must be maintained entire and incorrupt, not merely by external profession, but as under his eye, which penetrates the inmost recesses of his heart.

THE THIRD COMMANDMENT:

THE NAME OF GOD

*You shall not misuse the name of the LORD your God, for the LORD
will not hold anyone guiltless who misuses his name.*
—*Exodus 20:7, NIV*

In order that God may obtain due reverence for his name, he forbids its being taken in vain, especially in oaths. From this we infer, every oath should be a testimony of true piety, whereby the majesty of God himself should obtain its proper glory. Moreover, it is clear that not only when we swear by the name of God, but whenever mention of it is made, his name is to be reverently honored.

To swear by God's name is a species or part of religious worship, and this is obvious too from the words of Isaiah 45:23; for when he predicts that all nations shall devote themselves to pure religion, he says, "By myself I have sworn, my mouth has uttered in all integrity a word that will not be revoked: Before me every knee will bow; by me every tongue will swear." Now, if the bowing of the knees is a token of adoration, this swearing which is connected with it is equivalent to an acknowledgment that God is God.

Whereas God's essence is invisible, his name is set before us as an image, insofar as God manifests himself to us and is distinctly made known to us by his own marks, just as humans are known each by their names. Consequently, God's name is profaned whenever any detraction is made from his supreme wisdom, infinite power, justice, truth, mercy, and righteousness. God's name, then, is taken in vain, not only when any one abuses it by lying, but when it is lightly and disrespectfully brought out in proof of frivolous and trifling matters; I speak of oaths. In this, however, human ingratitude is very gross: When God grants us his name, as if at their request, to put an end to their troubles and to be a pledge of their truth, still it flies promiscuously from their mouths with manifest disrespect. We should only speak of God religiously, so that appropriate veneration of Him should be maintained among us.

SPEAKING WITH REVERENCE

You shall not misuse the name of the LORD your God, for the LORD
will not hold anyone guiltless who misuses his name.
—Exodus 20:7, NIV

The purpose of this commandment is that the majesty of the name of God is to be held sacred. In sum, therefore, it means that we must not profane it by using it irreverently or contemptuously. This prohibition implies a corresponding precept: It should be our study and care to treat his name with religious veneration. Wherefore, it becomes us to regulate our minds and our tongues so as never to think or speak of God and his mysteries without reverence and great humility, and never to have any feeling towards him but one of deep veneration.

We must steadily observe the three following things: First, whatever our mind conceives of him, whatever our tongue utters, must bespeak his excellence and correspond to the sublimity of his sacred name—in short, must be fitted to extol its greatness. Secondly, we must not rashly and preposterously pervert his sacred Word and adorable mysteries to purposes of ambition, or selfishness, or amusement, but (as they bear the impress of his dignity) must always maintain them in due honor and esteem. Lastly, we must not detract from or throw disgrace upon his works, as miserable men are wont insultingly to do, but must hail every action which we attribute to him as wise, and just, and good. This is to sanctify the name of God. When we act otherwise, his name is profaned with vain and wicked abuse because it is applied to a purpose foreign to that to which it is consecrated. In being deprived of its dignity it is gradually brought into contempt.

The commandment refers especially to the case of oaths and this it does the more effectually to deter us from every species of profanation. That the thing here commanded relates to the worship of God and the reverence due to his name, and not to the equity which men are to cultivate towards each other, is apparent from this: that God, for the meantime, vindicates his own right and defends his sacred name, but does not teach the duties which men owe to men.

THE FOURTH COMMANDMENT, PART 1:

SABBATH

Remember the Sabbath day by keeping it holy. Six days you shall labor and do all your work, but the seventh day is a Sabbath to the LORD your God. —Exodus 20:8, NIV

The object of this commandment is that believers should exercise themselves in the worship of God; for we know how prone humans are to fall into indifference, unless they have some props to lean on or some stimulants to arouse them to maintain care and zeal for religion.

God placed before their eyes as the perfection of sanctity that they should all cease from their work. Surely God has no delight in idleness and sloth, and therefore there was no importance in the simple cessation of the labors of their hands and feet. It would have been a childish superstition to rest for no other reason than to spend the rest-time worshipping God. Thus, so that we make no mistake in the meaning of this commandment, it is well to remember the thing it signifies: that the Jews would know that their lives could not be approved by God unless, by ceasing from their own works, they should rid themselves of their reason, counsels, and all

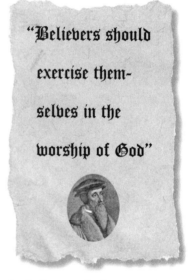

"Believers should exercise themselves in the worship of God"

the feelings and affections of the flesh. For they were not forbidden without exception from the performance of every work, since they were required both to circumcise their children, and to bring the victims into the court, and to offer them in sacrifice on that day; but they were only called away from their own works, that, as if dead to themselves and to the world, they might wholly devote themselves to God.

THE FOURTH COMMANDMENT, PART 2:
SABBATH

Remember the Sabbath day by keeping it holy. Six days you shall labor and do all your work, but the seventh day is a Sabbath to the LORD your God. —Exodus 20:8, NIV

We must see what is the entirety of this sanctification: the death of the flesh, when humans deny themselves and renounce their earthly nature, so that they may be ruled and guided by the Spirit of God. It is to be gathered without doubt from many passages that the keeping of the Sabbath was a serious matter, since God repeats no other commandment more frequently, nor more strictly requires obedience to any.

The legitimate use of the Sabbath must be supposed to be self-renunciation, since one is considered to have "ceased from his works" who is not led by his own will nor indulges his own wishes, but who suffers himself to be directed by the Spirit of God. And this emptying out of self must be taken so far that the Sabbath is violated even by good works, if we regard them as our own.

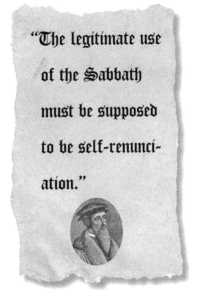

"The legitimate use of the Sabbath must be supposed to be self-renunciation."

RESTING IN GOD

Remember the Sabbath day by keeping it holy. Six days you shall labor and do all your work, but the seventh day is a Sabbath to the LORD your God. On it you shall not do any work, neither you, nor your son or daughter, nor your manservant or maidservant, nor your animals, nor the alien within your gates. For in six days the LORD made the heavens and the earth, the sea, and all that is in them, but he rested on the seventh day. Therefore the LORD blessed the Sabbath day and made it holy. —Exodus 20:8–11, NIV

The purpose of the commandment is that being dead to our own affections and works we meditate on the kingdom of God. Under the rest of the seventh days the divine Lawgiver meant to furnish the people of Israel with a type of the spiritual rest by which believers were to cease from their own works and allow God to work in them. Further, he meant that there should be a stated day on which they should assemble to hear the Law and perform religious rites, or which, at least, they should specially employ in meditating on his works and be thereby trained to piety. Moreover, he meant that servants and those who lived under the authority of others should be indulged with a day of rest, and thus have some intermission from labor.

This adumbration of spiritual rest held a primary place in the Sabbath. Indeed, there is no commandment the observance of which the Almighty more strictly enforces. In Nehemiah, the Levites, in the public assembly, thus speak: "Thou made known unto them thy holy Sabbath, and commanded them precepts, statutes, and laws, by the hand of Moses thy servant." You see the singular honor which it holds among all the precepts of the Law. The Sabbath is a sign by which Israel might know that God is their sanctifier. If our sanctification consists in the mortification of our own will, the analogy between the external sign and the thing signified is most appropriate. We must rest entirely, in order that God may work in us; we must resign our own will, yield up our heart, and abandon all the lusts of the flesh. In short, we must desist from all the acts of our own mind so that, God working in us, we may rest in him—as the Apostle also teaches (Heb. 3:13; 4:3, 9).

THE FIFTH COMMANDMENT:

HONORING PARENTS

Honor your father and your mother, so that you may live long in the land the LORD your God is giving you. —Exodus 20:12, NIV

uman society cannot be maintained in its integrity unless children modestly submit themselves to their parents, and unless those who are set over others by God's ordinance are even reverently honored.

Surely, since God would not have his servants comply with external ceremonies only, it cannot be doubted that all the duties of piety towards parents are here included, to which children are laid under obligation by natural reason itself, and these may be reduced to three heads: that they should regard them with reverence; that they should obediently comply with their commands, and allow themselves to be governed by them; and that they should endeavor to repay what they owe to them, and thus heartily devote themselves to them and their services. Since, therefore, the name of Father is a sacred one and is transferred to humans by the peculiar goodness of God, the dishonoring of parents redounds to the dishonor of God himself, nor can any one despise a father without being guilty of an offense against God. Therefore, however unworthy of honor a father may be, he still retains, inasmuch as he is a father, his right over his children, provided it does not in any way contradict the judgment of God. In condemning, therefore, the vices of a father, a truly pious child will subscribe to God's Law; and still, whatsoever this father may be, will acknowledge that he is to be honored, as being the father given by God.

Obedience comes next, which is also circumscribed by certain limits. Honor, therefore, includes obedience—so that someone who shakes off the yoke of a father, and won't be governed by the father's authority, is justly said to despise the father. Still, the power of a father is limited in that God, on whom all relationships depend, should have the rule over fathers as well as children; for parents govern their children only under the supreme authority of God. The third head of honor is that children should take care of their parents, and be ready and diligent in all their duties towards them.

RIGHTFUL HONOR

Honor your father and your mother, so that you may live long in the land the LORD your God is giving you. —Exodus 20:12, NIV

The end of this commandment is that, since the Lord takes pleasure in the preservation of his own ordinance, the degrees of dignity appointed by him must be held inviolable. The sum of the commandment, therefore, will be that we are to look up to those whom the Lord has set over us, yielding them honor, gratitude, and obedience. Hence, it follows that every thing in the way of contempt, ingratitude, or disobedience is forbidden—for the term honor has this extent of meaning in Scripture.

To those whom he raises to eminences he communicates his authority, in so far as necessary to maintain their station. The titles of Father, God, and Lord all meet in him alone; hence whenever any one of them is mentioned, our mind should be impressed with the same feeling of reverence. therefore, those to whom he imparts such titles, he distinguishes by some small spark of his brilliance, so as to entitle them to honor, each in his own place. In this way, we must consider that our earthly father possesses something of a divine nature in him—because there is some reason for his bearing a divine title—and that he who is our prince and ruler is admitted to some communion of honor with God.

Wherefore, we ought to have no doubt that the Lord here lays down this universal rule: Knowing how every individual is set over us by his appointment, we should pay him reverence, gratitude, obedience, and every duty in our power. And it makes no difference whether those on whom the honor is conferred are deserving or not. Be they what they may, the Almighty, by conferring their station upon them, shows that he would have them honored.

The commandment specifies the reverence due to those to whom we owe our being. This Nature herself should in some measure teach us. For they are monsters, and not men, who petulantly and contumeliously violate the paternal authority. Hence, the Lord orders all who rebel against their parents to be put to death, they being unworthy of the light in paying no deference to those to whom they are indebted for beholding it.

THE SIXTH COMMANDMENT:
NONVIOLENCE

You shall not murder. —*Exodus 20:13, NIV*

The sum of this commandment is that we should not unjustly do violence to any one. In order, however, that God can more completely restrain us from all injury of others, he sets out one particular form of it, which is abhorrent to human sense; for we all detest murder so as to recoil from those whose hands are polluted with blood, as if they carried disease with them. Undoubtedly God would have the remains of his image, which still shines forth in humans, to continue in some sense, so that all might feel that every homicide is an offense against God.

There are, consequently, two parts in the commandment: First, that we should not annoy, or oppress, or be at odds with anyone; and, secondly, that we should not only live at peace with others, without starting fights, but also should aid, as far as we can, the miserable who are unjustly oppressed, and should endeavor to defy the wicked, lest they should injure humans as the urge strikes them. Christ, therefore, in explaining the true sense of the Law, not only pronounces those who have committed murder to be sinners, but also that "anyone who is angry with his brother will be subject to judgment. Again, anyone who says to his brother, 'Raca,' is answerable to the Sanhedrin. But anyone who says, 'You fool!' will be in danger of the fire of hell" (Matt. 5:22). For Jesus does not, as some have ignorantly supposed, make some new law, but shows the folly and perversity of those interpreters of the Law who only insist on the external appearance, the husk of things.

By this law also, God exhorts his people to exercise the duties of humanity towards brute animals, in order that they may be the more ready to assist their siblings. Here God had another intention, that believers should testify their forgiveness of their enemies by being merciful to their animals. If it had been simply said that our enemies were to be helped, and that we must deal with them by acts of kindness to overcome their ill-will, all cruelty would have been condemned enough; but when God commands us not only to help our enemies but would also have us exercise these kindnesses to their very beasts, God more emphatically and strongly expresses how very far removed from hatred and the desire of revenge he desires his children to be.

PROTECTING BOTH THE BODY AND THE SOUL

You shall not murder. —Exodus 20:13, NIV

The purpose of this commandment, is that since the Lord has bound the whole human race by a kind of unity, the safety of all ought to be considered as entrusted to each. In general, therefore, all violence and injustice, and every kind of harm from which our neighbor's body suffers, is prohibited. Accordingly, we are required faithfully to do what in us lies to defend the life of our neighbor—to promote whatever tends to his tranquility, to be vigilant in warding off harm, and to assist in removing danger when it comes.

Remembering that the divine Lawgiver thus speaks, consider that he requires you to apply the same rule in regulating your mind. It were ridiculous that he, who sees the thoughts of the heart and has special regard to them, should train the body only to rectitude. Therefore, this commandment prohibits the murder of the heart, and requires a sincere desire to preserve our brother's life. Indeed, the hand commits the murder, but the mind, under the influence of wrath and hatred, conceives it. How can you be angry with your brother, without passionately longing to do him harm? If you must not be angry with him, neither must you hate him—hatred being nothing but longstanding anger.

Man is both the image of God and our flesh. Wherefore, if we would not violate the image of God, we must hold the person of man sacred.

To be clear of the crime of murder, it is not enough to refrain from shedding man's blood. If in act you perpetrate, if in endeavor you plot, if in wish and design you conceive what is adverse to another's safety, you have the guilt of murder. On the other hand, if you do not according to your means and opportunity study to defend his safety, by that inhumanity you violate the law. And if the safety of the body is so carefully provided for, we may hence infer how much care and exertion is due to the safety of the soul, which is of immeasurably higher value in the sight of God.

THE SEVENTH COMMANDMENT:

PRUDENCE VS. ADULTERY

You shall not commit adultery. —Exodus 20:14, NIV
Rather, clothe yourselves with the Lord Jesus Christ, and do not think
about how to gratify the desires of the sinful nature.
—Romans 13:14, NIV

Although one kind of impurity is referred to, it is sufficiently plain, from the principle laid down, that believers are generally exhorted to chastity. Furthermore, it is inarguable that God will never approve or excuse what the common sense of humankind declares to be obscene. For, although lewdness has everywhere been rampant in every age, still the opinion could never be utterly extinguished that fornication is a scandal and a sin. We know how unbridled was the licentiousness of the heathen; for, although God never allowed all shame to be extinguished together with purity, still, respect for what was right was stifled, and they avoided facing the grossness of the sin by vulgarity and scurrilous jokes.

Since, then, the minds of all humans were made stupid by indulgence, it was needful to arouse them by declaring the atrocity of the sin, so that they might learn to beware of all pollution. Unbridled lusts aren't condemned here alone, but God also instructs his people to cherish modesty and chastity. The sum is that those who desire to approve themselves to God should be pure "from everything that contaminates" (2 Cor. 7:1).

As long as we carry our flesh upon us, we cannot cast away every care for it; for though our thoughts be on heaven, we sojourn still on earth. The things, then, which belong to the body must be taken care of, but only so far as they are helps to us in our pilgrimage, and not that they may make us to forget our true country. Even heathens have said that a few things are enough to satisfy nature, but the appetites of the human body are insatiable. Everyone, then, who wishes to satisfy the desires of the flesh, must necessarily not only fall into, but be immersed, in a vast and deep gulf.

GUARDING PURITY

You shall not commit adultery. —*Exodus 20:14, NIV*

The purpose of this commandment is that, as God loves chastity and purity, we ought to guard against all uncleanness. Therefore, the substance of the commandment is that we must not defile ourselves with any impurity or libidinous excess. To this corresponds the affirmative, that we must regulate every part of our conduct chastely and abstinently. The thing expressly forbidden is adultery, to which lust naturally tends, that its filthiness may dispose us to abominate every form of lust. The law under which man was created was not to lead a life of solitude but rather to enjoy a help-meet for him, and ever since he fell under the curse the necessity for this mode of life is increased. Therefore, the Lord made the requisite provision for us in this respect by the institution of marriage, which, entered into under his authority, he has also sanctified with his blessing. Hence, it is evident that any mode of cohabitation different from marriage is cursed in his sight, and that the conjugal relation was ordained as a necessary means of preventing us from giving way to unbridled lust. Therefore, let us beware of yielding to indulgence, seeing we are assured that the curse of God lies on every man and woman cohabiting without marriage.

Virginity, I admit, is a virtue not to be despised. But since it is denied to some (and to others granted only for a season) those who are assailed by incontinence, and unable successfully to war against it, should retake themselves to the remedy of marriage and thus cultivate chastity in the way of their calling. Those incapable of self-restraint, if they apply not to the remedy allowed and provided for intemperance, war with God and resist his ordinance. And let no man tell me (as many in the present day do) that he can do all things God helping! The help of God is present only with those who walk in his ways (Ps. 91:14), that is, in his callings—from which all withdraw themselves who, omitting the remedies provided by God, vainly and presumptuously strive to struggle with and surmount their natural feelings. Our Lord affirms that continence is a special gift from God, and of the class of those which are not bestowed indiscriminately on the whole body of the Church, but only on a few of its members (Matt. 19:12).

THE EIGHTH COMMANDMENT:

GENEROSITY VS. THEFT

You shall not steal. —Exodus 20:15, NIV

Since kindness is the goal of the Law, we must seek the definition of theft from it. This, then, is the rule of charity: that everyone's rights should be safely preserved, and that none should do to another what he would not have done to himself. It follows, therefore, that not only are those thieves who secretly steal the property of others, but those also who seek for gain from others' losses, accumulate wealth by unlawful practices, and are more devoted to their private advantage than to equality. There is no difference between a person robbing her or his neighbor by fraud or by force. But, in order that God may better withhold his people from all fraudulent injustice, he uses the word "theft," which all naturally hate as something disgraceful. For we know how many coverings people use to bury their misdeeds, and not only so, but also how they convert their misdeeds into praise by false pretexts. Craftiness and cunning are called "prudence";

and someone is spoken of as wise and cautious for cleverly outdoing others, for taking in the simple, and subtly oppressing the poor. Since, therefore, the world boasts of vices as if they were virtues, and thus all people freely excuse themselves in sin, God wipes away all this gloss by pronouncing all unjust means of gain to be theft.

We must bear in mind also that an affirmative law is connected with the prohibition, because, even if we abstain from wrong-doing, we do not therefore satisfy God, who has put humans into mutual obligation to each other so that they may seek to benefit, care for, and help their neighbors. Thus God certainly lays down openhandedness and kindness, and the other duties that maintain human society; and hence, in order that we may not be condemned as thieves by God, we must endeavor, as far as possible to make our neighbor's advantage be promoted no less than our own.

GIVE EVERY MAN HIS DUE

You shall not steal. —*Exodus 20:15, NIV*

The purpose of this commandment is that, injustice being an abomination to God, we must render to every man his due. In substance, then, the commandment forbids us to long after other men's goods and, accordingly, requires every man to exert himself honestly in preserving his own. For we must consider that what each individual possesses has not fallen to him by chance, but by the distribution of the sovereign Lord of all, so that no one can pervert his means to bad purposes without committing a fraud on a divine dispensation. We know that all the ways by which we obtain possession of the goods and money of our neighbors through harm or deception is to be regarded as theft. Though they may be obtained by an action at law, a different decision is given by God. He sees the long train of deception by which the man of craft begins to lay nets for his more simple neighbor, until he entangles him in its meshes. He sees the harsh and cruel laws by which the more powerful oppresses and crushes the feeble. And he sees the enticements by which the more wily baits the hook for the less wary—though all these escape the judgment of man, and no awareness is taken of them. Nor is the violation of this commandment confined to money, or merchandise, or lands, but extends to every kind of right; for we defraud our neighbors to their hurt if we decline any of the duties which we are bound to perform towards them.

Therefore, we shall duly obey this commandment: if we study to acquire nothing but honest and lawful gain; if we long not to grow rich by injustice, nor to plunder our neighbor of his goods, that our own may thereby be increased; and if we hasten not to heap up wealth cruelly wrung from the blood of others. Let each of us consider how far he is bound in duty to others, and in good faith pay what we owe. In the same way, let the people pay all due honor to their rulers, submit patiently to their authority, obey their laws and orders, and decline nothing which they can bear without sacrificing the favor of God.

THE NINTH COMMANDMENT:

HONESTY

You shall not give false testimony against your neighbor.
—Exodus 20:16, NIV

lthough God seems only to prescribe that no one should go into court and lie publicly to injure the innocent, yet it is plain that the faithful are prohibited from all false accusations, and not only such as are circulated in the streets but also those which are stirred in private houses and secret corners. For it would be absurd, when God has already shown that he cares for the fortunes of human beings, for God to neglect their reputations, which are much more precious. Therefore, in whatever way we injure our neighbors by unjustly defaming them, we are accounted false witnesses before God.

We must now pass on from the prohibitive to the affirmative law. For it will not be enough for us to restrain our tongues from speaking evil, unless we are also kind and fair to our neighbors, candid interpreters of their acts and words, and do not allow them, as far as we can help, to be burdened with false accusations. Besides, God not only forbids us to invent accusations against the innocent, but also forbids us to give believability to reproaches

and bad reports about others out of malevolence or hatred. Some people may perhaps deserve their bad reputations, and we may truly accuse them of this or that; but if the reproach be the result of our anger, or if the accusation proceed from ill-will, it will be vain for us to excuse ourselves by saying that we have reported nothing but what is true.

In short, we must conclude that by these words a restraint is laid on all meanness of language which tends to bring disgrace on our siblings; and on all irritability also that causes their good name to suffer injury; and on all accusations which flow from hatred, or envy, or rivalry, or any other improper feeling. We must also go further and not be suspicious or too curious in observing the defects of others, for such eager curiosity betrays bad intentions, or at any rate bad dispositions. For, if love is not suspicious, he who condemns his neighbor falsely, or on trifling guesses, or who holds her or him in low esteem, undoubtedly sins against this commandment.

CULTIVATE THE TRUTH

You shall not give false testimony against your neighbor.
—Exodus 20:16, NIV

The purpose of the commandment is to cultivate genuine truth towards each other since God, who is truth, abhors falsehood. The sum, therefore, will be that we must not by malicious and false accusations injure our neighbor's name, or by falsehood impair his fortunes—in fine, that we must not injure any one from petulance, or a love of evil-speaking. To this prohibition corresponds the command that we must faithfully assist everyone, as far as in us lies, in asserting the truth, for the maintenance of his good name and his estate. Indeed, there can be no doubt that as in the previous commandment he prohibited cruelty, unchastity, and avarice, so here he prohibits falsehood. By malignant or vicious detraction, we sin against our neighbor's good name. By lying, sometimes even by casting a slur upon him, we injure him in his estate.

It makes no difference whether you suppose that formal and judicial testimony is here intended, or the ordinary testimony which is given in private conversation. For falsehood in a court of justice is always accompanied with perjury. But against perjury, insofar as it profanes and violates the name of God, there is a sufficient provision in the third commandment. Hence the legitimate observance of this precept consists in employing the tongue in the maintenance of truth, so as to promote both the good name and the prosperity of our neighbor. The equity of this is perfectly clear. For if a good name is more precious than riches, a man robbed of his good name is no less injured than if he were robbed of his goods; while, in the latter case, false testimony is sometimes not less injurious than robbery committed by the hand.

And yet it is strange, with what supine security men everywhere sin in this respect. Indeed, very few are found who do not notoriously labor under this disease—such is the envenomed delight we take both in prying into and exposing our neighbor's faults. He who forbids us to defame our neighbor's reputation by falsehood desires us to keep it untarnished in so far as truth will permit.

THE TENTH COMMANDMENT:

COVETING

Neither shalt thou desire thy neighbour's wife, neither shalt thou covet thy neighbour's house, his field, or his manservant, or his maidservant, his ox, or his ass, or any thing that is thy neighbour's.
—Deuteronomy 5:21, KJV

God had already sufficiently forbidden us to set our hearts on the property of others, to attempt the seduction of their spouses, or to seek for gain at another's loss and inconvenience. Now, as he lists off oxen and asses, and all other things as well as wives and servants, it is very clear that his Law is directed to the same things, but in a different way: to restrain all ungodly desires either of fornication or theft. Why does God now forbid in his people the lust for theft and fornication? For it seems to be a superfluous repetition. Still, on the other hand, it must be remembered that, although it was God's plan by the whole Law to arouse people's feelings to sincere obedience of it, yet such is their hypocrisy and indifference that it was necessary to stimulate them more sharply and to push them harder, lest they should seek loopholes. It was not then in vain that God, having dealt with piety and justice, gave a separate warning: that they were not only to abstain from evil doing but also that what he had commanded should be performed with the sincere affection of the heart. Hence Paul assumes from this commandment that the whole "Law is spiritual" (Rom. 7:7, 14), because God, by his condemnation of lust, sufficiently showed that he not only asks obedience from our hands and feet but also put restraint upon our minds, lest they should desire to do what is unlawful.

Therefore, we now see that there is nothing inappropriate in the general condemnation of envy by a distinct commandment. For after God has broadly and commonly laid down rules for moral integrity, at length God ascends to the fountain itself, and at the same time, as it were, points out with his finger the root from which evil and corrupt fruits spring forth. I admit, indeed, that the corrupt thoughts which arise spontaneously, and so also vanish before they affect the mind, do not come into account before God; yet, even though we do not actually acquiesce in the evil desire, still, if it affects us pleasantly, it is sufficient to render us guilty.

LET CHARITY REGULATE YOUR THOUGHTS

You shall not covet your neighbor's house. You shall not covet your neighbor's wife, or his manservant or maidservant, his ox or donkey, or anything that belongs to your neighbor. —Exodus 20:17, NIV

he purpose of the command is this: Since the Lord would have the whole soul pervaded with love, any feeling of an adverse nature must be banished from our minds. The sum, therefore, will be that no thought be permitted to insinuate itself into our minds, and inhale them with a noxious desire tending to our neighbor's loss. To this corresponds the contrary precept that every thing which we conceive, deliberate, will, or design, be conjoined with the good and advantage of our neighbor.

But here it seems we are met with a great and perplexing difficulty. For if it was correctly said elsewhere that (under the words "adultery" and "theft") lust and an intention to injure and deceive are prohibited, it may seem superfluous afterwards to employ a separate commandment to prohibit a covetous desire of our neighbor's goods. The difficulty will easily be removed by distinguishing between design and covetousness. Design, such as we have spoken of in the previous commandments, is a deliberate consent of the will, after passion has taken possession of the mind. Covetousness may exist without such deliberation and assent, when the mind is only stimulated and tickled by vain and perverse objects.

As the Lord previously ordered that charity should regulate our wishes, studies, and actions, so he now orders us to regulate the thoughts of the mind in the same way, that none of them may be depraved and distorted, so as to give the mind a contrary bent. Having forbidden us to turn and incline our mind to wrath, hatred, adultery, theft, and falsehood, he now forbids us to give our thoughts the same direction. He requires a mind so admirably arranged as not to be prompted in the slightest degree contrary to the law of love.

THE CHARACTER OF THE LAW

Behold, I have taught you statutes and judgments, even as the LORD my God commanded me, that ye should do so in the land whither ye go to possess it. Keep therefore and do them; for this is your wisdom and your understanding in the sight of the nations, which shall hear all these statutes, and say, Surely this great nation is a wise and understanding people. —Deuteronomy 4:5–6

In the Law, human life is instructed not merely in outward decency but in inward spiritual righteousness. Though none can deny this, yet very few duly attend to it because they do not consider the Lawgiver, by whose character that of the Law must also be determined. God, whose eye nothing escapes and who regards not the outward appearance so much as purity of heart, under the prohibition of murder, adultery, and thefts includes wrath, hatred, lust, covetousness, and all other things of a similar nature. Being a spiritual Lawgiver, he speaks to the soul not less than the body. The murder which the soul commits is wrath and hatred; the theft, covetousness and avarice; and the adultery, lust.

It may be alleged that human laws have respect to intentions and wishes, and not fortuitous events. They consider the animosity with which the act was done, but do not scrutinize the secret thoughts. Accordingly, their demand is satisfied when the hand merely refrains from transgression.

On the contrary, the law of heaven being enacted for our minds, the first thing necessary to a due observance of the Law is to put them under restraint. But the generality of men, even while they are most anxious to conceal their disregard of the Law, only frame their hands and feet and other parts of their body to some kind of observance, but in the meanwhile keep the heart utterly estranged from everything like obedience. With their whole soul they breathe out slaughter, boil with lust, cast a greedy eye at their neighbor's property, and in wish devour it. Here the principal thing which the Law requires is wanting, Paul strenuously protests, when he declares that the "law is spiritual" (Rom. 7:14) —intimating that it not only demands the homage of the soul, and mind, and will but also requires an angelic purity which, purified from all filthiness of the flesh, savors only of the Spirit.

ONLY ONE INTERCESSOR

This is good, and pleases God our Savior, who wants all men to be saved and to come to a knowledge of the truth. For there is one God and one mediator between God and men, the man Christ Jesus, who gave himself as a ransom for all men. —1 Timothy 2:3–6, NIV

If we attribute prayer to the saints who having died in the body live in Christ, let us not imagine that they have any other way of appealing to God than through Christ, who alone is the way, or that their prayers are accepted by God in any other name. Wherefore, since the Scripture calls us away from all others to Christ alone, since our heavenly Father is pleased to gather together all things in him, it would be the extreme of stupidity, aside from madness, to attempt to obtain access by means of others, so as to be drawn away from him without whom access cannot be obtained.

If we appeal to the consciences of all who take pleasure in the intercession of saints, we shall find that their only reason for it is that they are filled with anxiety, as if they supposed that Christ were insufficient or too rigorous. By this anxiety they dishonor Christ and rob him of his title of sole Mediator—a title which, being given him by the Father as his special privilege, ought not to be transferred to any other. By so doing they obscure the glory of his nativity and make void his cross; in short, they divest and defraud of due praise everything which he did or suffered, since all which he did and suffered goes to show that he is and ought to be deemed sole Mediator.

At the same time, they reject the kindness of God in manifesting himself to them as a Father, for he is not their Father if they do not recognize Christ as their brother. This they plainly refuse to do if they think not that he feels for them a brother's affection—affection than which none can be more gentle or tender. Wherefore Scripture offers him alone, sends us to him, and establishes us in him. "He," says Ambrose, "is our mouth by which we speak to the Father; our eye by which we see the Father; our right hand by which we offer ourselves to the Father. Save by his intercession neither we nor any saints have any intercourse with God" (Ambros. Lib. de Isaac et Anima).

PRAISE AND THANKSGIVING

Save us, O LORD our God, and gather us from the nations, that we may give thanks to your holy name and glory in your praise.
—Psalm 106:47, NIV

though prayer is properly confined to vows and supplications, yet so strong is the affinity between petition and thanksgiving that both may be conveniently comprehended under one name. By prayer and request we pour out our desires before God, asking as well those things which tend to promote his glory and display his name, as the benefits which contribute to our advantage. By thanksgiving we duly celebrate his kindnesses toward us, ascribing to his liberality every blessing which enters into our lot. We have already described the greatness of our want, while experience itself proclaims the straits which press us on every side to be so numerous and so great that all have sufficient ground to send forth sighs and groans to God without intermission. For even should they be exempt from adversity, still the holiest ought to be stimulated—first by their sins and, secondly, by the innumerable assaults of temptation—to long for a remedy. The sacrifice of praise and thanksgiving can never be interrupted without guilt, since God never ceases to load us with favor upon favor, so as to force us to gratitude, however slow and sluggish we may be. In short, so great and widely diffused are the riches of his charity towards us, so marvelous and wondrous the miracles which we behold on every side, that we never can want a subject and materials for praise and thanksgiving.

Since all our hopes and resources are placed in God, so that neither our persons nor our interests can prosper without his blessing, we must constantly submit ourselves and our all to him. Then whatever we deliberate, speak, or do, should be deliberated, spoken, and done under his hand and will—in fine, under the hope of his assistance. And since he receives the honor which is due when he is acknowledged to be the author of all good, it follows that we ought continually to express our thankfulness, and that we have no right to use the benefits which proceed from his charity if we do not diligently proclaim his praise and give him thanks.

PUBLIC AND PRIVATE PRAYER

Yet a time is coming and has now come when the true worshipers will worship the Father in spirit and truth, for they are the kind of worshipers the Father seeks. —John 4:23, NIV

he who neglects to pray alone and in private, however caringly he frequents public meetings, there gives his prayers to the wind, because he defers more to the opinion of man than to the secret judgment of God. Still, lest the public prayers of the Church should be held in contempt, the Lord anciently bestowed upon them the most honorable designation, especially when he called the temple the "house of prayer" (Isa. 56:7). For by this expression he both showed that the duty of prayer is a principal part of his worship, and that to enable believers to engage in it with one consent his temple is set up before them as a kind of banner. A noble promise was also added, "Praise waits for thee, O God, in Zion: and unto thee shall the vow be performed" (Ps. 65:1). By these words the Psalmist reminds us that the prayers of the Church are never in vain, because God always furnishes his people with materials for a song of joy.

There can be no doubt that the same promise belongs to us—a promise which Christ sanctioned with his own lips, and which Paul declares to be perpetually in force.

As God in his word enjoins common prayer, so public temples are the places destined for the performance of them; hence those who refuse to join with the people of God in this observance have no ground for the pretext that they enter their chamber in order that they may obey the command of the Lord. For he who promises to grant whatsoever two or three assembled in his name shall ask (Matt. 18:20) declares that he by no means despises the prayers which are publicly offered up—provided there be no pretension, or appeasement at human applause, and provided there be a true and sincere affection in the secret recesses of the heart. Seeing we are the true temples of God, we must pray in ourselves if we would invoke God in his holy temple.

FROM FORETASTE TO FRUITION

But for you who revere my name, the sun of righteousness will rise with healing in its wings. And you will go out and leap like calves released from the stall. —Malachi 4:2, NIV

Since God was pleased to testify in ancient times by means of amends and sacrifices that he was a Father, and to set apart for himself a chosen people, he was doubtless known even then in the same character in which he is now fully revealed to us. Accordingly Malachi, having enjoined the Jews to attend to the Law of Moses (because after his death there was to be an interruption of the prophetical office), immediately after declares that the sun of righteousness should arise (Mal. 4:2); thus intimating that though the Law had the effect of keeping the pious in expectation of the coming Messiah, there was ground to hope for much greater light on his advent. For this reason, Peter, speaking of the ancient prophets, says, "Unto whom it was revealed that not unto themselves, but unto us, they did minister the things which are now reported unto you by them that have preached the gospel unto you, with the Holy Ghost sent down from heaven" (1 Pet. 1:12).

Not that the prophetical doctrine was useless to the ancient people, or unavailing to the prophets themselves, but that they did not obtain possession of the treasure which God has transmitted to us by their hands. The grace of which they testified is now set familiarly before our eyes. They had only a slight foretaste; to us is given a fuller fruition. Our Savior, accordingly, while he declares that Moses testified of him, admirably praises the superior measure of grace bestowed upon us (John 5:46). Addressing his disciples, he says, "Blessed are your eyes, for they see, and your ears, for they hear. For verily I say unto you, That many prophets and righteous men have desired to see those things which ye see, and have not seen them, and to hear those things which ye hear, and have not heard them" (Matt. 13:16; Luke 10:23). It is no small acclamation of the Gospel revelation that God has preferred us to holy men of old, so much distinguished for piety.

THE GOSPEL AND DOCTRINE OF FAITH

Be thou partaker of the afflictions of the gospel according to the power of God; Who hath saved us, and called us with an holy calling, ... according to his own purpose and grace, which was given us in Christ Jesus before the world began, But is now made manifest by the appearing of our Savior Jesus Christ, who hath abolished death, and hath brought life and immortality to light through the gospel.
—2 Timothy 1:8–10

by the gospel, I take that to mean the clear manifestation of the mystery of Christ. I confess, indeed, that inasmuch as the term gospel is applied by Paul to the doctrine of faith (2 Tim. 4:10), it includes all the promises by which God reconciles men to himself and which occur throughout the Law. For Paul there opposes faith to those terrors which vex and torment the conscience when salvation is sought by means of works. Hence it follows that Gospel, taken in a large sense, comprehends the evidences of mercy and paternal favor which God bestowed on the Patriarchs.

Still, by way of excellence, it is applied to the promulgation of the grace manifested in Christ. This is not only founded on general use, but has the sanction of our Savior and his Apostles. Hence it is described as one of his peculiar characteristics that he preached the gospel of the kingdom (Matt. 4:23; 9:35; Mark 1:14). Mark, in his preface to the gospel, calls it "The beginning of the gospel of Jesus Christ." There is no use of collecting passages to prove what is already perfectly known. Christ at his advent "brought life and immortality to light through the gospel" (2 Tim. 1:10).

Paul does not mean by these words that the Fathers were plunged in the darkness of death before the Son of God became incarnate; but he claims for the Gospel the honorable distinction of being a new and extraordinary kind of embassy, by which God fulfilled what he had promised, these promises being realized in the person of the Son. For though believers have at all times experienced the truth of Paul's declaration that "all the promises of God in him are yea and amen" (inasmuch as these promises were sealed upon their hearts), yet because he has in his flesh completed all the parts of our salvation, this vivid manifestation of realities was justly entitled to this new and special distinction.

LAW AND THE GOSPEL

Now to him that is of power to stablish you according to my gospel, and the preaching of Jesus Christ, according to the revelation of the mystery, which was kept secret since the world began, But now is made manifest, and by the scriptures of the prophets, according to the commandment of the everlasting God, made known to all nations for the obedience of faith. —*Romans 16:25–26*

We see the error of those who, in comparing the Law with the Gospel, represent it merely as a comparison between the merit of works and the gratuitous imputation of righteousness. The contrast thus made is by no means to be rejected, because by the term "Law" Paul frequently understands that rule of holy living in which God exacts what is his due—giving no hope of life unless we obey in every respect and, on the other hand, denouncing a curse for the slightest failure. This Paul does when showing that we are freely accepted of God, and accounted righteous by being pardoned, because that obedience of the Law to which the reward is promised is nowhere to be found. Hence he appropriately represents the righteousness of the Law and the Gospel as opposed to each other. But the Gospel has not succeeded the whole Law in such a sense as to introduce a different method of salvation. It rather confirms the Law, and proves that everything which it promised is fulfilled. What was shadow, it has made substance.

When Christ says that the Law and the Prophets were until John, he does not consign the fathers to the curse, which, as the slaves of the Law, they could not escape. He intimates that they were only instilled with the rudiments, and remained far beneath the height of the Gospel doctrine. Accordingly Paul, after calling the Gospel "the power of God unto salvation to every one that believeth," adds that it was "witnessed by the Law and the Prophets" (Rom. 1:16; 3:21). Though he describes "the preaching of Jesus Christ" as "the revelation of the mystery which was kept secret since the world began," he modifies the expression by adding that it is "now made manifest...by the scriptures of the prophets" (Rom. 16:25–26). Hence we infer that when the whole Law is spoken of, the Gospel differs from it only in respect of clearness of manifestation.

THE BEST MODEL OF BELIEVING

The LORD had said to Abram, "Leave your country, your people and your father's household and go to the land I will show you.
—*Genesis 12:1, NIV*

braham alone ought to be to us equal to tens of thousands if we consider his faith, which is set before us as the best model of believing, to whose race also we must be held to belong in order that we may be the children of God. What could be more absurd than that Abraham should be the father of all the faithful, and not even occupy the meanest corner among them? He cannot be denied a place in the list; nay, he cannot be denied one of the most honorable places in it, without the destruction of the whole Church.

Now, as regards his experience in life, the moment he is called by the command of God, he is torn away from friends, parents, and country objects in which the chief happiness of life is deemed to consist, as if it had been the fixed purpose of the Lord to deprive him of all the sources of enjoyment. No sooner does he enter the land in which he was ordered to dwell than he is driven from it by famine. What is the happiness of inhabiting a land where you must so often suffer from hunger, nay, perish from famine, unless you flee from it? Wherever he goes, he meets with savage-hearted neighbors, who will not even allow him to drink of the wells which he has dug with great labor. At length Isaac is born, but in return, the first-born Ishmael is displaced and almost hostilely driven forth and abandoned. Isaac remains alone, and the good man, now worn out with age, has his heart upon him when shortly after he is ordered to offer him up in sacrifice. What can the human mind conceive more dreadful than for the father to be the murderer of his son? Had he been slain by some stranger, this would, indeed, have been much worse than natural death. But all these calamities are little compared with the murder of him by his father's hand.

Let it not be said that he was not so very distressed, because he at length escaped from all these tempests.

PROMISES FULFILLED

As for me, I will behold thy face in righteousness: I shall be satisfied,
when I awake, with thy likeness. —Psalm 17:15, NIV

Let us learn that the holy fathers under the Old Testament were not ignorant that in this world God seldom or never gives his servants the fulfillment of what is promised them, and therefore has directed their minds to his sanctuary, where the blessings not exhibited in the present shadowy life are treasured up for them. This sanctuary was the final judgment of God, which (as they could not at all discern it by the eye) they were contented to apprehend by faith. Inspired with this confidence, they doubted not that, whatever might happen in the world, a time would at length arrive when the divine promises would be fulfilled.

This is attested by such expressions as these: "As for me, I will behold thy face in righteousness: I shall be satisfied, when I awake, with thy likeness" (Ps. 17:15). "I am like a green olive tree in the house of God" (Ps. 52:8). And, "The righteous shall flourish like the palm tree: he shall grow like a cedar in Lebanon. Those that be planted in the house of the LORD shall flourish in the courts of our God. They shall still bring forth fruit in old age; they shall be fat and flourishing" (Ps. 92:12–14). He had exclaimed a little before "O Lord, how great are thy works! and thy thoughts are very deep." "When the wicked spring as the grass, and when all the workers of iniquity do flourish: it is that they shall be destroyed for ever."

Where was this splendor and beauty of the righteous, unless when the appearance of this world was changed by the manifestation of the heavenly kingdom? Lifting their eyes to the eternal world, they despised the momentary hardships and calamities of the present life and confidently broke out into these exclamations: "He shall never suffer the righteous to be moved. But thou, O God, shall bring them down into the pit of destruction: bloody and deceitful men shall not live out half their days" (Ps. 55:22–23).

GOD WITH US

Therefore, since we have a great high priest who has gone through the heavens, Jesus the Son of God, let us hold firmly to the faith we profess. For we do not have a high priest who is unable to sympathize with our weaknesses, but we have one who has been tempted in every way, just as we are—yet was without sin. —Hebrews 4:14–15, NIV

It deeply concerned us that he who was to be our Mediator should be very God and very man. Our iniquities—like a cloud intervening between him and us—having utterly alienated us from the kingdom of heaven, none but a person reaching to him could be the medium of restoring peace. But who could thus reach to him? Could any of the sons of Adam? All of them, with their parents, shuddered at the sight of God. Could any of the angels? They had need of a head, by connection with which they might adhere to their God entirely and inseparably. What then? The case was certainly desperate, if the Godhead itself did not descend to us, it being impossible for us to ascend.

Thus the Son of God properly became our Emmanuel, the God with us—and in such a way that by mutual union his divinity and our nature might be combined. Otherwise, neither was the proximity near enough, nor the affinity strong enough, to give us hope that God would dwell with us, so great was the repugnance between our pollution and the spotless purity of God. Had man remained free from all taint, he was of too humble a condition to penetrate to God without a Mediator. What, then, must it have been, when by fatal ruin he was plunged into death and hell, defiled by so many stains, made loathsome by corruption—in fine, overwhelmed with every curse?

Therefore, it is not without cause, that Paul, when he would set forth Christ as the Mediator, distinctly declares him to be man, "one Mediator between God and man, the man Christ Jesus" (1 Tim. 2:5). He might have called him God, or at least, omitting to call him God, he might also have omitted to call him man. But because the Spirit, speaking by his mouth, knew our infirmity, he opportunely provides for it by the most appropriate remedy: setting the Son of God familiarly before us as one of ourselves. Therefore, that no one may feel perplexed where to seek the Mediator or by what means to reach him, the Spirit reminds us that he is near, nay, beside us, inasmuch as he is our flesh.

SON OF GOD AND SON OF MAN

And if children, then heirs; heirs of God, and joint-heirs with Christ; if so be that we suffer with him, that we may be also glorified together.
—Romans 8:17

The work to be performed by the Mediator was of no common description. It was this: to restore us to the divine favor, so as to make us, instead of sons of men, sons of God; instead of heirs of hell, heirs of a heavenly kingdom. Who could do this unless the Son of God should also become the Son of man, and so receive what is ours as to transfer to us what is his, making that which is his by nature to become ours by grace? Relying on this earnest, we trust that we are the sons of God, because the natural Son of God assumed to himself a body of our body, flesh of our flesh, bones of our bones, that he might be one with us. He declined not to take what was peculiar to us, that he might in his turn extend to us what was peculiarly his own, and thus might be in common with us both Son of God and Son of man. Hence that holy brotherhood which he commends with his own lips, when he says, "I ascend to my Father, and your Father, to my God, and your God" (John 20:17).

In this way, we have a sure inheritance in the heavenly kingdom, because the only Son of God, to whom it entirely belonged, has adopted us as his brethren; and if brethren—then partners with him in the inheritance (Rom. 8:17). Moreover, it was especially necessary for this cause also that he who was to be our Redeemer should be truly God and man. It was his to swallow up death; who but Life could do so? It was his to conquer sin; who could do so save Righteousness itself? It was his to put to flight the powers of the air and the world; who could do so but the mighty power superior to both? But who possesses life and righteousness, and the dominion and government of heaven, but God alone? Therefore, God, in his infinite mercy, having determined to redeem us, became himself our Redeemer in the person of his only begotten Son.

LOOK TO HEAVEN

He that loveth his life shall lose it; and he that hateth his life in this world shall keep it unto life eternal. —John 12:25

his expression is used comparatively because we ought to despise life, so far as it hinders us from living to God for if meditation on the heavenly life were the prevailing sentiment in our hearts, the world would have no influence in detaining us. Hence, too, we obtain a reply to an objection that might be urged. "Many persons, through despair, or for other reasons, and chiefly from weariness of life, kill themselves; and yet we will not say that such persons provide for their own safety, while others are hurried to death by ambition, who also rush down to ruin."

But here Christ speaks expressly of that hatred or contempt of this fading life, which believers derive from the contemplation of a better life. Consequently, whoever does not look to heaven has not yet learned in what way life must be preserved. Besides, this lat-

> "whoever does not look to heaven has not yet learned in what way life must be preserved"

ter clause was added by Christ, in order to strike terror into those who are too desirous of the earthly life; for if we are overwhelmed by the love of the world, so that we cannot easily forget it, it is impossible for us to go to heaven. But since the Son of God arouses us so violently, it would be the height of folly to sleep a mortal sleep.

GOD'S WILL RULES

Now is my soul troubled, and what shall I say? Father, save me from this hour; but for this cause came I into this hour. —John 12:27

ow, if the feelings of Christ, which were free from all sin, needed to be restrained in this manner, how earnestly ought we to apply to this object, since the numerous affections which spring from our flesh are so many enemies to God in us! Let the godly, therefore, persevere in doing violence to themselves, until they have denied themselves.

It must also be observed that we ought to restrain not only those affections which are directly contrary to the will of God, but those which hinder the progress of our calling—though, in other respects, they are not wicked or sinful. To make this more fully evident, we ought to place in the first rank the will of God; in the second, the will of man pure and entire, such as God gave to Adam, and such as was in Christ; and, lastly, our own, which is infected by the contagion of sin. The will of God is the rule to which every thing that is inferior ought to be subjected. Now, the pure will of nature will not of itself rebel against God; but man, though he were wholly formed to righteousness, would meet with many obstructions, unless he subject his affections to God.

Christ, therefore, had but one battle to fight, which was to cease to fear what he naturally feared, as soon as he perceived that the pleasure of God was otherwise. We, on the other hand, have a twofold battle; for we must struggle with the obstinacy of the flesh. The consequence is that the most valiant combatants never vanquish without being wounded.

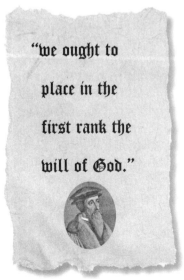

"we ought to place in the first rank the will of God."

THE PROFITABLE GOSPEL

Jesus cried and said, He that believeth on me, believeth not on me, but on him that sent me. —John 12:44

The object of Christ, in this statement, is to encourage his followers to a proper and unshaken steadfastness of faith. But it contains also an implied reproof, by which he intended to correct that perverse fear. The cry is expressive of vehemence; for it is not a simple doctrine, but an exhortation intended to excite them more powerfully. The statement amounts to this: Faith in Christ does not rely on any mortal man, but on God; for it finds in Christ nothing but what is divine, or rather, it beholds God in his face. Hence he infers that it is foolish and unreasonable for faith to be wavering or doubtful, for it is impossible to offer a greater insult to God than not to rely on his truth.

Who is it then that has duly profited by the Gospel? It is he who, relying on this confidence—that he does not believe men but God—quietly and steadily contends against all the machinations of Satan. If, then, we would render to God the

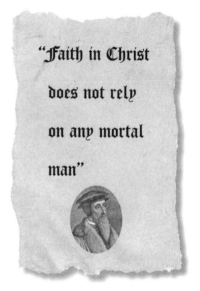

"Faith in Christ does not rely on any mortal man"

honor due to him, we must learn to remain firm in faith, not only though the world were shaken, but even though Satan should disturb and overturn all that is under heaven.

Believers are said "not to believe on Christ," when they do not fix their whole attention on his human countenance. Comparing himself with the Father, he bids us look at the power of God; for the weakness of the flesh has no firmness in itself.

CONVERSION OF THE WILL

A new heart also will I give you, and a new spirit will I put within you: and I will take away the stony heart out of your flesh, and I will give you an heart of flesh. And I will put my spirit within you, and cause you to walk in my statutes, and ye shall keep my judgments, and do them. —Ezekiel 36:26–27, NIV

Since the Lord, in bringing assistance, supplies us with what is lacking, the nature of that assistance will immediately make manifest its converse: our extreme poverty. When the Apostle says to the Philippians, "Being confident of this very thing, that he which has begun a good work in you, will perform it until the day of Jesus Christ" (Phil. 1:6), there cannot be a doubt that, by the good work thus begun, he means the very commencement of conversion in the will. God, therefore, begins the good work in us by exciting in our hearts a desire, a love, and a study of righteousness, or (to speak more correctly) by turning, training, and guiding our hearts toward righteousness; and he completes this good work by confirming us with perseverance.

But if anyone should complain that the good work thus begun by the Lord consists in aiding the will, which is in itself weak, the Spirit elsewhere declares what the will, when left to itself, is able to do. His words are, "A new heart also will I give you, and a new spirit will I put within you: and I will take away the stony heart out of your flesh, and I will give you a heart of flesh. And I will put my Spirit within you, and cause you to walk in my statutes, and ye shall keep my judgments, and do them" (Ezek. 36:26-27).

How can it be said that the weakness of the human will is aided so as to enable it to aspire to the choice of good, when the fact is that it must be wholly transformed and renovated? If it is like turning a stone into flesh when God turns us to the study of rectitude, everything proper to our own will is abolished, and that which succeeds in its place is wholly of God. I say the will is abolished, but not in so far as it is will, for in conversion everything essential to our original nature remains. I also say that it is created anew, not because the will then begins to exist, but because it is turned from evil to good.

DEPENDENT ON GOD'S GRACE

Create in me a clean heart, O God; and renew a right spirit within me. —Psalm 51:10, NIV

Solomon prays that the Lord may "incline our hearts unto him, to walk in his ways, and keep his commandments" (1 Kings 8:58), implying that our heart is perverse and naturally indulges in rebellion against the divine Law until it is turned. It is said in the Psalms, "Incline my heart unto thy testimonies" (Ps. 119:36). Feeling for the time that he was deprived of directing grace, David prays, "Create in me a clean heart, O God; and renew a right spirit within me" (Ps. 51:10). Speaking in the person of a man alienated from God, he properly prays for the blessings which God bestows upon his elect in regeneration. Accordingly, like one dead, he desires to be created anew, so as to become, instead of a slave of Satan, an instrument of the Holy Spirit. Strange and monstrous are the longings of our pride.

If arrogance did not stand in the way, we could not overlook the clear testimony which Christ has borne to the production of his grace. Thus he said, "I am the true vine, and my Father is the husbandman....As the branch cannot bear fruit of itself, except it abide in the vine; no more can you, except you abide in me" (John 15:1, 4). If we can no more bear fruit of ourselves than a vine can bud when rooted up and deprived of moisture, there is no longer any room to ask what the aptitude of our nature is for good. There is no ambiguity in the conclusion, "For without me you can do nothing." He says not that we are too weak to be enough for ourselves; but, by reducing us to nothing, he excludes the idea of our possessing any, even the least ability. If, when bound to Christ, we bear fruit like the vine, which draws its vegetative power from the moisture of the ground, and the dew of heaven, and the fostering warmth of the sun, I see nothing in a good work, which we can call our own, without trenching upon what is due to God.

EFFECTUAL GRACE

It is written in the prophets, And they shall be all taught of God. Every man therefore that hath heard, and hath learned of the Father, cometh unto me. —John 6:45

The movement of the will is not of that description which was for many ages taught and believed—a movement which thereafter leaves us the choice to obey or resist it—but rather one which affects us efficaciously. We must, therefore, strongly disapprove the commonly repeated sentiment of Chrysostom, "Whom he draws, he draws willingly," insinuating that the Lord only stretches out his hand and waits to see whether we will be pleased to take his aid. We grant that, as man was originally constituted, he could incline to either side. But since he has taught us by his example how miserable a thing free will is if God works not in us, of what use to us was grace imparted in such scanty measure? Nay, by our own ingratitude, we obscure and impair divine grace.

The Apostle's doctrine is not that the grace of a good will is offered to us if we will accept of it, but that God himself is pleased so to work in us as to guide, turn, and govern our heart by his Spirit, and reign in it as his own possession. Ezekiel promises that a new spirit will be given to the elect, not merely that they may be able to walk in his precepts, but that they may really walk in them (Ezek. 11:19; 36:27). And the only meaning which can be given to our Savior's words, "Every man, therefore, that has heard and learned of the Father, comes unto me" (John 6:45), is that the grace of God is effectual in itself. Men are indeed to be taught that the favor of God is offered, without exception, to all who ask it; but since those only begin to ask whom heaven inspires by grace, even this minute portion of praise must not be withheld from him. It is the privilege of the elect to be regenerated by the Spirit of God, and then placed under his guidance and government.

FAVORED OF GOD

Then Hezekiah turned his face toward the wall, and prayed unto the LORD, And said, Remember now, O LORD, I beseech thee, how I have walked before thee in truth and with a perfect heart, and have done that which is good in thy sight. And Hezekiah wept sore.
—*Isaiah 38:2–3*

Sometimes the saints—in humbly appealing to God —seem to appeal to their own righteousness, as when David says, "Preserve my soul; for I am holy" (Ps. 86:2). Also Hezekiah, "Remember now, O LORD, I beseech thee how I have walked before thee in truth, and with a perfect heart, and have done that which is good in thy sight" (Isa. 38:2). All they mean by such expressions is that regeneration declares them to be among the servants and children to whom God declares he will show favor.

We have already seen how he declares by the Psalmist that his eyes "are upon the righteous, and his ears are open unto their cry" (Ps. 34:16), and again by the Apostle that "whatsoever we ask of him we obtain, because we keep his commandments" (John 3:22). In these passages he does not fix a value on prayer as a meritorious work, but seeks to establish the confidence of those who are conscious of an unwavering integrity and innocence, such as all believers should possess.

Those appeals in which the saints allude to their purity and integrity correspond to such promises that they may have, in their own experience, a manifestation of that which all the servants of God are made to expect. Thus they almost always use this mode of prayer when before God they compare themselves with their enemies, from whose injustice they long to be delivered by his hand.

When making such comparisons, there is no wonder that they bring forward their integrity and simplicity of heart, and that by the justice of their cause the Lord may be the more disposed to give them relief. We rob not the pious breast of the privilege of enjoying a consciousness of purity before the Lord, and thus feeling assured of the promises with which he comforts and supports his true worshippers, but we would have them to lay aside all thought of their own merits and find their confidence of success in prayer solely on the divine mercy.

FEAR AND FAVOR

But I, by your great mercy, will come into your house; in reverence will I bow down toward your holy temple. —Psalm 5:7, NIV

notwithstanding our being belittled and truly humbled, we should be animated to pray with the sure hope of succeeding. There is, indeed, an appearance of contradiction between two things—between a sense of the just vengeance of God and firm confidence in his favor. And yet they are in perfect accord, if it is the mere goodness of God that raises up those who are overwhelmed by their own sins.

For repentance and faith go hand in hand, being united by an indissoluble tie—the former causing terror, the latter joy—so in prayer they must both be present. This concurrence David expresses in a few words: "But as for me, I will come into thy house in the multitude of thy mercy, and in thy fear will I worship toward thy holy temple" (Ps. 5:7). Under the goodness of God he comprehends faith, at the same time not excluding fear; for not only does his majesty compel our reverence but also our own unworthiness rids us of all pride and confidence, and keeps us in fear. The confidence of which I speak is not one which frees the mind from all anxiety and soothes it with sweet and perfect rest; such rest is peculiar to those who, while all their affairs are flowing to a wish, are annoyed by no care, stung with no regret, agitated by no fear.

But the best stimulus which the saints have to prayer is when, in consequence of their own necessities, they feel the greatest lack of peace and are all but driven to despair, until faith seasonably comes to their aid; because in such straits the goodness of God so shines upon them that while they groan, burdened by the weight of present calamities, and tormented with the fear of greater, they yet trust to this goodness—and in this way both lighten the difficulty of endurance—and take comfort in the hope of final deliverance.

It is necessary that the prayer of the believer should be the result of both feelings, and exhibit the influence of both; while he groans under present and anxiously dreads new evils, he should at the same time have recourse to God, not at all doubting that God is ready to stretch out a helping hand to him.

ASSURANCE AND PRAYER

Let thy mercy, O LORD, be upon us, according as we hope in thee.
—Psalm 33:22

When we say that believers ought to feel firmly assured, our opponents think we are saying the most absurd thing in the world. But if they had any experience in true prayer, they would assuredly understand that God cannot be duly invoked without this firm sense of the divine benevolence. But as no man can well perceive the power of faith, without at the same time feeling it in his heart, what profit is there in disputing with men of this character, who plainly show that they have never had more than a vain imagination? The value and necessity of that assurance for which we contend is learned chiefly from prayer. Everyone who does not see this gives proof of a very stupid conscience.

Therefore, leaving those who are thus blinded, let us fix our thoughts on the words of Paul, who says that God can only be invoked by such as have obtained a knowledge of his mercy from the Gospel and feel firmly assured that that mercy is ready to be bestowed upon them. The only prayer acceptable to God is that which springs (if I may so express it) from this presumption of faith and is founded on the full assurance of hope. He might have been contented to use the simple name of faith, but he adds not only confidence but also liberty or boldness, and by this mark he might distinguish us from unbelievers—who indeed like us pray to God, but pray at random. Hence, the whole Church thus prays, "Let thy mercy O LORD, be upon us, according as we hope in thee" (Ps. 33:22). The same condition is set down by the Psalmist in another passage, "When I cry unto thee, then shall mine enemies turn back: this I know, for God is for me" (Ps. 56:9). Again, "In the morning will I direct my prayer unto thee, and will look up" (Ps. 5:3). From these words we gather that prayers are vainly poured out into the air unless accompanied with faith, in which, as from a watchtower, we may quietly wait for God.

THE PRECEPT AND THE PROMISE

Ask, and it shall be given you; seek, and ye shall find; knock, and it shall be opened unto you: For every one that asketh receiveth; and he that seeketh findeth; and to him that knocketh it shall be opened.
—Matthew 7:7–8

In enjoining us to pray, God convicts us of impious rebelliousness if we obey not. He could not give a more precise command than that which is contained in the psalms: "Call upon me in the day of trouble" (Ps. 50:15). But as there is no office of piety more frequently enjoined by Scripture, there is no occasion for here dwelling longer upon it.

"Ask," says our Divine Master, "and it shall be given you; seek, and ye shall find; knock, and it shall be opened unto you" (Matt. 7:7). Here, indeed, a promise is added to the precept, and this is necessary. For though all confess that we must obey the precept, yet the greater part would shun the invitation of God, did he not promise that he would listen and be ready to answer.

These two positions being laid down, it is certain that all who trivially allege that they are not to come to God direct-ly, are not only rebellious and disobedient but are also convicted of unbelief, inasmuch as they distrust the promises. Hypocrites, under a pretense of humility and modesty, proudly condemn the precept, as well as deny all credit to the gracious invitation of God—nay, rob him of a principal part of his worship. For when he rejected sacrifices, in which all holiness seemed to consist, he declared that the chief thing, which above all others is precious in his sight, is to be invoked in the day of necessity.

Therefore, when he demands that which is his own and urges us to readiness in obeying, no pretexts for doubt (how specious they may be) can excuse us. Hence, all the passages throughout Scripture in which we are commanded to pray are set up before our eyes as so many banners, to inspire us with confidence.

GOD'S DELIGHTFUL PROMISES

And it shall come to pass, that before they call, I will answer; and while they are yet speaking, I will hear. —Isaiah 65:24

t is strange that God's delightful promises affect us coldly, or scarcely at all, so that men prefer to wander up and down—forsaking the fountain of living waters—and hewing out to themselves broken cisterns—rather than embrace the divine liberality voluntarily offered to them (Jer. 2:13). "The name of the LORD," says Solomon, "is a strong tower; the righteous runs into it, and is safe" (Prov. 18:10). After predicting the fearful disaster which was at hand, Joel subjoins the following memorable sentence: "And it shall come to pass, that whosoever shall call on the name of the LORD shall be delivered" (Joel 2:32). This we know properly refers to the course of the Gospel.

Scarcely one in a hundred is moved to come into the presence of God, though he himself exclaims by Isaiah, "And it shall come to pass, that before they call, I will answer; and while they are yet speaking, I will hear" (Isa. 65:24). This

honor he elsewhere bestows upon the whole Church in general, as belonging to all the members of Christ: "He shall call upon me, and I will answer him; I will be with him in trouble; I will deliver him, and honor him" (Ps. 91:15).

However, as I already observed, my intention is not to enumerate all, but only to select some admirable passages as a specimen of how kindly God allures us to himself and how extreme our ingratitude must be when with such powerful motives our sluggishness still retards us. Wherefore, let these words always resound in our ears: "The LORD is nigh unto all them that call upon him, to all that call upon him in truth" (Ps. 145:18). Likewise those passages which we have quoted from Isaiah and Joel— in which God declares that his ear is open to our prayers, and that he is delighted as with a sacrifice of sweet savor when we cast our cares upon him— should continue to resound.

RIGHTEOUSNESS

And those he predestined, he also called; those he called, he also justified; those he justified, he also glorified. —Romans 8:30, NIV

Some say that unless virtue and vice proceed from free choice, it is absurd either to punish man or reward him. With regard to punishment, I answer that it is properly inflicted on those by whom the guilt is contracted. What matters it whether you sin with a free or an enslaved judgment, so long as you sin voluntarily, especially when man is proved to be a sinner because he is under the bondage of sin? In regard to the rewards of righteousness, is there any great absurdity in acknowledging that they depend on the kindness of God rather than our own merits? How often do we meet in Augustine with this expression, "God crowns not our merits but his own gifts; and the name of reward is given not to what is due to our merits, but to the recompense of grace previously bestowed"?

Some seem to think there is sharpness in the remark that there is no place at all for the mind if good works do not spring from free will as their proper source; but in thinking this so very unreasonable they are widely mistaken. Augustine does not hesitate uniformly to describe as necessary the very thing which they count it impious to acknowledge. Thus he asks, "What is human merit? He who came to bestow not due recompense but free grace, though himself free from sin, and the giver of freedom, found all men sinners" (Augustine in Ps. 31). Again, "You are nothing in yourself, sin is yours, merit God's. Punishment is your due; and when the reward shall come, God shall crown his own gifts, not your merits."

On what ground, then, are believers crowned? Because by the mercy of God, not their own exertions, they are predestinated, called, and justified. So away with the vain fear that unless free will stand there will no longer be any merit! "If thou didst receive it, why dost thou glory as if thou has not received it?" (1 Cor. 4:7). Everything is denied to free will for the very purpose of leaving no room for merit. And yet, as the beneficence and liberality of God are manifold and inexhaustible, the grace which he bestows upon us gives compensation as if the virtuous acts were our own.

DIVINE ADVICE

I will give them an undivided heart and put a new spirit in them; I will remove from them their heart of stone and give them a heart of flesh. Then they will follow my decrees and be careful to keep my laws.
—Ezekiel 11:19–20, NIV

though they would gladly evade divine advice, the ungodly are forced, whether they will or not, to feel its power. But its chief use is to be seen in the case of believers, in whom the Lord, while he always acts by his Spirit, also omits not the instrumentality of his Word, but employs it, and not without effect. Let this, then, be a standing truth: the whole strength of the godly consists in the grace of God, according to the words of the prophet, "I will give them one heart, and I will put a new spirit within you; and I will take the stony heart out of their flesh, and will give them a heart of flesh, that they may walk in my statutes" (Ezek. 11:19–20). If, in order to prepare us for the grace which enables us to obey divine advice, God seeks to employ divine advice, what is there in such an arrangement for you to carp and scoff at? Had divine advice and warning no other profit with the godly than to convince them of sin, they could not be deemed altogether useless. Now, when, by the Spirit of God acting within, they have the effect of inflaming their desire of good, of arousing them from lethargy, of destroying the pleasure and honeyed sweetness of sin (making it hateful and loathsome) who will presume to cavil at them as superfluous?

God works in his elect in two ways: inwardly by his Spirit and outwardly by his Word. By his Spirit illuminating their minds and training their hearts to the practice of righteousness, he makes them new creatures, while, by his Word, he stimulates them to long and seek for this renovation. In both, he exerts the might of his hand in proportion to the measure in which he dispenses them. The Word urges their consciences now, and will render them more inexcusable on the day of judgment. Thus, while declaring that none can come to him but those whom the Father draws and that the elect come after they have heard and learned of the Father (John 6:44–45), our Savior does not lay aside the office of teacher, but carefully invites those who must be taught inwardly by the Spirit before they can make any profit.

ELECTION'S PROGRESS

I speak not of you all; I know whom I have chosen; but that the Scripture may be fulfilled, He who eateth bread with me hath lifted up his heel against me. —John 13:18

This very circumstance—that they will persevere—he ascribes to their election; for the virtue of men, being frail, would tremble at every breeze and would be laid down by the feeblest stroke, if the Lord did not uphold it by his hand. But as he governs those whom he has elected, all the engines which Satan can employ will not prevent them from persevering to the end with unshaken firmness. And not only does he ascribe to election their perseverance, but likewise the commencement of their piety.

Whence does it arise that one man, rather than another, devotes himself to the Word of God? It is because he was elected. Again, whence does it arise that this man makes progress and continues to lead a good and holy life, but because the purpose of God is unchangeable, to complete the work which was begun by his hand? In short, this is the source of the distinction between the children of God and unbelievers: The former are drawn to salvation by the Spirit of adoption, while the latter are hurried to destruction by their flesh, which is under no restraint. Otherwise Christ might have said, "Know what kind of person each of you will be." But that they may not claim anything for themselves—but, on the contrary, may acknowledge that, by the grace of God alone and not by their own virtue—they differ from Judas, he places before them that election by free grace on which they are founded. Let us, therefore, learn that every part of our salvation depends on election.

79

A FIXED FAITH

Let not your heart be troubled—you believe in God, believe also in me.
—John 14:1

All acknowledge that we ought to believe in God, and this is an admitted principle to which all assent without contradiction; and yet there is scarce one in a hundred who actually believes it, not only because the naked majesty of God is at too great a distance from us but also because Satan interposes clouds of every description to hinder us from contemplating God. The consequence is that our faith, seeking God in his heavenly glory and inaccessible light, vanishes away; and even the flesh, of its own accord, suggests a thousand imaginations to turn away our eyes from beholding God in a proper manner.

The Son of God, then, who is Jesus Christ, holds out himself as the object to which our faith ought to be directed, and by means of which it will easily find that on which it can rest; for he is the true Immanuel, who answers us within, as soon as we seek him by faith. It is one of the

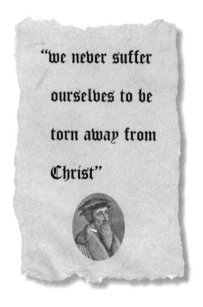

"we never suffer ourselves to be torn away from Christ"

leading articles of our faith— that our faith ought to be directed to Christ alone, that it may not wander through long windings, and that it ought to be fixed on him, that it may not waver in the midst of temptations. And this is the true proof of faith: when we never suffer ourselves to be torn away from Christ and from the promises which have been made to us in him.

A SURE PLEDGE

As the Father hath loved me, so have I loved you; abide in my love.
—John 15:9

It was rather the design of Christ to lay, as it were, in our bosom a sure pledge of God's love towards us. The love which is here mentioned must be understood as referring to us, because Christ testifies that the Father loves him, as he is the Head of the Church. And this is highly necessary for us; for he who, without a Mediator, inquires how he is loved by God, involves him in a labyrinth, in which he will neither discover the entrance nor the means of extricating himself.

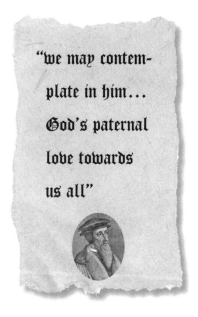

"we may contemplate in him... God's paternal love towards us all"

We ought therefore to cast our eyes on Christ, in whom will be found the testimony and pledge of the love of God; for the love of God was fully poured out on him, that from him it might flow to his members. He is distinguished by this title, that he is the beloved Son, in whom the will of the Father is satisfied (Matt. 3:17). But we ought to observe the end, which is that God may accept us in him. So, then, we may contemplate in him, as in a mirror, God's paternal love towards us all; because he is not loved apart, or for his own private advantage, but that he may unite us with him to the Father.

A CHRISTIAN EXAMPLE

At Caesarea there was a man named Cornelius, a centurion in what was known as the Italian Regiment. He and all his family were devout and God-fearing; he gave generously to those in need and prayed to God regularly. —Acts 10:1–2, NIV

Luke says that Cornelius was a godly man, and one who feared God and that like a good householder he took care to instruct his families. Then Luke praises him for the offices of love, because he was charitable toward all the people and, lastly, that he prayed to God continually. And because the Law is contained in two tables, Luke commends, in one place, Cornelius's godliness; then he goes into the second part, that Cornelius exercised the offices of love toward people. This is very profitable to notice, because we have, in the person, a way to live well described. Thus, in ordering the life well, let faith and religion be the foundation, which, if these be taken away, all other virtues are nothing else but smoke. Luke reckons up the fear of God and prayer as fruits and testimonies of godliness and of the worship of God. For religion cannot be separated from the fear of God and the reverence of him, neither can anyone be counted godly except those who,

acknowledging God Father and Lord, addict themselves wholly to him. Let every one of us exhort ourselves to persevere in prayer by the example of Cornelius.

Like Cornelius, our godliness ought so to appear to others, that we declare that we fear God by using generosity and justice. For from this fountain springs true and well-ordered generosity: If the troubles and sorrows of our brothers do move us to compassion; if, considering the unity which is amongst us, we foster and cherish them as we would cherish our own selves, and study to help them as we would help our own members; and if it be true that he was such an excellent mirror of godliness and holiness, even when he had but a small smattering of faith, ought not we to be ashamed who seem learned in the faith, and are yet so cold in the exercises of godliness? If a small sparkle of faith prevailed so much in him, what ought the full brightness of knowledge to work in us?

THE POOR IN SPIRIT

Blessed are the poor in spirit, for theirs is the kingdom of heaven.
—*Matthew 5:3, NIV*

Now let us see, in the first place, why Christ spoke to his disciples about true blessedness. We know that not only do most people, but even the educated, hold this error: that someone who is free from annoyance, attains all their wishes, and leads a joyful and easy life is happy. Therefore, in order to get his people used to bearing the cross, Christ exposes the mistaken opinion that those are happy who lead an easy and prosperous life according to the flesh. The only consolation which softens and even sweetens the bitterness of the cross and of afflictions is the conviction that we are happy in the midst of miseries; for our patience is blessed by the Lord, and will soon be followed by a happy result. This doctrine, I admit, is widely removed from the common opinion. But the disciples of Christ must learn the philosophy of placing their happiness beyond the world and above the affections of the flesh. Though human reason will never admit what is here taught by Christ, yet he does not bring forward any imaginary thing. Let us therefore remember that the main goal of Christ's discourse is to show that those who are oppressed by the reproaches of the wicked, and victims of various calamities, are not unhappy.

Many are pressed down by troubles, and yet continue to swell inwardly with pride and cruelty. But Christ pronounces those to be happy who, chastened and subdued by their problems, submit themselves wholly to God and, with inward humility, commend themselves to him for protection.

We see that Christ does not swell the minds of his own people by some untrue belief or harden them into unfeeling stubbornness, but leads them to keep the hope of eternal life and stimulates them to patience by assuring them that in this way they will pass into the heavenly kingdom of God. It deserves our attention that only those who are reduced to nothing in themselves, and rely on the mercy of God, are poor in spirit: For those who are broken or overwhelmed by despair complain against God, and this proves them to be of a proud and haughty spirit.

THE MEEK

Blessed are the meek, for they will inherit the earth.
—Matthew 5:5, NIV

y "the meek," he means persons of mild and gentle dispositions, who are not easily made angry by injuries, who are not ready to take offense, but are prepared to endure anything rather than do the same actions to wicked persons. When Christ promises the inheritance of the earth to the meek, we might think it silly. Those who angrily repel any attacks, and whose hands are always ready to revenge injuries, are more the persons who claim for themselves the dominion of the earth. And experience certainly shows that, the more kindly one endures their wickedness, the more bold and insolent it becomes. Hence arises the evil proverb that "We must howl with the wolves, because the wolves will immediately devour every one who makes himself a sheep." But Christ places his own protection and that of the Father, in contrast with the fury and violence of the wicked, and declares, on good grounds, that the meek will be the lords and heirs of the earth. The children of this world never think themselves safe, but they fiercely revenge the injuries that are done them and defend their life by the "weapons of war" (Ezek. 32:27). But as we must believe that Christ alone is the guardian of our life, all that remains for us is to "hide ourselves under the shadow of his wings" (Ps. 17:8). We must be sheep if we wish to be reckoned a part of his flock.

I first suggest that it be considered how much ferocious people are troubled by their own restlessness. While they lead so stormy a life, though they were a hundred times lords of the earth, though they possess all, they certainly possess nothing. For the children of God, on the other hand, I say that though they may not put their feet down on what is their own, they enjoy a quiet residence on the earth. And this is no imaginary possession; for they know that the earth, which they inhabit, has been granted to them by God. Besides, the hand of God is interposed to protect them against the violence and fury of the wicked. Though exposed to every species of attack, subject to the malice of evil people, surrounded by all kinds of danger, they are safe under the divine protection.

HUNGERING FOR RIGHTEOUSNESS

Blessed are those who hunger and thirst for righteousness, for they will be filled. Blessed are the merciful, for they will be shown mercy.
—*Matthew 5:6–7, NIV*

To "hunger and thirst" here is, I think, used as a figurative expression, and means to suffer poverty, to lack the necessaries of life, and even to be defrauded of one's rights. It might be paraphrased as: "Happy are they who, though their wishes are so moderate that they desire nothing but what is reasonable, are yet languishing, like persons who are famished with hunger." Though their distressing anxiety exposes them to the ridicule of others, yet it is a certain preparation for happiness, for at length they shall be satisfied. God will one day listen to their groans and satisfy their just desires. For to him, as we learn from the song of Mary, it belongs to fill the hungry with good things (Luke 1:53).

When Christ says, "Blessed are the merciful," this paradox, too, contradicts human judgment. The world reckons people to be happy when they give themselves no concern about the distresses of others, but worry about their own ease. Christ says that those are happy who are not only prepared to endure their own troubles but to take a share in the troubles of others who assist the wretched who willingly take part with those who are in distress who clothe themselves, as it were, with the same troubled emotions so that they may be more ready to render others assistance. He adds, "For they will be shown mercy"—not only with God but also among people, whose minds God will influence in the direction of exercising humanity. Though the whole world may sometimes be ungrateful, and may return the very worst reward to those who have done acts of kindness, it ought to be reckoned enough that grace is laid up with God for the merciful and humane— so that they, in their turn, will find him to be gracious and merciful.

PURITY AND PEACE

Blessed are the pure in heart, for they will see God. Blessed are the peacemakers, for they will be called sons of God.
—Matthew 5:8–9, NIV

When Christ says, "Blessed are the pure in heart," we might be apt to think that it is in accordance with the judgment of all. Purity of heart is universally acknowledged to be the mother of all virtues. And yet there is hardly one person in a hundred who does not put slyness in the place of the greatest virtue. Hence those persons are commonly thought to be happy whose cleverness is exercised in the successful practice of deceit, who gain crafty advantages, by indirect means, over those with whom they come in contact. Christ does not at all agree with human reason when he pronounces those to be happy who take no delight in cunning, but deal sincerely with men, and express nothing, by word or look, which they do not feel in their heart. Simple people are ridiculed for lacking caution and for not taking enough thought for themselves. But Christ directs them to higher views and bids them to consider that, if they lack the wisdom to deceive in this world, they will enjoy the sight of God in heaven.

By peacemakers he means those who not only seek peace and avoid quarrels, as far as lies in their power, but who also labor to settle differences among others, who advise all people to live at peace, and take away every occasion of hatred and strife. There are good grounds for this statement. As it is hard and irritating work to reconcile those who are at odds, persons who have a mild disposition, who study to promote peace, are compelled to put up with the indignity of hearing reproaches, complaints, and protestations on all sides. The reason is that every one wants advocates who will defend only their own cause. That we may not depend on the favor of people, Christ bids us look up to the judgment of his Father, who is the God of peace (Rom. 15:33) and who accounts us his children when we cultivate peace—though our endeavors may not be acceptable to other people—for to be called means to be accounted the children of God.

PERSECUTION

Blessed are those who are persecuted because of righteousness, for theirs is the kingdom of heaven. Blessed are you when people insult you, persecute you and falsely say all kinds of evil against you because of me. Rejoice and be glad, because great is your reward in heaven, for in the same way they persecuted the prophets who were before you.
—*Matthew 5:10–12, NIV*

The disciples of Christ have very great need of this instruction and the more hard and disagreeable it is for the flesh to admit it, the more earnestly ought we to make it the subject of our meditation. We cannot be Christ's soldiers in any other condition: than to have the greater part of the world rising in hostility against us and pursuing us even to death. The state of the matter is this. Satan, the prince of the world, will never cease to fill his followers with rage to carry on hostilities against the members of Christ. It is, no doubt, monstrous and unnatural that people who study to live a righteous life should be attacked and tormented in a way they do not deserve. Yet, because of the unbridled wickedness of the world, it too frequently happens that good people, through a zeal of righteousness, arouse against them the resentments of the ungodly. Above all, it is, as

we may say, the ordinary lot of Christians to be hated by the majority of mankind. For the flesh cannot endure the doctrine of the Gospel; none can endure to have their vices reproved.

"Righteousness" describes those who inflame the hatred and provoke the rage of the wicked against them because, through an earnest desire to do what is good and right, they oppose bad causes and defend good ones as far as lies in their power. Now, in this respect, the truth of God justly holds the first rank. But if, at any time, the Lord spares our weakness and does not permit the ungodly to torment us as they would desire, yet, during the season of rest and leisure, it is proper for us to meditate on this doctrine so that we may be ready, whenever it shall be necessary, to enter the field, and may not engage in the contest till we have been well prepared.

WOE TO THE RICH

But woe to you who are rich, for you have already received your comfort. Woe to you who are well fed now, for you will go hungry. Woe to you who laugh now, for you will mourn and weep. Woe to you when all men speak well of you, for that is how their fathers treated the false prophets. —Luke 6:24–26, NIV

As Luke has related not more than four kinds of blessings, so he now contrasts with them four curses, so that the clauses match. This contrast not only tends to strike terror into the ungodly, but to arouse believers, that they may not be lulled to sleep by the vain and deceitful seductions of the world. We know how prone people are to be intoxicated by material comfort or ensnared by flattery, and on this account the children of God often envy non-believers, when they see everything go on prosperously and smoothly with them.

Jesus pronounces a curse on the rich—not on all the rich, but on those who receive their consolation in the world; that is, who are so completely occupied with their worldly possessions that they forget the life to come. The meaning is: Riches are so far from making someone happy that they often become the means of a person's destruction. In any other point of view, the rich are not excluded from the kingdom of heaven, provided they do not become snares for themselves or fix their hope on the earth, so as to shut against them the kingdom of heaven. Augustine finely illustrates this when he, in order to show that riches are not in themselves a hindrance to the children of God, reminds his readers that poor Lazarus was received into the bosom of rich Abraham.

In the same sense, Jesus pronounces a curse on those who are satiated and full, because they are lifted up by confidence in the blessings of the present life and reject those blessings which are of a heavenly nature. A similar view must be taken of what he says about laughter. For by those who laugh he means those who are plunged in carnal pleasures and spurn every kind of trouble which would be found necessary for maintaining the glory of God.

The last woe is intended to correct ambition. For nothing is more common than to seek the applause of people, or, at least, to be carried away by them; and, in order to guard his disciples against such a course, Jesus points out to them that the favor of men would prove to be their ruin.

THE LIGHT OF THE WORLD

You are the light of the world. A city on a hill cannot be hidden. Neither do people light a lamp and put it under a bowl. Instead they put it on its stand, and it gives light to everyone in the house. In the same way, let your light shine before men, that they may see your good deeds and praise your Father in heaven. —Matthew 5:14–16, NIV

We are all the children of light, after having been enlightened by faith, and are commanded to carry in our hands "burning lamps" (so that we will not wander in darkness) and even to point out to others the way of life (Luke 12:35). But as the preaching of the Gospel was committed to the Apostles more than others, and is now committed to the pastors of the Church, this designation is given to them in particular by Christ. They are placed in this rank on the condition that they shall shine, as from an elevated situation, on all others.

He joins two comparisons: A city placed on a mountain cannot be concealed, and a candle, when it has been lit, is not usually concealed. This means that they ought to live in such a manner as if the eyes of all were upon them. And certainly the more eminent a person is, the more injury he does by a bad example if he acts improperly. Therefore, Christ, informs the Apostles that they must be more careful to live a devout and holy life than unknown persons of the common rank, because the eyes of all are directed to them as to lighted candles; and they must not be endured if their devotion and uprightness of conduct do not correspond to the doctrine of which they are ministers.

After having taught the apostles that, in consequence of the rank in which they are placed, both their vices and their virtues are better known for a good or bad example, he now tells them to regulate their life so as to excite all to glorify God by saying, "Let your light shine before men" (2 Cor. 8:21).

HARMONY BETWEEN SIBLINGS IN CHRIST

Therefore, if you are offering your gift at the altar and there remember that your brother has something against you, leave your gift there in front of the altar. First go and be reconciled to your brother; then come and offer your gift. —Matthew 5:23–24, NIV

The precept of the Law that forbids murder (Ex. 20:13) is obeyed when we maintain agreement and familial kindness with our neighbor. To impress this more strongly upon us, Christ declares that even the duties of religion are displeasing to God and are rejected by him if we are at variance with each other. When he commands those who have injured any of their brethren to be reconciled to them before they offer their gifts, his meaning is that, so long as a difference with our neighbor is kept up by our fault, we have no access to God. But if the worship which men render to God is polluted and corrupted by their resentments, this enables us to see how highly he holds mutual agreement among ourselves.

For the words of Christ mean nothing more than this. It is a false and empty profession of worshipping God which is made by those who, after acting unjustly towards their siblings, treat them with haughty disdain. The outward exercises of divine worship are in many people the pretenses, rather than the true expressions, of godliness. Whatever we offer to God is polluted unless, at least as much as is up to us (Rom. 12:18), we are at peace with our siblings.

Lastly, God does not receive and acknowledge any as his children who do not, in their turn, show themselves to be siblings to each other. Although it is only to those who have injured their brethren that these words are addressed, telling them to do their best to be reconciled to them, yet with one example he points out how highly the harmony of brethren is esteemed by God.

90

THE SPIRIT'S ORGANS

And ye also shall bear witness, because ye have been with me from the beginning. —John 15:27

We now see in what way faith is by hearing (Rom. 10:17), and yet it derives its certainty from the seal and earnest of the Spirit (Eph. 1:13–14). Those who do not sufficiently know the darkness of the human mind imagine that faith is formed naturally by hearing and preaching alone; and there are many fanatics who disdain the outward preaching, and talk in lofty terms about secret revelations and inspirations. But we see how Christ joins these two things together; and, therefore, though there is no faith till the Spirit of God seal our minds and hearts, still we must not go to seek visions or oracles in the clouds, but rather the Word, which is near us, in our mouth and heart (Rom. 10:8), must keep all our senses bound and fixed on itself, as Isaiah says beautifully:

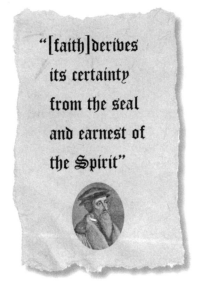

"[faith] derives its certainty from the seal and earnest of the Spirit"

"'My Spirit that is upon thee, and my words which I have put in thy mouth, shall not depart out of thy mouth, nor out of the mouth of thy seed, nor out of the mouth of thy seed's seed,' saith the Lord, 'from henceforth and forever'" (Isa. 59:21).

TRADING THE WORST FOR THE BEST

Verily, verily, I say unto you, He that heareth my word, and believeth on him that sent me, hath everlasting life, and shall not come into condemnation; but is passed from death unto life. —John 5:24

There is no impropriety in saying that we have already passed from death to life. For the incorruptible seed of life (1 Peter 1:23) resides in the children of God, and they already sit in the heavenly glory with Christ by hope (Col. 3:3), and they have the kingdom of God already established within them (Luke 17:21). For though their life be hidden, they do not on that account cease to possess it by faith. And though they are besieged on every side by faith, they do not cease to be calm on this account, that they know that they are in perfect safety through the protection of Christ.

Yet let us remember that believers are now in life in such a manner that they always carry about with them the cause of death. But the Spirit, who dwells in us, is life, which will at length destroy the remains of death; for it is a true saying of Paul that death is the last enemy that shall be destroyed (1 Cor. 15:26).

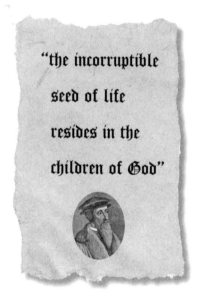

"the incorruptible seed of life resides in the children of God"

And, indeed, this passage contains nothing that relates to the complete destruction of death, or the entire manifestation of life. But though life be only begun in us, Christ declares that believers are so certain of obtaining it, that they ought not to fear death. And we need not wonder at this, since they are united to him who is the inexhaustible fountain of life.

THE GOSPEL'S MEANING IN CHRIST

For I am not ashamed of the gospel of Christ: for it is the power of God unto salvation to every one that believeth; to the Jew first, and also to the Greek. —Romans 1:16

he meaning of the word "Gospel" is well-known. In Scripture it denotes, by way of eminence, the glad and delightful message of the grace exhibited to us in Christ—in order to instruct us, by despising the world and its fading riches and pleasures, to desire with our whole heart, and to embrace when offered to us, this invaluable blessing. God expressly bestows the name Gospel on the message which he orders to be proclaimed concerning Christ; for he thus reminds us that nowhere else can we obtain true and solid happiness, and that in him we have all that is necessary for a happy life.

Some consider the word "Gospel" to mean all the gracious promises of God which are found scattered even in the Law and the Prophets. But as it is the ordinary declaration made by the Holy Spirit in the Scriptures that the Gospel was first proclaimed when Christ came, let us

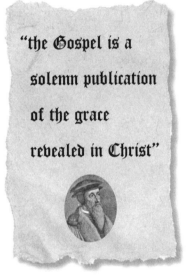

"the Gospel is a solemn publication of the grace revealed in Christ"

keep by that definition of the Gospel which I have given; for it is a solemn publication of the grace revealed in Christ. On this account the Gospel is called the power of God to salvation to everyone who believes (Rom. 1:16), because in it God displays his righteousness. As Christ is the pledge of the mercy of God, and of his fatherly love towards us, so he is, in a peculiar manner, the subject of the Gospel.

LIFE AND DEATH

But the righteousness that is by faith says: "Do not say not in your heart, 'Who will ascend into heaven?' " (that is, to bring Christ down) "or 'Who will descend into the deep?' " (that is, to bring up Christ up from the dead). —Romans 10:6–7, NIV

In the passages Paul is quoting from, Moses mentions heaven and the sea, places remote and difficult for people to reach. But Paul, as though there was some spiritual mystery concealed under these words, applies them to the death and resurrection of Christ. Paul does not, therefore, repeat verbally what Moses has said, but makes changes, accommodating Moses' testimony to his own purpose. Moses spoke of inaccessible places; Paul refers to those which are indeed hid from the sight of us all, but which can be seen by faith.

Let us now then simply explain the words of Paul. The assurance of our salvation lies on two foundations that is, when we understand that life has been obtained for us and that death has been conquered for us. Paul teaches us that faith through the word of the Gospel is sustained by both of these; for Christ, by dying, destroyed death, and by rising again he obtained life in his own power. The benefit of Christ's death and resurrection is now communicated to us by the Gospel. There is no reason for us to seek anything farther. The meaning of the words "Who will ascend into heaven?" is the same as if he'd said: "Who knows whether the inheritance of eternal and celestial life is ours?" And the words: "Who will descend into the deep?" mean, "Who knows whether the everlasting destruction of the soul follows the death of the body?" Paul teaches us that doubt on those two points is removed by the righteousness of faith; for the one doubt would draw down Christ from heaven, and the other would bring him up again from death. Christ's ascension into heaven ought indeed fully to confirm our faith as to eternal life. For anyone who doubts whether the inheritance of heaven is prepared for the faithful, in whose name and on whose account Jesus has entered that place, in a way removes Christ himself from the possession of heaven. Since in like manner Jesus underwent the horrors of hell to deliver us from them, to doubt whether the faithful are still exposed to this misery is to render void and, as it were, to deny his death.

THE ETERNAL LIFE

That which was from the beginning, which we have heard, which we have seen with our eyes; which we have looked at and our hands have touched—this we proclaim concerning the Word of life. The life appeared; we have seen it and testify to it, and we proclaim to you the eternal life, which was with the Father and has appeared to us.
—*1 John 1:1–2, NIV*

hen John says, "which was with the Father," this is true, not only from the time when the world was formed but also from eternity, for Jesus was always God—the fountain of life. And the power of making life was possessed by his eternal wisdom, but he did not actually use it before the creation of the world. And from the time when God began to exhibit the Word, that power which before was hid, diffused itself over all created things.

Life was then at length manifested in Christ, when he in our flesh completed the work of redemption. For though the fathers of the faith before Christ were, even under the Law, associates and partakers of the same life, we know that they were shut up under the hope that was to be revealed. It was necessary for them to seek life from the death and resurrection of Christ, but the event was not only far remote from their eyes but also hid from their minds. They depended, then, on the hope of revelation, which at length in due time followed. They could not, indeed, have obtained life, except it was in some way manifested to them; but the difference between us and them is that we hold him already revealed, as it were, in our hands whom they sought, obscurely promised to them in types.

John's idea here is to remove the idea that the Gospel is brand-new, which might have lessened its dignity. He therefore says that life had not, finally, just then began to be, having but lately appeared, for it was always with the Father.

WALK IN THE LIGHT

But if we walk in the light, as he is in the light, we have fellowship with one another, and the blood of Jesus, his Son, purifies us from all sin. —1 John 1:7, NIV

John says that the proof of our union with God is certain if we are conformable to God. He is not saying that purity of life reconciles us to God, as the prior cause. But John means that our union with God is made evident by the effect; that is, when God's purity shines forth in us. And, doubtless, such is the fact: Wherever God comes, all things are so imbued with his holiness that he washes away all filth; for without him we have nothing but filth and darkness. It is hence evident that no one leads a holy life, except she or he is united to God. It may, however, be asked, "Who among us can so exhibit the light of God in her or his life that this likeness which John talks about should exist? That would mean being wholly pure and free from darkness." To this I answer that sayings like John's are accommodated to our human capacities. Thus anyone is said to be like God who aspires to God's likeness, however distant from it he may as yet be. They walk in darkness who are not ruled by the fear of God, and who do not, with a pure conscience, devote themselves wholly to God and seek to promote God's glory.

Then, on the other hand, those who in sincerity of heart spend their lives in the fear and service of God and faithfully worship God, walk in the light; for these people keep the right way, though they may in many things offend and sigh under the burden of the flesh.

After having taught what is the bond of our union with God, now John shows what fruit flows from it: that our sins are freely remitted by the blood of Jesus. This passage is remarkable. From it we first learn that the expiation of Christ, effected by his death, properly belongs to us when we, in uprightness of heart, do what is right and just; for Christ is no redeemer except to those who turn from iniquity and lead a new life. If, then, we desire to have God favorable to us, so as to forgive our sins, we should not forgive ourselves. In short, remission of sins cannot be separated from repentance, nor can the peace of God be in those hearts where the fear of God does not prevail. Secondly, the gratuitous pardon of sins is given us not only once, but that it is a benefit perpetually residing in the church and daily offered to the faithful.

HOPING AGAINST HOPE

So Joshua son of Nun called the priests and said to them, "Take up the ark of the covenant of the LORD and have seven priests carry trumpets in front of it." And he ordered the people, "Advance! March around the city, with the armed guard going ahead of the ark of the LORD."
—Joshua 6:6–7, NIV

God's promise was, indeed, enough in itself to give the Israelites hope of victory, but the method of acting was so strange as almost to destroy the promise's credibility. God orders them to make one circuit round the city daily until the seventh day, on which they are told to go round it seven times, sounding trumpets and shouting. The whole affair looked like nothing other than child's play; and yet it was a proper test for their faith, since it proved their willingness to consent to the divine message even when they saw in the act itself nothing but disappointment. With the same intention, the Lord often, for a time, conceals his own might under weakness and seems to play with mere toys, so that his weakness will at length appear stronger than all strength and his folly superior to all wisdom.

While the Israelites thus abandon reason and depend implicitly on his words, they gain much more by trifling than they could have done by making a full-on assault. It was good for them to play the fool for a short time, and not display too much acuteness in asking cautious and probing questions about how their victory over the city would work. For that would have been, in a manner, to obstruct the course of divine omnipotence.

There was another reason for doubt that might have crept into their minds. If the inhabitants of the city had suddenly sallied forth, the Israelites would easily have lost, proceeding around the city in long straggling lines without any regular military arrangement that might have enabled it to repel a hostile assault. But here, also, whatever anxiety they might have felt, they decided to cast it upon God; for sacred is the security which rests on God's providence.

BEING TESTED

Some time later God tested Abraham. He said to him, "Abraham!"
"Here I am," he replied. —Genesis 22:1, NIV

y the words "some time later," the author of Genesis intended to contain in one phrase the various events by which Abraham had been tossed up and down and, the somewhat more quiet state of life which, in his old age, he had begun to obtain. He had spent an unsettled life in continued exile up to his eightieth year; harassed with many injuries, he had endured with difficulty a miserable and anxious existence, in continual trouble. Famine had driven him out of the land where he had gone, by God's command, into Egypt. Twice his wife had been taken from him. He had been separated from his nephew. He had saved this nephew when captured in war, at the peril of his own life. He had lived childless with his wife, when all his hopes were suspended upon his having a child. Having at length gotten a son, he was forced to disown him and to drive him far from home. Isaac alone remained—Abraham's special, and only, consolation. He was enjoying peace at home, but now God suddenly thundered out of heaven, denouncing the sentence of death upon this son. The meaning, therefore, of the passage is that by this temptation, as if by the last act, the faith of Abraham was far more severely tried than before.

The author of Genesis soon tells us how God would tempt Abraham; namely, that God would shake the faith the holy man had placed in God's own word, by a counter assault of that word itself. God therefore addresses Abraham by name so that there would be no doubt about the Author of the command. For unless Abraham had been fully persuaded that it was the voice of God commanding him to slay his son Isaac, he would have been easily released from anxiety. Relying on the certain promise of God that Isaac would continue Abraham's seed, Abraham would have rejected the suggestion as the fallacy of Satan, and thus, without any difficulty, the temptation would have been shaken off. But now all occasion of doubt is removed, so that, without argument, Abraham acknowledges the oracle to be from God.

ABSOLUTE FAITH

(PART ONE)

Then God said, "Take your son, your only son, Isaac, whom you love, and go to the region of Moriah. Sacrifice him there as a burnt offering on one of the mountains I will tell you about." —Genesis 22:2, NIV

It was difficult and painful to Abraham to forget that he was a father and a husband; to cast off all human affections; and to endure, before the world, the disgrace of shameful cruelty, by becoming the executioner of his son. But the other was a far more severe and horrible thing; namely, that he seems to see God contradicting himself and his own word, and then that he supposes the hope of the promised blessing to be cut off from him when Isaac is torn away from his embrace. For what more could he have to do with God, when the only pledge of grace is taken away? But as before—when he expected the seed of Isaac from his own withered body—Abraham, by hope, rose above what it seemed possible to hope for; so now—when in the death of his son he believes in the life-giving power of God so much as to promise himself a blessing out of the ashes of his son—he emerges from the labyrinth of temptation.

It remains for every one of us to apply this example to himself. The Lord, indeed, is so indulgent to our sickness that he does not so severely and sharply test our faith; yet he intended to offer an example by which he might call us to a general trial of faith through Abraham, the father of all the faithful. For the faith, which is more precious than gold and silver, should not lie idle, without trial; and experience teaches that everyone will be tried by God according to the measure of his faith. At the same time, we may also observe that God tempts his servants, not only by overcoming the natural affections of the flesh, but by reducing all their senses to nothing, so that God may lead them to a complete renunciation of themselves.

ABSOLUTE FAITH

(PART TWO)

And he said, Take now thy son, thine only son Isaac, whom thou lovest,
and get thee into the land of Moriah; and offer him there for a burnt
offering upon one of the mountains which I will tell thee of.
—Genesis 22:2

As if it were not enough to command in one word the sacrifice of his son, God pierces, as with fresh strokes, the mind of the holy man. By calling Isaac "his only son," God again irritates the wound recently indicted by the banishment of the other son. He then looks forward into the future, because no hope of offspring would remain. If the death of a firstborn son is horrible, what must the mourning of Abraham be? Each word which follows emphasizes and aggravates Abraham's grief. "Slay," God says, "the one you love." And God does not here refer merely to paternal love, but to that which sprung from faith. Abraham loved his son—not only as nature dictates and as parents commonly do, taking delight in their children, but because Abraham saw the paternal love of God in his son. From this God seems not so much to assault the paternal love of Abraham as to trample upon God's own benevolence. It was just as if God should condemn Abraham to eternal torment.

By telling him to go to the region of Moriah, the bitterness of grief is more than a little increased. For God does not require him to put his son immediately to death, but forces him to turn this execution over and over in his mind during three whole days—that in preparing himself to sacrifice his son, he torture his own senses all the more severely. Before, when God commanded Abraham to leave his country, he held his mind in suspense as to the location Abraham would move to. But in this case, the delay which most cruelly tormented the holy man, as if he were being tortured, was intolerable. God had a purpose in mind with this suspense, however. For there is nothing to which we are more prone than to be wise beyond our measure. Therefore, in order that we may become docile and obedient to God, it is good for us to be deprived of our own wisdom, and that nothing should be left us but to resign ourselves to be led according to God's will.

PROMPT OBEDIENCE

Early the next morning Abraham got up and saddled his donkey. He took with him two of his servants and his son Isaac. When he had cut enough wood for the burnt offering, he set out for the place God had told him about. On the third day Abraham looked up and saw the place in the distance. He said to his servants, "Stay here with the donkey while I and the boy go over there. We will worship and then we will come back to you." —Genesis 22:3–5, NIV

The author of Genesis says, "Early the next morning Abraham got up and saddled his donkey." This promptness shows the greatness of Abraham's faith. Innumerable thoughts must have oppressed the mind of the holy man, and surely any one of them would have been enough to overwhelm his spirit unless he had fortified it by faith. And there is no doubt that Satan, during the darkness of the night, would heap upon Abraham a vast mass of worries and cares. Only the courage of a hero could have allowed Abraham to overcome each care gradually, by wrestling with them and wearing them down. But once they had been overcome, then to immediately set himself to the task of fulfilling the command of God, even to rise early the next morning to do so, was a remarkable effort. Other men, brought low by a message so dire and terrible, would have fainted, and have lain prostrate, as if deprived of life. But the first dawn of morning was scarcely early enough for Abraham's haste. Therefore, in a few words, the author of Genesis highly praises Abraham's faith when he declares that it surmounted, in so short a space of time, so enormous and labyrinthine a temptation.

On the third day, Abraham saw, indeed, with his eyes, the place which before had been shown him in secret vision. But when it is said that he "looked up," the author of Genesis seems to be telling us that Abraham had been very anxious during the whole of the three days. And here his greatness appears, that he makes his thoughts so well composed and tranquil that he does nothing in an agitated manner. When, however, he says that he will return with the boy, he seems to lie. But since it is certain that he never lost sight of what had been promised about the raising up of his seed in Isaac, it may be that Abraham, trusting in the providence of God, believed his son would survive even in death itself.

SORROW TO JOY

But the angel of the LORD called out to him from heaven, "Abraham! Abraham!" "Here I am," he replied. —Genesis 22:11, NIV

braham's inward temptations had been already overcome by the time Abraham intrepidly raised his hand to slay his son. And it was by the special grace of God that he obtained such a victory. But now Moses tells us that suddenly, beyond all hope, Abraham's sorrow was changed into joy.

But it is our business with earnest minds to consider how wonderfully God, in the very moment of death, both recalled Isaac from death to life and restored to Abraham his son, as one who had risen from the tomb. The author of Genesis also describes the voice of the angel as sounding out of heaven, to give assurance to Abraham that the voice had come from God, in order that he might withdraw his hand under the direction of the same faith by which he had stretched it out. For, in a cause of such magnitude, it was not lawful for him either to start or to stop anything, except under the

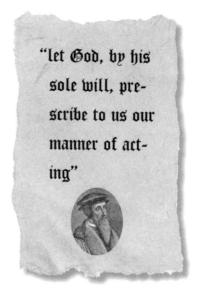

"let God, by his sole will, prescribe to us our manner of acting"

authority of God.

Let us, therefore, learn from his example. Not to pursue what our carnal sense may declare to be our right course, but rather let God, by his sole will, prescribe to us our manner of acting and of ceasing to act. And truly Abraham does not charge God with inconstancy, because he considers that there had been just cause for the exercising of his faith.

GOD'S CERTAINTY

Wherein God, willing more abundantly to shew unto the heirs of promise the immutability of his counsel, confirmed it by an oath.
—Hebrews 6:17

See how kindly God as a gracious Father accommodates himself to our slowness to believe; as he sees that we rest not on his simple word, that he might more fully impress it on our hearts, he adds an oath.

Hence also it appears how much it concerns us to know that there is such a certainty respecting his goodwill towards us that there is no longer any occasion for wavering or for trembling. For when God forbids his name to be taken in vain or on a slight occasion and denounces the severest vengeance on all who rashly abuse it, when he commands reverence to be rendered to his majesty, he thus teaches us that he holds his name in the highest esteem and honor.

The certainty of salvation is then a necessary thing; for he who forbids to swear without reason has been pleased to

> " I seek those tears shed, not for display, but in repentance."

swear for the sake of rendering it certain. And we may hence also conclude what great account he makes of our salvation; for in order to secure it, he not only pardons our unbelief, but giving up as it were his own right and yielding to us far more than what we could claim, he kindly provides a remedy for it.

FAITH'S FOUNDATION

Let us hold fast the profession of our hope without wavering; for He who promised is faithful. —Hebrews 10:23, NASB

s he exhorts here the Jews to persevere, he mentions hope rather than faith; for as hope is born of faith, so it is fed and sustained by it to the last. He requires also profession or confession, for it is not true faith except it shows itself before men. And he seems indirectly to touch the dissimulation of those who paid too much attention, in order to please their own nation, to the ceremonies of the Law. He therefore bids them not only to believe with the heart but also to show and to profess how much they honored Christ.

But we ought carefully to notice the reason which he subjoins: for he is faithful that promised. For we hence first learn that our faith rests on the foundation that God is true; that is, true to his promise, which his Word contains. For that we may believe, the voice

> "as hope is born of faith, so it is fed and sustained by it to the last"

or Word of God must precede. But it is not every kind of word that is capable of producing faith; a promise alone is that on which faith may develop. And so from this passage we may learn the mutual relation between the faith of men and the promise of God—for except God promises, no one can believe.

THE SIMPLE PURITY

He shall glorify me: for he shall receive of mine, and shall shew it unto you. —John 16:14

hrist now reminds them that the Spirit will not come to erect any new kingdom, but rather to confirm the glory which has been given to him by the Father. For many foolishly imagine that Christ taught only so as to lay down the first lessons, and then to send the disciples to a higher school. In this way they make the Gospel to be of no greater value than the Law, of which it is said that it was a schoolmaster of the ancient people (Gal. 3:24). By a false pretense of the Spirit, the world was bewitched to depart from the simple purity of Christ; for, as soon as the Spirit is separated from the word of Christ, the door is open to all kinds of delusions and impostures.

We now see that the information given by Christ, that he would be glorified by the Spirit whom he should send, is far from being superfluous; for it was intended to inform us that the office of the Holy Spirit was

> "the world was bewitched to depart from the simple purity of Christ"

nothing else than to establish the kingdom of Christ and to maintain and confirm forever all that was given him by the Father. Why then does he speak of the Spirit's teaching? Not to withdraw us from the school of Christ, but rather to ratify that word by which we are commanded to listen to him, otherwise he would diminish the glory of Christ.

THE FRUIT OF PERSEVERANCE

See that what you have heard from the beginning remains in you. If it does, you also will remain in the Son and in the Father.
—1 John 2:24, NIV

here is the fruit of perseverance: They in whom God's truth remains, remain in God. We hence learn what we are to seek in every truth pertaining to religion. Those therefore do the best in this life, who makes such progress as to cleave totally to God. But those in whom the Father doesn't dwell through his Son are altogether vain and empty, whatever knowledge they may possess. Moreover, this is the highest compliment for sound doctrine: that it unites us to God, and that in it is found whatever has to do with the fullness of God. In the last place, John reminds us that it is real happiness when God dwells in us.

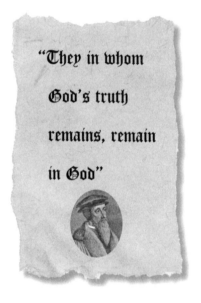

"They in whom God's truth remains, remain in God"

The sum of what is said is that we cannot live except by nourishing to the end the seed of life sown in our hearts. John insists much on this point—that not only the beginning of a blessed life is to be found in the knowledge of Christ but also its perfection. But no repetition of this fact can be too much, since it is well known that it has always been a cause of ruin to all people, that being not content with Christ, they have had a hankering to wander beyond the simple doctrine of the Gospel.

A TRIAL OF OBEDIENCE

When the woman saw that the fruit of the tree was good for food and pleasing to the eye, and also desirable for gaining wisdom, she took some and ate it. She also gave some to her husband, who was with her, and he ate it. —Genesis 3:6, NIV

a s the act which God pun-ished so severely must have been not a trivial fault, but a heinous crime, it will be necessary to attend to the peculiar nature of the sin which produced Adam's fall and provoked God to inflict such fearful vengeance on the whole human race. The common idea of sensual intemperance is childish. The sum and substance of all virtues could not consist in abstinence from a single fruit amid a general abundance of every delicacy that could be desired, since the earth, with happy fertility, yields not only abundance but also endless variety. We must, therefore, look deeper than sensual intemperance.

The prohibition to touch the tree of the knowledge of good and evil was a trial of obedience—that Adam, by observing it, might prove his willing submission to the command of God. For the very term shows the end of the precept to have been to keep him contented with his lot, and not allow him arrogantly to aspire beyond it. The promise—which gave him hope of eternal life as long as he should eat of the tree of life and, on the other hand, the fearful denunciation of death the moment he should taste of the tree of the knowledge of good and evil—was meant to prove and exercise his faith.

Assuredly, when the Word of God is despised, all reverence for him is gone. His majesty cannot be duly honored among us, nor his worship maintained in its integrity, unless we hang as it were upon his lips. Hence infidelity was at the root of the revolt. From infidelity, again, sprang ambition and pride, together with ingratitude; because Adam, by longing for more than was allotted him, manifested contempt for the great liberality with which God had enriched him. Man, when carried away by the blasphemies of Satan, did his very utmost to annihilate the whole glory of God.

THE CONTAGION OF SIN

Behold, I was shapen in iniquity; and in sin did my mother conceive me. —Psalm 51:5

As Adam's spiritual life would have consisted in remaining united and bound to his Maker, so estrangement from him was the death of his soul. Nor is it strange that he who perverted the whole order of nature in heaven and earth deteriorated his race by his revolt. "The whole creation groans," says Paul, "being made subject to vanity, not willingly" (Rom. 8:20, 22).

If the reason is asked, there cannot be a doubt that creation bears part of the punishment deserved by man, for whose use all other creatures were made. Therefore, since through man's fault a curse has extended above and below, over all the regions of the world, there is nothing unreasonable in its extending to all his offspring. After the heavenly image in man was effaced, he not only was himself punished by a withdrawal of the ornaments in which he had been arrayed—wisdom, virtue, justice, truth, and holiness—and by the substitution in their place of those dire pests—blindness, impotence, vanity, impurity, and unrighteousness—but he involved his posterity also and plunged them in the same wretchedness.

Surely there is no ambiguity in David's confession, "I was shaped in iniquity; and in sin did my mother conceive me," (Ps. 51:5). His object in the passage is not to throw blame on his parents; but the better to commend the goodness of God towards him, he properly reiterates the confession of impurity from his very birth.

As it is clear that there was no peculiarity in David's case, it follows that it is only an instance of the common lot of the whole human race. All of us, therefore, descending from an impure seed, come into the world tainted with the contagion of sin. Nay, before we behold the light of the sun we are in God's sight defiled and polluted. "Who can bring a clean thing out of an unclean? Not one," says the Book of Job (Job 14:4).

Lost in Adam, Received in Christ

For as by one man's disobedience many were made sinners, so by the obedience of one shall many be made righteous. —Romans 5:19

the impurity of parents is transmitted to their children, so that all, without exception, are originally depraved. The beginning of this depravity will not be found until we ascend to the first parent of all as the fountain head. We must, therefore, hold it for certain that, in regard to human nature, Adam was not merely a progenitor but also, a root, and by his corruption the whole human race was deservedly compromised. This is plain from the contrast which the Apostle draws between Adam and Christ, "Wherefore, as by one man sin entered into the world, and death by sin; and so death passed upon all men, for that all have sinned; even so might grace reign through righteousness unto eternal life by Jesus Christ our Lord" (Rom. 5:19-21).

Out of all controversy, the righteousness of Christ, and thereby life, is ours by solely as a gift from God; it follows that both of these were lost in Adam that they might be recovered in Christ, whereas sin and death were brought in by Adam that they might be abolished in Christ. There is no obscurity in the words, "As by one man's disobedience many were made sinners, so by the obedience of one shall many be made righteous."

Accordingly, the relation subsisting between the two is this: As Adam, by his ruin, involved and ruined us, so Christ, by his grace, restored us to salvation. Adam, when he corrupted himself, transmitted the contagion to all his posterity. For a heavenly Judge, our Savior himself, declares that all are by birth vicious and depraved, when he says that "that which is born of the flesh is fleshy" (John 3:6), and that therefore the gate of life is closed against all until they have been regenerated.

HUMBLE PRAYER

*All of us have become like one who is unclean, and all our righteous
acts are like filthy rags; we all shrivel up like a leaf, and like the wind
our sins sweep us away. No one calls on your name or strives to lay
hold of you; for you have hidden your face from us and made us waste
away because of our sins. Yet, O LORD, you are our Father. We are the
clay, you are the potter; we are all the work of your hand. Do not be
angry beyond measure, O LORD; do not remember our sins forever. Oh,
look upon us, we pray, for we are all your people.*
—Isaiah 64:6–9, NIV

he who comes into the presence of God to pray must divest himself of all vainglorious thoughts, lay aside all idea of worth; in short, he must discard all self-confidence, humbly giving God the whole glory, lest by claiming any right or power himself, vain pride cause him to turn away his face. Of this submission, which casts down all haughtiness, we have numerous examples in the servants of God.

Thus Daniel, on whom the Lord himself bestowed such high commendation, says, "We do not present our supplications before you for our righteousness but for your great mercies. O LORD, hear; O LORD, forgive; O LORD, hearken and do; defer not, for your own sake, O my God: for your city and your people are called by your name."

This he does not indirectly in the usual manner, as if he were one of the individuals in a crowd. He rather confesses his guilt apart, and as a beggar committing himself to the asylum of pardon, he distinctly declares that he was confessing his own sin, and the sin of his people Israel (Dan. 9:18-20).

David also sets us an example of this humility: "Enter not into judgment with thy servant: for in thy sight shall no man living be justified" (Ps. 143:2). You see how they put no confidence in anything but this: Considering that they are the Lord's, they despair not of being the objects of his care.

In the same way, Jeremiah says, "O LORD, though our iniquities testify against us, do thou it for thy name's sake" (Jer. 14:7).

PARDONED FIRST

Remember not the sins of my youth, nor my transgressions: according to thy mercy remember thou me for thy goodness' sake, O LORD.
—Psalm 25:7

Supplication for pardon, with humble and sincere confession of guilt, forms both the preparation and commencement of right prayer. For the holiest of men cannot hope to obtain anything from God until he has been freely reconciled to him. God cannot be the friend of any but those whom he pardons. Hence it is not strange that this is the key by which believers open the door of prayer, as we learn from several passages in Psalms. David, when presenting a request on a different subject, says, "Remember not the sins of my youth, nor my transgressions; according to your mercy remember me, for your goodness sake, O LORD" (Ps. 25:7).

Here also we see that it is not sufficient to call ourselves to account for the sins of each passing day; we must also call to mind those which might seem to have been long before buried in oblivion. Although the saints do not always in express terms ask forgiveness of sins, yet if we carefully ponder those prayers as given in Scripture, the truth of what I say will readily appear; namely, that their courage to pray was derived solely from the mercy of God, and that they always began with appeasing him. For when a man interrogates his conscience, so far is he from presuming to lay his cares too casually before God, that if he did not trust to mercy and pardon, he would tremble at the very thought of approaching him.

There is, indeed, another special confession. When believers long for deliverance from punishment, they at the same time pray that their sins may be pardoned; for it were absurd to wish that the effect should be taken away while the cause remains. For we must beware of imitating foolish patients who, anxious only about curing accidental symptoms, neglect the root of the disease. Nay, our endeavor must be to have friendship with God even before he attests his favor by external signs, because this is the order which he himself chooses. It were of little avail to experience his kindness, did not conscience feel that he is appeased, and thus enable us to regard him as altogether lovely.

FAITH'S ORIGIN

I pray for them: I pray not for the world, but for them which thou hast given me; for they are thine. —John 17:9

We learn from these words that God chooses out of the world those whom he thinks fit to choose to be heirs of life, and that this distinction is not made according to the merit of men, but depends on his mere good-pleasure. For those who think that the cause of election is in men must begin with faith. Now, Christ expressly declares that they who are given to him belong to the Father; and it is certain that they are given so as to believe, and that faith flows from this act of giving. If the origin of faith is this act of giving, and if election comes before it in order and time, what remains but that we acknowledge that those whom God wishes to be saved out of the world are elected by free grace?

Now since Christ prays for the elect only, it is necessary for us to believe the doctrine of election, if we wish that he should plead with the Father for our salvation. A grievous injury, therefore, is inflicted on

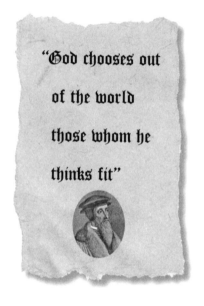

"God chooses out of the world those whom he thinks fit"

believers by those persons who endeavor to blot out the knowledge of election from the hearts of believers, because they deprive them of the pleading and intercession of the Son of God. These words serve also to expose the stupidity of those who, under the pretence of election, give themselves up to the indolence—whereas it ought rather to arouse us to earnestness in prayer, as Christ teaches us by his example.

STRENGTH SUPPLIED

That the saying might be fulfilled, which he spake, Of them which thou gavest me have I lost none. —John 18:9

Christ did not keep the Apostles safe to the last, but this he accomplished: Amid incessant dangers, and even in the midst of death, still their eternal salvation was secured. I reply, the Evangelist does not speak merely of their bodily life, but rather means that Christ, sparing them for a time, made provision for their eternal salvation. Let us consider how great their weakness was. What do we think they would have done, if they had been brought to the test? While, therefore, Christ did not choose that they should be tried beyond the strength which he had given to them, he rescued them from eternal destruction.

And hence we may draw a general doctrine, that, though he try our faith by many temptations, still he will never allow us to come into extreme danger without supplying us also with strength to overcome. And, indeed, we see how he continually bears with our weakness,

> "Amid incessant dangers, and even in the midst of death, still their eternal salvation was secured"

when he puts himself forward to repel so many attacks of Satan and wicked men, because he sees that we are not yet able or prepared for them. In short, he never brings his people into the field of battle till they have been fully trained, so that even in perishing they do not perish, because there is gain provided for them both in death and in life.

LOFTY TALK

Then saith the damsel that kept the door unto Peter, Art not thou also one of this man's disciples? He saith, I am not. —John 18:17

Peter is introduced into the high priest's hall; but it cost him very dear, for, as soon as he sets his foot within it, he is constrained to deny Christ. When he stumbles so shamefully at the first step, the foolishness of his boasting is exposed. He had boasted that he would prove to be a valiant champion, and able to meet death with firmness; and now, at the voice of a single maid, and that voice unaccompanied by threatening, he is confounded and throws down his arms.

Such is a demonstration of the power of man. Certainly, all the strength that appears to be in men is smoke, which a breath immediately drives away. When we are out of the battle, we are too courageous; but experience shows that our lofty talk is foolish and groundless; and, even when Satan makes no attacks, we contrive for ourselves idle alarms which disturb us before the time.

The voice of a feeble woman terrified Peter. And what is the case with us? Do we not continually tremble at the rustling of a falling leaf? A false appearance of danger, which was still distant, made Peter tremble. And are we not every day led away from Christ by childish absurdities? In short, our courage is of such a nature that, of its own accord, it gives way where there is no enemy; and thus does God revenge the arrogance of men by reducing fierce minds to a state of weakness. A man, filled not with fortitude but with wind, promises that he will obtain an easy victory over the whole world; and yet, no sooner does he see the shadow of a thistle, than he immediately trembles. Let us therefore learn not to be brave in any other than the Lord.

DIVINE FAVOR

Blessed is the nation whose God is the LORD, the people he chose for his inheritance. —Psalm 33:12, NIV

The divine favor to which faith is said to have respect, we understand to include in it the possession of salvation and eternal life. For if, when God is propitious, no good thing can be wanting to us, we have ample security for our salvation when assured of his love. "Turn us again, O God, and cause thy face to shine," says the Prophet, "and we shall be saved" (Ps. 80:3). Hence the Scriptures make the sum of our salvation to consist in the removal of all enmity and our admission into favor, thus intimating that when God is reconciled all danger is past and every thing good will befall us. Wherefore, faith, apprehending the love of God, has the promise both of the present and the future life, and ample security for all blessings (Eph. 2:14).

The nature of this must be ascertained from the Word. Faith does not promise us length of days, riches, and honors (the Lord not having been pleased that any of these should be appointed us); but is contented with the assurance that however poor we may be in regard to present comforts, God will never fail us. The chief security lies in the expectation of future life, which is placed beyond doubt by the Word of God. Whatever be the miseries and calamities which await the children of God in this world, they cannot make his favor cease to be complete happiness. Hence, when we were desirous to express the sum of blessedness, we designated it by the favor of God, from which, as their source, all kinds of blessings flow. And we may observe throughout the Scriptures that they refer us to the love of God, not only when they treat of our eternal salvation, but of any blessing whatever—for which reason David sings that the loving-kindness of God experienced by the pious heart is sweeter and more to be desired than life itself (Ps. 63:3).

In short, if we have every earthly comfort to a wish, but are uncertain whether we have the love or the hatred of God, our felicity will be cursed and therefore miserable. But if God lift on us the light of his fatherly countenance, our very miseries will be blessed, inasmuch as they will become helps to our salvation.

FREE PROMISE

But what does it say? "The word is near you; it is in your mouth and in your heart," that is, the word of faith we are proclaiming.
—Romans 10:8, NIV

free promise we make the foundation of faith, because in it faith properly consists. For though it holds that God is always true, whether in ordering or forbidding, promising or threatening; though it obediently receives his commands, observes his prohibitions, and gives heed to his threatening; yet it properly begins with promise, continues with it, and ends with it. It seeks life in God, life which is not found in commands or the denunciations of punishment, but in the promise of mercy. And this promise must be gratuitous; for a conditional promise, which throws us back upon our works, promises life only insofar as we find it existing in ourselves.

Therefore, if we would not have faith to waver and tremble, we must support it with the promise of salvation, which is offered by the Lord spontaneously and freely, from a regard to our misery rather than our worth. Hence the Apostle bears this testimony to the Gospel that it is the word of faith (Rom. 10:8). This he concedes not either to the precepts or the promises of the Law, since there is nothing which can establish our faith, but that free embassy by which God reconciles the world to himself. Hence he often uses faith and the Gospel as correlative terms, as when he says that the ministry of the Gospel was committed to him for "obedience to the faith;" that "it is the power of God unto salvation to every one that believeth;" that "therein is the righteousness of God revealed from faith to faith" (Rom. 1:5, 16–17).

Therefore, when we say that faith must rest on a free promise, we deny not that believers accept and embrace the Word of God in all its parts, but we point to the promise of mercy as its special object. Believers, indeed, ought to recognize God as the judge and avenger of wickedness; and yet mercy is the object to which they properly look, since he is exhibited to their contemplation as "good and ready to forgive," "plenteous in mercy," "slow to anger," "good to all," and shedding "his tender mercies over all his works" (Ps. 86:5; 103:8; 145:8–9).

ALL THE PROMISES

For he himself is our peace, who has made the two one and has
destroyed the barrier, the dividing wall of hostility, by abolishing in his
flesh the law with its commandments and regulations. His purpose was
to create in himself one new man out of the two, thus making peace.
—Ephesians 2:14–15, NIV

We have good ground for comprehending all the promises in Christ since the Apostle comprehends the whole Gospel under the knowledge of Christ, and declares that all the promises of God are in him yea, and amen. The reason for this is obvious. Every promise which God makes is evidence of his good will. This is invariably true, and is not inconsistent with the fact that the large benefits which the divine liberality is constantly bestowing on the wicked are preparing them for heavier judgment. As they neither think that these proceed from the hand of the Lord, nor acknowledge them as his (or if they do so acknowledge them, never regard them as proofs of his favor) they are in no respect more instructed thereby in his mercy than brute beasts, which, according to their condition, enjoy the same liberality and yet never look beyond it. Still it is true that by rejecting the promises generally offered to them, they subject themselves to severer punishment. For though it is only when the promises are received in faith that their effectiveness is manifested, still their reality and power are never extinguished by our infidelity or ingratitude.

Therefore, when the Lord by his promises invites us not only to enjoy the fruits of his kindness but also to meditate upon them, he at the same time declares his love. Without controversy, God loves no man out of Christ. He is the beloved Son, in whom the love of the Father dwells, and from whom it afterwards extends to us. Thus Paul says, "In whom he has made us accepted in the Beloved" (Eph. 1:6). It is by his intervention, therefore, that love is diffused so as to reach us. Accordingly, in another passage, the Apostle calls Christ "our peace" (Eph. 2:14), and also represents him as the bond by which the Father is united to us in paternal affection (Rom. 8:3). It follows that whenever any promise is made to us, we must turn our eyes toward Christ. Hence, with good reasons Paul declares that in him all the promises of God are confirmed and completed (Rom. 15:8).

THOSE TO WHOM IT IS GIVEN

This only would I learn of you, Received ye the Spirit by the works of the law, or by the hearing of faith? —Galatians 3:2

a simple external manifestation of the word ought to be amply sufficient to produce faith, did not our blindness and perverseness prevent. But such is the proneness of our mind to vanity that it can never adhere to the truth of God, and such its dullness that it is always blind even in his light. Hence, without the illumination of the Spirit, the Word has no effect; and hence also it is obvious that faith is something higher than human understanding. Nor were it sufficient for the mind to be illumined by the Spirit of God unless the heart also were strengthened and supported by his power. Here the Schoolmen go completely astray, dwelling entirely in their consideration of faith, on the bare simple assent of the understanding, and altogether overlooking confidence and security of heart.

Faith is the special gift of God in both ways—in purifying the mind so as to give it a relish for divine truth, and afterwards in establishing it therein. For the Spirit does not merely originate faith, but gradually increases it, until by its means he conducts us into the heavenly kingdom. "That good thing which was committed unto thee," says Paul, "keep by the Holy Ghost which dwells in us" (2 Tim. 1:14).

In what sense Paul says (Gal. 3:2) that the Spirit is given by the hearing of faith, may be easily explained. If there were only a single gift of the Spirit, he who is the author and cause of faith could not without absurdity be said to be its effect; but after celebrating the gifts with which God decorates his church, and by successive additions of faith leads it to perfection, there is nothing strange in his ascribing to faith the very gifts which faith prepares us for receiving.

It seems to some paradoxical, when it is said that none can believe Christ save those to whom it is given; but this is partly because they do not observe how obscure and sublime heavenly wisdom is, or how dull the mind of man in discerning divine mysteries, and partly because they pay no regard to that firm and stable constancy of heart which is the chief part of faith.

SEALED WITH THE SPIRIT

In whom ye also trusted, after that ye heard the word of truth, the gospel of your salvation: in whom also after that ye believed, ye were sealed with that holy Spirit of promise, Which is the earnest of our inheritance until the redemption of the purchased possession, unto the praise of his glory. —Ephesians 1:13–14

The Word is not received in faith when it merely flutters in the brain, but when it has taken deep root in the heart, and become an invincible bulwark to withstand and repel all the assaults of temptation. But if the illumination of the Spirit is the true source of understanding in the intellect, much more manifest is his agency in the confirmation of the heart—inasmuch as there is more distrust in the heart than blindness in the mind—and it is more difficult to inspire the soul with security than to imbue it with knowledge. Hence the Spirit performs the part of a seal, sealing upon our hearts the very promises, the certainty of which was previously impressed upon our minds. It also serves as an earnest in establishing and confirming these promises. Thus the Apostle says, "In whom also, after that ye believed, ye were sealed with that holy Spirit of promise, which is the earnest of our inheritance" (Eph. 1:13–14). You see how he teaches that the hearts of believers are stamped with the Spirit as with a seal, and calls it the Spirit of promise, because it ratifies the Gospel to us.

Yet I know that faith is subject to various doubts, so that the minds of believers are seldom at rest, or at least are not always tranquil. Still, whatever be the engines by which they are shaken, they either escape from the whirlpool of temptation, or remain steadfast in their place. Faith finds security and protection in the words of the Psalm, "God is our refuge and strength, a very present help in trouble; therefore will not we fear, though the earth be removed, and the mountains be carried into the midst of the sea" (Ps. 46:1–2). This delightful tranquility is elsewhere described: "I laid me down and slept; I awaked, for the Lord sustained me" (Ps. 3:5). Not that David was uniformly in this joyful frame; but insofar as the measure of his faith made him sensible of the divine favor, he glories in intrepidly despising every thing that could disturb his peace of mind.

THE HOPE OF ETERNAL LIFE

For we are saved by hope: but hope that is seen is not hope: for what a man seeth, why doth he yet hope for? —Romans 8:24

Wherever living faith exists, it must have the hope of eternal life as its inseparable companion, or rather must of itself beget and manifest it; where it is wanting, however clearly and elegantly we may discourse of faith, it is certain we have it not. For if faith is (as has been said) a firm persuasion of the truth of God—a persuasion that it can never be false, never deceive, never be in vain—those who have received this assurance must at the same time expect that God will perform his promises, which in their conviction are absolutely true; so that in one word hope is nothing more than the expectation of those things which faith previously believes to have been truly promised by God. Thus, faith believes that God is true; hope expects that in due season he will manifest his truth. Faith believes that he is our Father; hope expects that he will always act the part of a Father towards us. Faith believes that eternal life has been given to us; hope expects that it will one day be revealed. Faith is the foundation on which hope rests; hope nourishes and sustains faith.

For as no man can expect any thing from God without previously believing his promises, so, on the other hand, the weakness of our faith, which might grow weary and fall away, must be supported and cherished by patient hope and expectation. For this reason Paul justly says, "We are saved by hope" (Rom. 8:24). For while hope silently waits for the Lord, it restrains faith from hastening on with too much precipitation, confirms it when it might waver in regard to the promises of God or begin to doubt of their truth, refreshes it when it might be fatigued, extends its view to the final goal, so as not to allow it to give up in the middle of the course, or at the very outset. In short, by constantly renovating and reviving, it is ever and anon furnishing more vigor for perseverance.

PERFECTLY SAVED

When Jesus therefore had received the vinegar, he said, It is finished: and he bowed his head, and gave up the ghost. —John 19:30

ow this word, which Christ employs, well deserves our attention; for it shows that the whole accomplishment of our salvation, and all the parts of it, are contained in his death. His resurrection is not separated from his death, but Christ only intends to keep our faith fixed on himself alone and not to allow it to turn aside in any direction whatever. The meaning, therefore, is that everything which contributes to the salvation of men is to be found in Christ and ought not to be sought anywhere else—or (which amounts to the same thing) that the perfection of salvation is contained in him. There is also an implied contrast for Christ contrasts his death with the ancient sacrifices and with all the figures. It is as if he had said, "Of all that was practiced under the Law, there was nothing that had any power in itself to make atonement for sins, to appease the wrath of God, and to obtain justification;

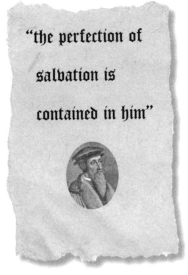

"the perfection of salvation is contained in him"

but now the true salvation is exhibited and manifested to the world." On this doctrine depends the abolition of all the ceremonies of the Law, for it would be absurd to follow shadows since we have the body in Christ. If we give our assent to this word which Christ pronounced, we ought to be satisfied with his death alone for salvation, and we are not at liberty to apply for assistance in any other quarter.

THE ONLY DELIVERER

Who in the days of his flesh, when he had offered up prayers and supplications with strong crying and tears unto him that was able to save him from death, and was heard in that he feared. —Hebrews 5:7

It is indeed certain that he was reduced to great straits; and being overwhelmed with real sorrows, he earnestly prayed his Father to bring him help. And what application is to be made of this? Even this: whenever our evils press upon us and overwhelm us, we may call to mind the Son of God who labored under the same; and since he has gone before us there is no reason for us to faint.

We are at the same time reminded that deliverance from evils can be found from no other but from God alone, and what better guidance can we have as to prayer than the example of Christ? He betook himself immediately to the Father. And thus the Apostle indicates what ought to be done by us when he says that he offered prayers to him who

"deliverance from evils can be found from no other but from God alone"

was able to deliver him from death. For by these words he intimates that he rightly prayed, because he fled to God the only Deliverer. His tears and crying recommend to us ardor and earnestness in prayer, for we ought not to pray to God formally, but with ardent desires.

ACCESS TO HEAVEN

*Wherefore he is able also to save them to the uttermost that come unto
God by him, seeing he ever liveth to make intercession for them.*
—Hebrews 7:25

though the high priest carried the names of the twelve tribes on his shoulders and symbols on his breast, yet he alone entered the sanctuary while the people stood in the court. But now by relying on Christ the Mediator we enter by faith into heaven; for there is no longer any veil intervening, but God appears to us openly, and lovingly invites us to a familiar access.

Christ ever liveth to make intercession; what sort of pledge and how great is this of love towards us! Christ lives for us, not for himself! That he was received into a blessed immortality to reign in heaven, this has taken place, as the Apostle declares, for our sake. Then the life, and the kingdom, and the glory of Christ are all destined for our salvation as to their object—nor has Christ anything which may not be applied to our benefit. For he has been given to us by the Father once for all on this condition: that all

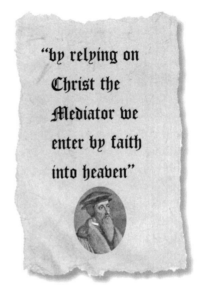

"by relying on Christ the Mediator we enter by faith into heaven"

his should be ours.

He at the same time teaches us by what Christ is doing, that he is performing his office as a priest; for it belongs to a priest to intercede for the people, that they may obtain favor with God. This is what Christ is ever doing, for it was for this purpose that he rose again from the dead. Then of right, for his continual intercession, he claims for himself the office of the priesthood.

BOUND TO SIN

I have surely heard Ephraim bemoaning himself thus; Thou hast chastised me, and I was chastised, as a bullock unaccustomed to the yoke: turn thou me, and I shall be turned; for thou art the LORD my God. Surely after that I was turned, I repented; and after that I was instructed, I smote upon my thigh: I was ashamed, yea, even confounded, because I did bear the reproach of my youth. —Jeremiah 31:18–19

When the will is chained as the slave of sin, it cannot make a movement towards goodness, far less steadily pursue it. Every such movement is the first step in that conversion to God, which in Scripture is entirely ascribed to divine grace. Thus Jeremiah prays, "Turn thou me, and I shall be turned" (Jer. 31:18). Hence, too, in the same chapter, describing the spiritual redemption of believers, the Prophet says, "The LORD has redeemed Jacob, and ransomed him from the hand of him that was stronger than he" (Jer. 31:11); he intimates how close the fetters are with which the sinner is bound, so long as he is abandoned by the Lord, and acts under the yoke of the devil.

Nevertheless, there remains a will which both inclines and rushes on with the strongest affection towards sin. Man, when placed under this bondage, is deprived not of will but of soundness of will. Thus simply to will is the part of man, to will ill the part of corrupt nature, to will well the part of grace.

Moreover, when I say that the will, deprived of liberty, is led or dragged by necessity to evil, it is strange that any should deem the expression harsh, seeing there is no absurdity in it, and it is not inconsistent with pious use. If the free will of God in doing good is not impeded, because he necessarily must do good, and if the devil, who can do nothing but evil, nevertheless sins voluntarily, can it be said that man sins less voluntarily because he is under a necessity of sinning?

Since he was corrupted by the fall, man sins—not forced or unwilling—but voluntarily, by a most forward bias of the mind, not by violent compulsion, or external force, but by the movement of his own passion. And yet such is the depravity of his nature: that he cannot move and act except in the direction of evil. If this is true, the thing not obscurely expressed is that he is under a necessity of sinning.

POWER TO OBEY

Now may our God and Father himself and our Lord Jesus clear the way for us to come to you. May the Lord make your love increase and over-flow for each other and for everyone else, just as ours does for you. May he strengthen your hearts so that you will be blameless and holy in the presence of our God and Father when our Lord Jesus comes with all his holy ones. —1 Thessalonians 3:11–13, NIV

Scripture has taught more on the subject than that the Law is a rule of life by which we ought to regulate our pursuits; it carefully and clearly explains that the use of the Law is manifold, the proper course is to learn what the power of the Law is in man. It explains what our duty is and it teaches that the power of obeying it is derived from the goodness of God, and it accordingly urges us to pray that this power may be given us. If there were merely a command and no promise, it would be necessary to try whether our strength were suffi-cient to fulfill the command. But since promises are annexed, which proclaim not only that aid but also that our whole power is derived from divine grace, they at the same time abundantly testify that we are not only unequal to the obser-vance of the Law but also mere fools in regard to it. Therefore, let us hear no more of a propor-tion between our ability and the divine precepts, as if the Lord had accommodated the stan-dard of justice which he was to give in the Law to our feeble capacities.

But some say, "Who will believe that the Lord designed his Law for blocks and stones?" There is no wish to make any one believe this. The ungodly are neither blocks nor stones when, taught by the Law that their lusts are offensive to God, they are proved guilty by their own confession; nor are the godly blocks or stones when, admonished of their powerless-ness, they take refuge in grace. To this effect are the mighty say-ings of Augustine, "God orders what we cannot do, that we may know what we ought to ask of him. There is a great utility in precepts, if all that is given to free will is to do greater honor to divine grace. Faith acquires what the Law requires; nay, the Law requires, in order that faith may acquire what is thus required; nay, more, God demands of us faith itself, and finds not what he thus demands, until by giv-ing he makes it possible to find it."

GOVERNED BY GOD

The LORD your God will circumcise your hearts and the hearts of your descendants, so that you may love him with all your heart and with all your soul, and live. —Deuteronomy 30:6, NIV

It appears that the grace of God is the rule of the Spirit in directing and governing the human will. Govern he cannot, without correcting, reforming, renovating (hence we say that the beginning of regeneration consists in the abolition of what is ours). In like manner, he cannot govern without moving, impelling, urging, and restraining. Accordingly, all the actions which are afterwards done are truly said to be wholly his.

Meanwhile, we deny not the truth of Augustine's doctrine that the will is not destroyed, but rather repaired, by grace—the two things being perfectly consistent. The human will may be said to be renewed when it is conformed to the true standard of righteousness and, at the same time, the will may be said to be made new, being so invalidated and corrupted that its nature must be entirely changed. There is nothing then to prevent us from saying that our will does what the Spirit does in us, although the will contributes nothing of itself apart from grace.

We must, therefore, remember what we quoted from Augustine that some men labor in vain to find in the human will some good quality properly belonging to it. Any intermixture which men attempt to make by conjoining the effort of their own will with divine grace is corruption, just as when unwholesome and muddy water is used to dilute wine. But though everything good in the will is entirely derived from the influence of the Spirit, yet, because we have naturally an innate power of willing, we are not improperly said to do the things of which God claims for himself all the praise; first, because every thing which his kindness produces in us is our own (only we must understand that it is not of ourselves); and, secondly, because it is our mind, our will, and our study which are guided by him to what is good.

PURPOSE OF PREACHING

Whose soever sins ye remit, they are remitted unto them; and whose soever sins ye retain, they are retained. —John 20:23

The principal design of preaching the Gospel is that men may be reconciled to God, and this is accomplished by the unconditional pardon of sins; as Paul also informs us, when he calls the Gospel, on this account, "the ministry of reconciliation," (2 Cor. 5:18). Many other things, undoubtedly, are contained in the Gospel, but the principal object which God intends to accomplish by it is to receive men into favor by not imputing their sins.

If, therefore, we wish to show that we are faithful ministers of the Gospel, we must give our most earnest attention to this subject. For the chief point of difference between the Gospel and heathen philosophy lies in this: that the Gospel makes the salvation of men to consist in the forgiveness of sins through free grace. This is the source of the other blessings which God bestows—such as, that God enlightens and regenerates us by his Spirit, that he forms us anew to his image, that he arms us with unshaken firmness against the world and Satan. Thus the whole doctrine of godliness, and the spiritual building of the Church, rests on this foundation: that God, having acquitted us from all sins, adopts us to be his children by free grace.

While Christ enjoins the Apostles to "forgive sins," he does not convey to them what is peculiar to himself. It belongs to him to "forgive sins." This honor, so far as it belongs peculiarly to himself, he does not surrender to the Apostles, but enjoins them, in his name, to proclaim "the forgiveness of sins," that through their agency he may reconcile men to God. In short, properly speaking, it is he alone who "forgives sins" through his Apostles and ministers.

DO YOU HEAR THE BELLS RINGING?

Verily, verily, I say unto you, The hour is coming, and now is, when the dead shall hear the voice of the Son of God: and they that hear shall live. —John 5:25

When the Evangelist represents the Son of God as swearing so frequently in reference to our salvation, hence we perceive: first, how eagerly he desires our welfare, and next, of how great importance it is that the faith of the Gospel should be deeply fixed and thoroughly confirmed. The statement has indeed some appearance of being incredible, when we are told that this is the effect of the faith of which Christ speaks; and therefore he confirms by an oath that the voice of his Gospel has such power of giving life that it is powerful to raise the dead.

I readily acknowledge that in the soul of man there remains some remnant of life—for understanding, and judgment, and will, and all our senses, are so many parts of life—but as there is no part which rises to the desire of the heavenly life, we need not wonder if the whole man, so far as relates to the kingdom of God, is accounted dead. And this death Paul explains more fully when he says that we are alienated from the pure and sound reason of the understanding, that we are enemies to God and opposed to his righteousness, in every affection of our heart, and that we wander in darkness like blind persons and are given up to wicked lusts (Eph. 2:1; 4:17). If a nature so corrupted has no power to desire righteousness, it follows that the life of God is extinguished in us.

Thus the grace of Christ is a true resurrection from the dead.

THE EVIDENCE SPEAKS

Search the scriptures; for in them ye think ye have eternal life: and they are they which testify of me. —John 5:39

again, we are taught by this passage that if we wish to obtain the knowledge of Christ, we must seek it from the Scriptures; for they who imagine whatever they choose concerning Christ will ultimately have nothing instead of him but a shadowy phantom.

First, then, we ought to believe that Christ cannot be properly known in any other way than from the Scriptures and if it be so, it follows that we ought to read the Scriptures with the express design of finding Christ in them. Whoever shall turn aside from this object, though he may weary himself throughout his whole life in learning, will never attain the knowledge of the truth. For what wisdom can we have without the wisdom of God?

Next, as we are commanded to seek Christ in the Scriptures, so he declares in this passage that our labors shall not be fruitless; for the Father testifies in them concerning his Son in such a manner that he will manifest him to us beyond all doubt. But what hinders the greater part of men from profiting is that they give to the subject nothing more than a superficial and cursory glance. Yet it requires the utmost attention, and, therefore, Christ enjoins us to search diligently for this hidden treasure.

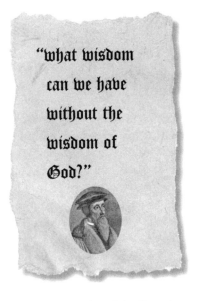

"what wisdom can we have without the wisdom of God?"

129

CONFESSING SINS

We have sinned, and have committed iniquity, and have done wickedly, and have rebelled, even by departing from thy precepts and from thy judgments. —Daniel 9:5

There is, indeed, but one prescribed method of confessing sins. Since it is the Lord who forgives, forgets, and wipes away sins, to him let us confess them that we may obtain pardon. He is the physician, therefore let us show our wounds to him. He is hurt and offended, let us ask peace of him. He is the discerner of the heart and knows all of one's thoughts, let us hasten to pour out our hearts before him. It is he, in fine, who invites sinners; let us delay not to draw near to him. "I acknowledge my sin unto thee," says David, "and mine iniquity have I not hid. I said, I will confess my transgressions unto the LORD; and thou forgave the iniquity of my sin" (Ps. 32:5). The following is Daniel's confession: "We have sinned, and have committed iniquity, and have done wickedly, and have rebelled, even by departing from thy precepts and thy judgments" (Dan. 9:5). To whom are we to confess? We are to confess to him; surely, that is, we are to fall down before him with a grieved and humbled heart and, sincerely accusing and condemning ourselves, seek forgiveness of his goodness and mercy.

He who has adopted this confession from the heart in the presence of God will doubtless have a tongue ready to confess whenever there is occasion among men to publish the mercy of God. He will not be satisfied to whisper the secret of his heart for once into the ear of one individual, but will often, and openly, and in the hearing of the whole world, ingenuously make mention both of his own ignominy and of the greatness and glory of the Lord. In this way David, after he was accused by Nathan, being stung in his conscience, confesses his sin before God and men. "I have sinned unto the LORD," says he (2 Sam. 12:13); that is, I have now no excuse, no evasion; all must judge me a sinner; and that which I wished to be secret with the Lord must also be made manifest to men. And it is proper that by confession of our misery, we should manifest the mercy of our God both among ourselves and before the whole world.

SCRIPTURE AND THE VIRTUOUS LIFE

Not only so, but we also rejoice in our suffering, because we know that suffering produces perseverance; perseverance, character; and character, hope. —Romans 5:3–4, NIV

We have said that the object of regeneration is to bring the life of believers into concord and harmony with the righteousness of God, and so confirm the adoption by which they have been received as sons. But although the Law comprehends within it that new life by which the image of God is restored in us, yet, as our sluggishness stands greatly in need both of helps and incentives it will be useful to collect out of Scripture a true account of this reformation lest any who have a heartfelt desire of repentance should in their zeal go astray. We see the length to which the Fathers, in treating of individual virtues, extend their exhortations. This they do, not from mere talkativeness; for whatever be the virtue which you undertake to recommend, your pen is spontaneously led by the abundance of the matter so to amplify that you seem not to have discussed it properly if you have not done it at length.

My intention, however, in the plan of life which I now propose to give, is not to extend it so far as to treat of each virtue specially, and expatiate in exhortation. For me it will be sufficient to point out the method by which a pious man may be taught how to frame his life aright, and briefly lay down some universal rule by which he may not improperly regulate his conduct. As philosophers have certain definitions of rectitude and honesty, from which they derive particular duties and the whole train of virtues; so in this respect Scripture is not without order, but presents a most beautiful arrangement, one too which is every way much more certain than that of philosophers. The only difference is that they, under the influence of ambition, constantly affect an exquisite eloquence of arrangement, which may serve to display their genius; whereas the Spirit of God, teaching without affectation, is not so perpetually observant of exact method, and yet by observing it at times sufficiently intimates that it is not to be neglected.

CHRISTIAN VIRTUE

But just as he who called you is holy, so be holy in all you do; for it is written: "Be holy, because I am holy." —1 Peter 1:15–16, NIV

The love of righteousness, to which we are by no means naturally inclined, may be instilled and implanted into our minds through the scriptural system. Moreover, it will prescribe a rule which will prevent us while in the pursuit of righteousness from going astray. It has numerous admirable methods of recommending righteousness. Many have been already pointed out in different parts of this work, but we shall here also briefly advert to some of them.

With what better foundation can it begin than by reminding us that we must be holy, because God is holy? (Lev. 19:1; 1 Pet. 1:16). For when we were scattered abroad like lost sheep, wandering through the labyrinth of this world, he brought us back again to his own fold. When mention is made of our union with God, let us remember that holiness must be the bond; not that by the merit of holiness we come into communion with him (we ought rather first to cleave to him, in order that, pervaded with his holiness, we may follow whither he calls), but because it greatly concerns his glory not to have any fellowship with wickedness and impurity. Wherefore he tells us that this is the end of our calling, the end to which we ought ever to have respect, if we would answer the call of God. For to what end were we rescued from the iniquity and pollution of the world into which we were plunged, if we allow ourselves, during our whole lives, to wallow in them?

Besides, we are at the same time admonished that if we would be regarded as the Lord's people, we must inhabit the holy city Jerusalem; which, as he hath consecrated it to himself, it were impious for its inhabitants to profane by impurity. Hence the expressions, "Who shall abide in thy tabernacle? Who shall dwell in thy holy hill? He that walks uprightly, and works righteousness" (Ps. 15:1–2; 24:3–4); for the sanctuary in which he dwells certainly ought not to be like an unclean stall.

CERTAINTY FROM THE GOSPEL

That ye put off concerning the former conversation the old man, which is corrupt according to the deceitful lusts. —Ephesians 4:22

this is the place to address those who, having nothing of Christ but the name and sign, would yet be called Christians. How dare they boast of this sacred name? None have certainty of Christ but those who have acquired the true knowledge of him from the Gospel. The Apostle denies that any man truly has learned Christ who has not learned to put off "the old man, which is corrupt according to the deceitful lusts, and put on Christ" (Eph. 4:22). They are convicted, therefore, of falsely and unjustly pretending a knowledge of Christ, whatever be the volubility and eloquence with which they can talk of the Gospel. Doctrine is not an affair of the tongue, but of the life; it is not apprehended by the intellect and memory merely, like other branches of learning, but is received only when it possesses the whole soul and finds its seat and habitation in the inmost recesses of the heart. Let them, therefore, either cease to insult God (by boasting that they are what they are not) or let them show themselves not unworthy disciples of their divine Master. To doctrine in which our religion is contained we have given the first place, since by it our salvation commences; but it must be inscribed into the breast, and pass into the conduct, and so transform us into itself, as not to prove unfruitful. If philosophers are justly offended and banish from their company with disgrace those who, while professing an art which ought to be the mistress of their conduct, convert it into mere rambling dialect, with how much better reason shall we detest those flimsy philosophers who are contented to let the Gospel play upon their lips when, from its efficacy, it ought to penetrate the inmost affections of the heart, fix its seat in the soul, and pervade the whole man a hundred times more than the frigid discourses of philosophers?

LIFE'S GOAL

We are therefore Christ's ambassadors, as though God were making his appeal through is. We implore you on Christ's behalf: Be reconciled to God. God made him who had no sin to be sin for us, so that in him we might become the righteous of God. —2 Corinthians 5:20–21, NIV

I insist not that the life of the Christian shall breathe nothing but the perfect Gospel, though this is to be desired and ought to be attempted. I insist not so strictly on evangelical perfection, as to refuse to acknowledge as a Christian any man who has not attained it. In this way all would be excluded from the Church, since there is no man who is not far removed from this perfection, while many, who have made but little progress, would be undeservedly rejected. What then?

Let us set this before our eye as the end at which we ought constantly to aim. Let it be regarded as the goal towards which we are to run. In the first place, God uniformly recommends integrity as the principal part of his worship, meaning by integrity real singleness of mind, devoid of gloss and fiction, and to this is opposed a double mind—as if it had been said that the spiritual commencement of a good life is when the internal affections are sincerely devoted to God, in the cultivation of holiness and justice.

But seeing that, in this earthly prison of the body, no man is supplied with strength sufficient to hasten in his course with due readiness, while the greater number are so oppressed with weakness that hesitating, and halting, and even crawling on the ground, they make little progress, let every one of us go as far as his humble ability enables him, and prosecute the journey once begun. No one will travel so badly as not daily to make some degree of progress.

This, therefore, let us never cease to do, so we may daily advance in the way of the Lord; and let us not despair because of the slender measure of success. How little, then, the success may correspond with our wish, our labor is not lost when today is better than yesterday—provided with true singleness of mind we keep our aim and aspire to the goal, not speaking flattering things to ourselves, nor indulging our vices, but making it our constant endeavor to become better, until we attain to goodness itself.

NOT OUR OWN

I have been crucified with Christ and I no longer live, but Christ lives in me. The life I live in the body, I live by faith in the Son of God, who loved me and gave himself for me. —Galatians 2:20, NIV

The great point is that we are consecrated and dedicated to God and, therefore, should not think, speak, design, or act, without a view to his glory. What he has made sacred cannot, without insult to him, be put to ill use. But if we are not our own, but the Lord's, it is plain both what error is to be shunned and to what end the actions of our lives ought to be directed. We are not our own; therefore, neither is our own reason or will to rule our acts and counsels. We are not our own; therefore, let us not make it our end to seek what may be agreeable to our carnal nature. We are not our own; therefore, as far as possible, let us forget ourselves and the things that are ours. On the other hand, we are God's; let us, therefore, live and die to him (Rom. 14:8). We are God's; therefore, let his wisdom and will preside over all our actions. We are God's; to him, then, as the only legitimate end, let every part of our life be directed.

Oh how great the proficiency of him who, taught that he is not his own, has withdrawn the dominion and government of himself from his own reason that he may give them to God! For as the surest source of destruction to men is to obey themselves, so the only haven of safety is to have no other will, no other wisdom, than to follow the Lord wherever he leads. Let this, then be the first step: to abandon ourselves and devote the whole energy of our minds to the service of God. By service, I mean not only that which consists in verbal obedience, but that by which the mind, divested of its own carnal feelings, implicitly obeys the call of the Spirit of God. This transformation, though it is the first entrance to life, was unknown to all the philosophers. They give the government of man to reason alone, thinking that she alone is to be listened to; in short, they assign to her the sole direction of the conduct. But Christian philosophy bids her give place and yield complete submission to the Holy Spirit, so that the man himself no longer lives, but Christ lives and reigns in him (Gal. 2:20).

DISGRACE OF VAINGLORY

Then Jesus said to his disciples, "If anyone would come after me, he must deny himself and take up his cross and follow me."
—Matthew 16:24, NIV

Indeed, we are not to seek our own, but the Lord's will, and act with a view to promote his glory. Great is our proficiency, when, almost forgetting ourselves, certainly postponing our own reason, we faithfully make it our study to obey God and his commandments. For when Scripture enjoins us to lay aside private regard to ourselves, it not only divests our minds of an excessive longing for wealth, or power, or human favor, but eradicates all ambition and thirst for worldly glory and other more secret pests. The Christian ought to be so trained and disposed as to consider that during his whole life he has to do with God.

For this reason, as he will bring all things to the disposal and estimate of God, so he will religiously direct his whole mind to him. For he who has learned to look to God in everything he does is at the same time diverted from all vain thoughts. This is that self-denial which Christ so strongly enforces on his disciples from the very outset (Matt. 16:24). As soon as it takes hold of the mind, it leaves no place either for pride, show, and ostentation; or for avarice, lust, luxury, effeminacy, or other vices which are prescribed by self-love. On the contrary, wherever it reigns not, the foulest vices are indulged in without shame; or, if there is some appearance of virtue, it is vitiated by a depraved longing for applause.

Show me, if you can, an individual who, unless he has renounced himself in obedience to the Lord's command, is disposed to do good for its own sake. Those who have not so renounced themselves have followed virtue at least for the sake of praise. The philosophers who have contended most strongly that virtue is to be desired on her own account, were so inflated with arrogance as to make it apparent that they sought virtue for no other reason than as a ground for indulging in pride. So far, therefore, is God from being delighted with these hunters after popular applause with their swollen breasts that he declares they have received their reward in this world (Matt. 6:2).

GOD'S FIRST PLAN FOR OUR LIVES

Jesus answered and said unto them, This is the work of God, that ye believe on him whom he hath sent. —John 6:29

They had spoken of works. Christ reminds them of one work: faith. By this he means that all that men undertake without faith is vain and useless, but that faith alone is sufficient, because this alone does God require from us—that we believe. For there is here an implied contrast between faith and the works and efforts of men. It is as if he had said, "Men toil to no purpose, when they endeavor to please God without faith, because by running, as it were, out of the course, they do not advance towards the goal." This is a remarkable passage, showing that—though men torment themselves wretchedly throughout their whole life— still they lose their pains if they have not faith in Christ as the rule of their life.

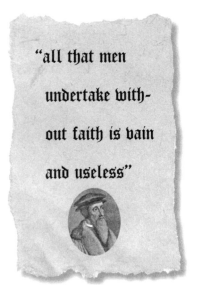

"all that men undertake with- out faith is vain and useless"

But we may think it strange that God approves of nothing but faith alone; for the love of our neighbor ought not to be despised, and the other exercises of religion do not lose their place and honor. So then, though faith may hold the high- est rank, still other works are not superfluous. The reply is easy: for faith does not exclude either the love of our neighbor or any other good work, because it con- tains them all within itself. Faith is called the only work of God, because by means of it we pos- sess Christ, and thus become the sons of God, so that he governs us by his Spirit. So then, because Christ does not separate faith from its fruits, we need not won- der if he make it to be the first and the last.

LIVING ALL THE WAY HOME

And this is the will of him that sent me, that every one which seeth the Son, and believeth on him, may have everlasting life: and I will raise him up at the last day. —John 6:40

h e had said that the Father had committed to him the protection of our salvation and now he likewise describes the manner in which it is accomplished. The way to obtain salvation, therefore, is to obey the Gospel of Christ. This point he had, indeed, glanced at a little before, but now he expresses more fully what he had spoken somewhat obscurely. And if it is the will of God that those whom he has elected shall be saved, and if in this manner he ratifies and executes his eternal decree, whoever he be that is not satisfied with Christ, but indulges in curious inquiries about eternal predestination, such a person (as far as lies in his power), desires to be saved contrary to the purpose of God. The election of God is in itself hidden and secret; the Lord manifests it by calling, that is, when he bestows on us this blessing of calling us.

They are madmen, therefore, who seek their own salvation or that of others in the whirlpool of predestination,

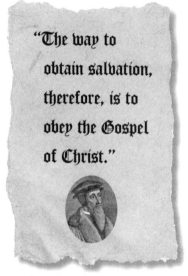

"The way to obtain salvation, therefore, is to obey the Gospel of Christ."

not keeping the way of salvation which is exhibited to them. Nay more, by this foolish speculation, they endeavor to overturn the force and effect of predestination. For if God has elected us to this end—that we may believe—take away faith, and election will be imperfect. But we have no right to break through the order and succession of the beginning and the end, since God, by his purpose, hath decreed and determined that it shall proceed unbroken.

HOW TO FIND JESUS

It is written in the prophets, And they shall be all taught of God.
Every man therefore that hath heard, and hath learned of the Father,
cometh unto me. —John 6:45

again, as Christ formerly affirmed that men are not fitted for believing until they have been drawn, so he now declares that the grace of Christ, by which they are drawn, is efficacious, so that they necessarily believe.

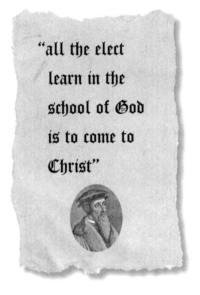

"all the elect learn in the school of God is to come to Christ"

These two clauses utterly overturn the whole power of free will. For if it be only when the Father has drawn us that we begin to come to Christ, there is not in us any commencement of faith, or any preparation for it. On the other hand, if all come whom the Father hath taught, he gives to them not only the choice of believing, but faith itself. Therefore, when we willingly yield to the guidance of the Spirit, this is a part and, as it were, a sealing of grace; because God would not draw us, if he were only to stretch out his hand and leave our will in a state of suspense. But in strict propriety of language he is said to draw us when he extends the power of his Spirit to the full effect of faith. They are said to hear God, who willingly assent to God speaking to them within, because the Holy Spirit reigns in their hearts.

When he says, "Cometh to me," he shows the inseparable connection that exists between him and the Father. For the meaning is that it is impossible that any who are God's disciples shall not obey Christ, and that they who reject Christ refuse to be taught by God—because the only wisdom that all the elect learn in the school of God is to come to Christ—for the Father, who sent him, cannot deny himself.

WHO IS GOD?

And he passed in front of Moses, proclaiming, "The LORD, the LORD, the compassionate and gracious God, slow to anger, abounding in love and faithfulness, maintaining love to thousands, and forgiving wickedness, rebellion and sin. Yet he does not leave the guilty unpunished; he punishes the children and their children for the sin of the fathers to the third and fourth generation." —Exodus 34:6–7, NIV

there are certain passages which contain especially vivid descriptions of God's character, setting it before us as if his true face were visibly portrayed. The author of Exodus, indeed, seems to have intended to briefly comprehend whatever may be known of God by humans when he wrote these verses. From this we may observe, first, that God's eternity and self-sufficiency are declared by his magnificent name twice repeated; and, secondly, that in the listing of God's perfections, God is described not as he is in himself, but as he is in relation to us, so that our acknowledgement of him may be more a vivid, actual impression than empty, visionary speculation. Moreover, the perfections listed are exactly the ones we see shining in the heavens and on the earth: compassion, goodness, mercy, justice, judgment, and truth. Still, however, every perfection listed in the Bible can be seen in creation.

Whatever we feel God to be when experience is our guide, such he declares himself to be by his Word. Assuredly, the attributes which it is most necessary for us to know are these three: loving-kindness, on which alone our entire safety depends; judgment, which is daily exercised on the wicked, and awaits them in a severer form, even for eternal destruction; righteousness, by which the faithful are preserved, and most lovingly cherished. The prophet declares that when you understand these, you have all you need to glory in God. Nor is there any omission of his truth, or power, or holiness, or goodness. For how could this knowledge of his loving-kindness, judgment, and righteousness exist if it were not founded on his inviolable truth? How could it be believed that he governs the earth with judgment and righteousness without presupposing his mighty power? Where, too, does his loving-kindness originate, but from his goodness?

In fine, if all his ways are loving-kindness, judgment, and righteousness, his holiness also is also conspicuous. Moreover, the knowledge of God, which is

CONTEMPLATING GOD'S WORK

They will speak of the glorious splendor of your majesty, and I will meditate on your wonderful works. —Psalm 145:5, NIV

Undoubtedly, one who attempts to give fit words to the inestimable wisdom, power, justice, and goodness of God in the formation of the world, no grace or splendor of diction could equal the greatness of the subject. Still there can be no doubt that the Lord wants us constantly occupied with this holy meditation, so that, as we contemplate the immense treasures of wisdom and goodness exhibited in God's creatures, as if they were so many mirrors, we won't just run our eye over them with a hasty and evanescent glance, but dwell long upon them, seriously and faithfully turn them in our minds, and every now and then recollect them.

Know that you genuinely understand the character of God as the Creator of the world if you do two things: first, if you attend to the general rule of God in the cosmos: never thoughtlessly or obliviously to overlook the glorious perfections which God displays in his creatures, secondly: if you apply what you see to yourself so as to fix it deeply in your heart. We do this first when we consider how great the Architect must be who framed and ordered the multitude of the stars so admirably that it is impossible to imagine a more glorious sight: so stationing some, fixing them to particular spots, that they cannot move; giving a free course to others yet setting limits to their wanderings; so tempering the movement of the whole as to measure out day and night, months, years, and seasons, and at the same time so regulating the unequal length of days as to prevent every thing like confusion. And we also do this when we attend to God's power in sustaining the vast mass, and guiding the swift orbits of the heavenly bodies. If we attempted to go over the whole subject we would never come to a conclusion, since there are as many miracles of divine power, as many striking evidences of wisdom and goodness, as there are classes of objects, nay, as there are individual objects, great or small, throughout the universe.

Praising God's Work

My mouth will speak in praise of the LORD. Let every creature praise his holy name for ever and ever. —Psalm 145:21, NIV

While we observe how God has destined all things for our good and salvation, we at the same time feel his power and grace, both in ourselves and in the great blessings which he has bestowed upon us. This stirs us up to place confidence in him, to invocation, to praise and love. The Lord himself, by the very order of creation, has demonstrated that he created all things for the sake of man.

It is worth noting that God divided the formation of the world into six days, though he would have had no more difficulty completing the whole work, in all its parts, in one moment than by a gradual progression. But God was pleased to display his providence and paternal care towards us in this: Before making humanity, God provided whatever he foresaw would be useful and healthful to him. How ungrateful, then, it would be to doubt whether we are cared for by this most excellent Parent who cared for us even before we were born! How impious to tremble in distrust, lest we should one day be abandoned in need by that kindness which, antecedent to our existence, displayed itself in a complete supply of all good things!

Moreover, the author of Genesis tells us that everything which the world contains is liberally placed at our disposal. As often as we call God the Creator of heaven and earth, let us remember that the distribution of all the things which he created are in his hand and power, but that we are his children, whom he has undertaken to nourish and bring up in allegiance to him. Let us remember this so that we may expect the substance of all good from him alone, and have full hope that he will never let us be in need of things necessary to salvation, so as to leave us dependent on some other source. Let us remember this so that in everything we desire we may address our prayers to him and, in every benefit we receive, acknowledge his hand and give him thanks. And let us remember this so that thus allured by his great goodness and beneficence, we may study with our whole heart to love and serve him.

RESISTING THE DEVIL

Be self-controlled and alert. Your enemy the devil prowls around like a roaring lion looking for someone to devour. Resist him, standing firm in the faith, because you know that your brothers throughout the world are undergoing the same kind of sufferings. —1 Peter 5:8–9, NIV

The tendency of all that Scripture teaches concerning devils is to put us on our guard against their tricks and manipulation, so that we may provide ourselves with weapons strong enough to drive away the most formidable foes. For when Satan is called the god and ruler of this world, the strong man armed, the prince of the power of the air, and the roaring lion, the object of all these descriptions is to make us more cautious and vigilant, and more prepared for the contest. Sometimes this is stated in distinct terms. Peter, after describing the devil as a roaring lion looking for someone to devour, immediately adds the exhortation, "Resist him, standing firm in the faith." And Paul, after reminding us that we wrestle not against flesh and blood, but against principalities, against powers, against the rulers of the darkness of this world, and against spiritual wickedness in high places, immediately enjoins us to put on armor equal to a great and perilous contest (Eph. 6:12).

So let this be the use to which we turn all these statements. Being forewarned of the constant presence of an enemy most daring, most powerful, most crafty, most unflagging, most weaponed, most expert in war, let us not allow ourselves to be overtaken by sloth or cowardice, but, on the contrary, with minds aroused and ever on the alert, let us stand ready to resist. And, knowing that this warfare is terminated only by death, let us learn to persevere. Above all, fully conscious of our weakness and lack of skill, let us invoke the help of God and attempt nothing without trusting in him, since it is his alone to supply counsel, and strength, and courage, and arms.

TRUSTING THE FUTURE TO GOD

So when they met together, they asked him, "Lord, are you at this time going to restore the kingdom to Israel?" He said to them: "It is not for you to know the times or dates the Father has set by his own authority."
—Acts 1:6–7, NIV

esus' answer is a general rejection of the whole question for they were too curious, desiring to know when their Master would have them be ignorant. But this is the true way to become wise: namely, to go as far forward in learning as our Master Christ goes in teaching, and willingly to be ignorant of those things which he conceals from us. But as there is naturally produced in us a certain foolish and vain curiosity, and also a certain rash kind of boldness, we must diligently observe this admonition of Christ in which he corrects both these vices. We must see this as a universal precept: being contented with the revelation of God, it is a heinous crime to inquire any further. Therefore, whenever we are vexed with this foolish desire to know more than we

ought, let us call to mind this saying of Christ, "It is not for you to know."

It is truth itself that God has winter and summer in his own power, and the rest of the seasons of the year, cold and heat, fair weather and foul. But we must be ignorant of the secret events of things, as of what will happen in times to come; for there is nothing which may make us more slack in doing our duties than speculating too subtly on it, for we will always take counsel according to the future events of things; but the Lord, by hiding the same from us, prescribes unto us what we ought to do. A conflict arises here, because we will not willingly suffer God to have that which is his own, namely, the sole government and direction of the days to come.

LIVING IN THE PRESENT

"But you will receive power when the Holy Spirit comes on you; and you will be my witnesses in Jerusalem, and in all Judea and Samaria, and to the ends of the earth." After he said this, he was taken up before their very eyes, and a cloud hid him from their sight.
—Acts 1:8–9, NIV

esus corrects two of the Disciples' errors in this one sentence "You will be my witnesses." First, he shows that they must fight before they can triumph; and, second, that the nature of Christ's kingdom was of another sort than they judged it to have been. Therefore, he says, "You shall be my witnesses"—that is, the planter must first work before he can reap his fruits. Hence, let us learn that we must first study how we may come unto the kingdom of God, before we begin to dispute about the state of the life to come.

Many there are who curiously inquire what manner of blessedness they shall enjoy upon their reception into the everlasting kingdom of heaven, while not having any care how they may come to enjoy the same. They reason concerning the quality of the life to come

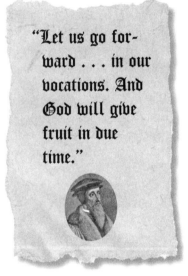

"Let us go forward . . . in our vocations. And God will give fruit in due time."

which they shall have with Christ, but they never think that they must be partakers of his death to live together with him (2 Tim. 2:11). Let each of us apply ourselves to the work at hand; let us fight stoutly under Christ's banner. Let us go forward maturely and courageously in our vocations. And God will give fruit in due time.

Praying
Faithfully

These all abode together with one accord in prayer and supplication,
with the wives, and Mary the mother of Jesus, and with his brethren.
—Acts 1:14, NIV

Luke shows that the Disciples looked diligently for the coming of the Holy Spirit. Furthermore, Luke expresses two things proper to true prayer—namely, that they persisted, and that they were all of one mind. This was an exercise of their patience, in that Christ made them wait a while, when he could straightway have sent the Holy Spirit. So God oftentimes drives off and, as it were, allows us to languish, so that he may train us to persevere. God trains us to be constant in prayer. Therefore, if we wish not to pray in vain, let us not be weary with the delay of time.

About the unity of their minds "with one accord," this is contrasted with the scattering abroad, which fear had caused before when the disciples scattered after Jesus' crucifixion. But we may easily gather, even from this, how important it is to pray generally, in that Christ

> "if we wish not to pray in vain, let us not be weary with the delay of time"

commands every one to pray for the whole body of Christ and generally for all people: "Our Father, give us this day," etc. (Matt. 6:9). Where does this unity of their tongues come from but from one Spirit? And truly it is needful that we be as siblings, and agree together like siblings, so that we may rightly call God Father.

DOUBT AND DISCIPLINE

Then said Jesus unto the twelve, Will ye also go away? —John 6:67

s the faith of the apostles might be greatly shaken, when they saw that they were so small a remnant of a great multitude, Christ directs his discourse to them and shows that there is no reason why they should allow themselves to be hurried away by the lightness and unsteadiness of others. When he asks them if they also wish to go away, he does so in order to confirm their faith; for, by exhibiting to them himself, that they may remain with him, he likewise exhorts them not to become the companions of apostates. And, indeed, if faith be founded on Christ, it will not depend on men and will never waver, though it should see heaven and earth mingling.

We ought also to observe this circumstance: that Christ, when deprived of nearly all his

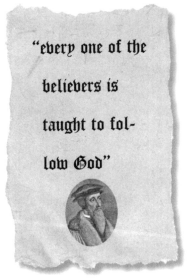

"every one of the believers is taught to follow God"

disciples, retains the twelve only, in like manner as Isaiah was formerly commanded to bind the testimony and seal the law among the disciples (Isa. 8:16).

By such examples, every one of the believers is taught to follow God, even though he should have no companion.

147

WHERE ELSE TO GO?

Then Simon Peter answered him, Lord, to whom shall we go? thou hast the words of eternal life. —John 6:68

It is a remarkable commendation bestowed on the Gospel, that it administers to us eternal life, as Paul testifies, that it is the power of God for salvation to every one who believeth (Rom. 1:16).

True, the Law also contains life, but because it denounces against all transgressors the condemnation of eternal death, it can do nothing but kill. Widely different is the manner in which life is offered to us in the Gospel, that is, when God reconciles us to himself through free grace, by not imputing our sins (2 Cor. 5:19). It is no ordinary assertion that Peter makes concerning Christ, when he says that he has the words of eternal life; but he ascribes this to Christ as belonging to him alone. Hence follows the second statement which I glanced

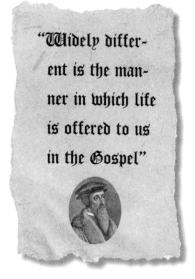

"Widely different is the manner in which life is offered to us in the Gospel"

at a little ago, that as soon as they have gone away from Christ, there remains for them everywhere nothing but death. Certain destruction, therefore, awaits all who, not satisfied with that Teacher, fly to the inventions of men.

Speaking the Truth

And we believe and are sure that thou art that Christ, the Son of the living God. —John 6:6

In these words, Peter gives a brief summary of faith. But the confession appears to have nothing to do with the matter in hand, for the question had been raised about eating the flesh of Christ. I reply, although the twelve did not at once comprehend all that Christ had taught, yet it is enough that, according to the capacity of their faith, they acknowledge him to be the Author of salvation and submit themselves to him in all things.

The word "believe" is put first, because the obedience of faith is the commencement of right understanding, or rather, because faith itself is truly the eye of the understanding. But immediately afterwards knowledge is added, which distinguishes faith from erroneous

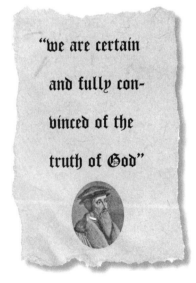

"we are certain and fully convinced of the truth of God"

and false opinions. Knowledge is connected with faith, because we are certain and fully convinced of the truth of God, not in the same manner as human sciences are learned, but when the Spirit seals it on our hearts.

THE KNOWLEDGE OF GOD

We know that we have come to know him if we obey his commands.
—1 John 2:3, NIV

aving discussed the gratuitous forgiveness of sins, John comes to the exhortations which belong to that doctrine, and which depend on it. And first indeed he reminds us that the knowledge of God, derived from the Gospel, is not ineffectual, but that obedience proceeds from it. He then shows what God especially requires from us, what is the chief thing in life: love to God.

What we read here of the living knowledge of God, the Scripture has a reason for repeating everywhere; for nothing is more common in the world than to turn the doctrine of religion into frigid speculation. In this way theology has been adulterated by certain kinds of philosophers, so that from their whole body of work not even the least spark of true religion shines forth. And curious people do everywhere learn just enough from God's

Word, as enables them to prattle for the sake of showing off. In short, no evil has been more common in all ages than vainly professing God's name. John then takes this principle as granted: that the knowledge of God is efficacious. He hence concludes that they by no means know God who keep not his precepts or commandments.

At the same time, the knowledge of God leads us to fear him and to love him. For we cannot know him as Lord and Father, as he shows himself, without being dutiful children and obedient servants. In short, the doctrine of the Gospel is a lively mirror in which we contemplate the image of God and are transformed into that image, as Paul teaches us in 2 Corinthians 3:18. Therefore, where there is no pure conscience, nothing can be there but an empty phantom of knowledge.

LOVING GOD

But if anyone obeys his word, God's love is truly made complete in him.
This is how we know we are in him: whoever claims to live in him
must walk as Jesus did. —1 John 2:5–6, NIV

ohn now defines what a true keeping of God's law is: to love God. Take this as its meaning—"to love God in sincerity of heart, is to keep his commandments." For John intended briefly to show what God requires from us, and what is the holiness of the faithful. Moses also said the same thing when he stated the sum of the law, "And now, O Israel, what does the LORD your God ask of you but to fear the LORD your God, to walk in all his ways, to love him" (Deut. 10:12). For the Law, which is spiritual, does not command only external works, but asks this especially: to love God with the whole heart. That no mention is here made of what we owe to people should not be viewed as unreasonable, for brotherly love flows immediately from the love of God.

Whosoever, then, desires that his life should be approved by God must have all his doings directed to this goal. If anyone objects and says that no one has ever been found who loved God this perfectly, I reply that it is sufficient for every one to aspire to this perfection according to the measure of grace given unto her or him. In the meantime, the definition is that the perfect love of God is the complete keeping of his Law. To make progress in this, as in knowledge, is what we ought to do. Hereby know we that we are in God. John refers to that fruit of the Gospel which he had already mentioned, which is fellowship with the Father and the Son; and he thus confirms the former sentence by stating what follows from it, as a consequence. For if it is the meaning of the Gospel to hold communion with God, and no communion can be without love, then no one makes a real progress in faith except he who cleaves from the heart to God.

A "NEW" COMMAND

Dear friends, I am not writing you a new command but an old one,
which you have had since the beginning. This old command is the mes-
sage you have heard. Yet I am writing you a new command; its truth is
seen in him and you, because the darkness is passing and the true light
is already shining. —1 John 2:7–8, NIV

Other interpreters do not, in my opinion, understand John's meaning here. He says "new" because God, as it were, renews the "new commandment" by daily suggesting it, so that the faithful may practice it through their whole life; for nothing more excellent can be sought by them. When children learn in school, each lesson gives its place in time to things that are higher and more solid. But John denies that the doctrine of brotherly love is of this kind (of the kind of things that grow old with time) but says that it is perpetually in force, so that it is no less the highest perfection than it is the very beginning.

It was, however, necessary that this should be added; for as people are always more curious than they should be, there are many who always seek something new. Hence there is a weariness among Christians for simple doctrines, which pro-

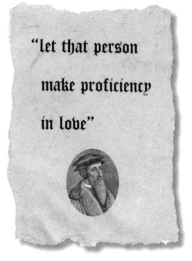

"let that person make proficiency in love"

duces innumerable prodigies of errors, when every person gapes continually after new mysteries. Now, when it is known that the Lord proceeds unchanging in the same even way, in order to keep us all through life in the doctrines which we have learned, a bridle needs to be put on desires of this kind. Thus, let anyone who would reach the goal of wisdom about the right way of living, let that person make proficiency in love.

THE RULE OF LIFE

Anyone who claims to be in the light but hates his brother is still in the darkness. —1 John 2:9, NIV

ohn pursues the same metaphor here as in the last verse. John had said that love is the only true rule to form our life around; he said that this rule or law is presented to us in the Gospel; he said, lastly, that it is there as the guiding light which ought to be continually looked on. Now, on the other hand, he concludes that all who are strangers to love walk in darkness. But the fact that he mentioned the love of God and then the love of others involves no more contradiction than there is between the effect and its cause. These are so connected together that they cannot be separated. John says in the third chapter that we falsely boast of love to God unless we love our brethren, and this is most true. But he now takes love for others as a testimony by which we prove that we love God.

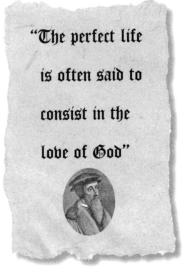

"The perfect life is often said to consist in the love of God"

In short, since love so admires God that in God it embraces all people, it should refer at one time to God, and at another to other people; and this is what is commonly done in Scripture. The perfect life is often said to consist in the love of God. Again, Paul teaches us that the whole law is fulfilled by those who love their neighbors (Rom. 13:8); and Christ declares that the main points of the law are righteousness, judgment, and truth (Matt. 23:23). Both these things are true and agree well together. For the love of God teaches us to love people, and we also in reality prove our love to God by loving other people at God's command. However this may be, it remains certain that love is the rule of life.

THE HEART IS DECEITFUL

The heart is deceitful above all things and beyond cure. Who can understand it? I the LORD search the heart and examine the mind, to reward a man according to his conduct, according to what his deeds deserve. —Jeremiah 17:9–10, NIV

What is taught here depends on what is said before in the chapter, and therefore they ought to be read together. Jeremiah's declaration that all who trust in the flesh are cursed, that we can expect no blessing unless we rely on God, ought to have been sufficient to move his hearers. But when he saw that this wasn't enough, he added, "I see how it is—the heart is deceitful above all things—so you who think yourselves so clever that you can deceive God and his ministers, 'I,' says Jehovah, 'I will search and examine the mind, for it belongs to me to examine the hearts of men.'"

Grant, Almighty God, that because we are wholly nothing and less than nothing, we may know our nothingness And having cast away all confidence in the world as well as in ourselves, we may learn to come to you suppliant and put our trust in you for our present life and for our eternal salvation, so that you

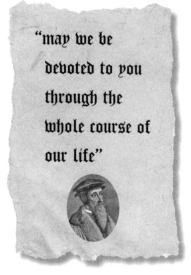

"may we be devoted to you through the whole course of our life"

alone will be glorified. And may we be devoted to you through the whole course of our life, and so persevere in humility and in calling on your name, that you may not only for once bring us help, but that we may know that you are always present with those who truly and from the heart call upon you—until we shall at length be filled with the fullness of all those blessings which are laid up for us in heaven by Christ our Lord. Amen.

GOD'S PROVIDENCE

Then they cried out to the LORD in their trouble, and he delivered them from their distress. —Psalm 107:6, NIV

The Psalmist mentions how God, in a wondrous manner, often brings sudden and unexpected relief to the miserable when almost on the brink of despair; whether in protecting them when they stray in deserts and at length leading them back into the right path, or supplying them with food when starving, or delivering them when captive from iron fetters and foul dungeons, or conducting them safe into harbor after shipwreck, or bringing them back from the gates of death by curing their diseases, or (after burning up the fields with heat and drought) fertilizing them with the river of his grace, or exalting the smallest of the people and casting down the mighty from their lofty seats. The Psalmist, after bringing forward examples of this description, infers that those things which we often call "luck" are so many proofs of divine providence—and more especially of fatherly mercy—furnishing ground for joy to the righteous and, at the same time, stopping the mouths of the ungodly.

But as the greater part of mankind, enslaved by error, walk blindfold in this glorious theater, the Psalmist exclaims that it is a rare and singular wisdom to meditate carefully on these works of God, which many apparently intelligent people behold without profit. Still, neither God's power nor God's wisdom are shrouded in darkness. His power is strikingly displayed when the rage of the wicked, to all appearance irresistible, is crushed in a single moment; their arrogance subdued, their strongest fortress overthrown, their armor dashed to pieces, their strength broken, their schemes defeated without an effort, and cockiness which set itself above the heavens is precipitated to the lowest depths of the earth. On the other hand, the poor are raised up out of the dust and the needy lifted out of the dung hill, the oppressed and afflicted are rescued in extremity, the despairing are animated with hope, the unarmed defeat the armed, the few defeated the many, and the weak defeated the strong.

THE SOUL

Remember him—before the silver cord is severed, or the golden bowl is broken; before the pitcher is shattered at the spring, or the wheel broken at the well, and the dust returns to the ground it came from, and the spirit returns to God who gave it. —Ecclesiastes 12:6–7, NIV

There can be no question that each person consists of a body and a soul, with "soul" meaning an immortal though created essence which is the nobler part. Sometimes it is called a spirit—as when Solomon, speaking of death, says that the spirit returns to God who gave it. And Christ, in commending his spirit to the Father, and Stephen commending his to Christ, simply mean that when the soul is freed from the prison-house of the body, God becomes its perpetual keeper.

It is true, indeed, that people who cleave too much to the earth are dull of apprehension; nay, being alienated from the Father of Lights, are so immersed in darkness as to imagine that they will not survive the grave. Still the light is not so completely quenched in darkness that all sense of immortality is lost. Conscience, in distinguishing between good and evil, responds to the Judgment of God, which makes it an undoubted sign of an immortal spirit. The body cannot be affected by any fear of spiritual punishment. This is competent only to the soul, which must therefore be endued with essence.

Then the mere knowledge of a God sufficiently proves that souls which rise higher than the world must be immortal, since it's impossible for anything else to reach the very fountain of life. In fine, while the many noble faculties given to the human mind proclaim that something divine is engraved on it, they are so many evidences of an immortal essence. The senses that the lower animals possess do not go beyond the body, or at least not beyond the objects actually presented to them. But the swiftness with which the human mind glances from heaven to earth, scans the secrets of nature, and, after it has searched all the ages, uses intellect and memory to digest each in its proper order (and reads the future in the past), clearly demonstrates that there lurks in man a something separated from the body.

GOD IS ACTIVE

By the word of the LORD were the heavens made, their starry host by the breath of his mouth. —Psalm 33:6, NIV
From heaven the LORD looks down and sees all mankind.
—Psalm 33:13, NIV

It is cold and lifeless to represent God as a momentary Creator who completed his work once for all and then left it. Here, especially, we must dissent from the irreligious and maintain that the presence of divine power is conspicuous, as much in the present condition of the world as in its first creation. Without appealing to God's Providence, we cannot understand the full force of what is meant by God being the Creator, however much we may seem to comprehend it with our mind and confess it with our tongue. Faith must penetrate deeper. After learning that there is a Creator, faith must infer that he is also a Governor and Preserver—who doesn't use a kind of general motion in the machine of the globe and its parts, but uses a special providence that sustains, cherishes, superintends, all the things which he has made, to the very smallest, even to a sparrow.

Thus the Psalmist, having assumed that the world was created by God, immediately assumes the continual movement of Providence: By the word of the LORD were the heavens made, their starry host by the breath of his mouth; immediately adding, From heaven the LORD looks down and sees all mankind. He joins other things to the same effect. For although everyone does not reason so accurately, it is not credible that human affairs could be superintended by God unless he made the world; and no one could seriously believe that God is Creator without feeling convinced that he takes care of his works. So the Psalmist, with good reason, and in admirable order, leads us from the one to the other.

SCRIPTURE ANCHORS US

Consequently, you are no longer foreigners and aliens, but fellow citizens with God's people and members of God's household, built on the foundation of the apostles and prophets, with Christ Jesus himself as the chief cornerstone. In him the whole building is joined together and rises to become a holy temple in the Lord. And in him you too are being built together to become a dwelling in which God lives by his Spirit.
—*Ephesians 2:20, NIV*

Paul testifies that the Church is "built on the foundation of the apostles and prophets." If the doctrine of the Apostles and Prophets is the foundation of the Church, the former must have had its certainty before the latter began to exist. For if the Christian Church was founded at first on the writings of the Prophets and the preaching of the Apostles, that doctrine (wherever it may be found) was certainly prior to the Church since, but for this, the Church herself never could have existed. When the Church receives it and gives it the stamp of her authority, she does not make something authentic which was otherwise doubtful; but, acknowledging it as the truth of God, she, out of duty, shows her reverence by an unhesitating assent. As to the question of how we shall be persuaded that it came from

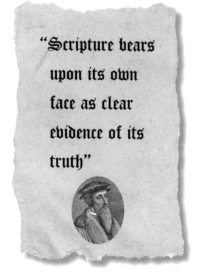

"**Scripture bears upon its own face as clear evidence of its truth**"

God without recurring to a decree of the Church: It is just the same as if it were asked how we learn to distinguish light from darkness, white from black, sweet from bitter. Scripture bears upon its own face as clear evidence of its truth, as white and black do of their color, sweet and bitter of their taste.

THE FINAL GOSPEL

God, who at sundry times and in divers manners spake in time past unto the fathers by the prophets, Hath in these last days spoken unto us by his Son, whom he hath appointed heir of all things, by whom also he made the worlds. —Hebrews 1:1–2

When he speaks of the last times, he intimates that there is no longer any reason to expect any new revelation; for it was not a word in part that Christ brought, but the final conclusion. It is in this sense that the Apostles take the last times and the last days. And Paul means the same when he says, "Upon whom the ends of the world are come" (1 Cor. 10:11). If God then has spoken now for the last time, it is right to advance thus far; so also when you come to Christ, you ought not to go farther. And these two things it is very needful for us to know. For it was a great hindrance to the Jews that they did not consider that God had deferred a fuller revelation to another time. Hence, being satisfied with their own Law, they did not hasten forward to the goal.

"the limit of our wisdom is made here to be the Gospel"

But since Christ has appeared, an opposite evil began to prevail in the world; for men wished to advance beyond Christ. As, then, the Spirit of God in this passage invites all to come as far as Christ, so he forbids them to go beyond the last time which he mentions. In short, the limit of our wisdom is made here to be the Gospel.

VALUE THE GIFT

*For if the word spoken by angels was steadfast, and every transgression
and disobedience received a just recompense of reward; How shall we
escape, if we neglect so great salvation; which at the first began to
be spoken by the Lord, and was confirmed unto us by them that
heard him. —Hebrews 2:2–3*

Not only the rejection of the Gospel, but also its neglect, deserves the heaviest punishment, and that on account of the greatness of the grace which it offers; hence he says, so great a salvation. God would indeed leave his gifts valued by us according to their worth. Then the more precious they are, the baser is our ingratitude when we do not value them. In a word, in proportion to the greatness of Christ will be the severity of God's vengeance on all the despisers of his Gospel.

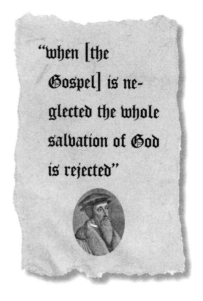

"when [the Gospel] is neglected the whole salvation of God is rejected"

And observe that the word "salvation" here is used to refer to the doctrine of salvation. For as the Lord would not have men otherwise saved than by the Gospel, so when that is neglected the whole salvation of God is rejected; for it is God's power unto salvation to those who believe (Rom. 1:16). Hence, he who seeks salvation in any other way, seeks to attain it by another power than that of God—which is an evidence of extreme madness.

But this high tribute is not only a commendation of the Gospel, but is also a wonderful support to our faith. For it is a testimony that the Word is by no means unprofitable, but that a sure salvation is conveyed by it.

WHO'S REALLY IN CHARGE?

Then they sought to take him: but no man laid hands on him, because his hour was not yet come. —John 7:30

hey had no want of will to do him mischief; they even made the attempt, and they had strength to do it. Why, then, amidst so much ardor, are they benumbed, as if they had their hands and feet bound? The Evangelist replies, because Christ's hour was not yet come; by which he means that, against all their violence and furious attacks, Christ was guarded by the protection of God. And at the same time he meets the offense of the cross. For we have no reason to be alarmed when we learn that Christ was dragged to death, not through the caprice of men, but because he was destined for such a sacrifice by the decree of the Father.

And hence we ought to infer a general doctrine; for though we live from day to day, still the time of every man's death has been fixed by God. It is difficult to believe that, while we are subject to so many accidents, exposed to so many open and concealed attacks both from men and beasts, and liable to so many diseases, we are safe from all risk until God is pleased to call us away.

But we ought to struggle against our own distrust. And we ought to attend first to the doctrine itself which is here taught, and next; to the object at which it aims, and the exhortation which is drawn from it namely, that each of us, casting all his cares on God (Ps. 55:22; 1 Peter 5:7), should follow his own calling and not be led away from the performance of his duty by any fears. Yet let no man go beyond his own bounds, for confidence in the providence of God must not go farther than God himself commands.

RIVERS OF LIFE

He that believeth on me, as the scripture hath said, out of his belly
shall flow rivers of living water. —John 7:38

he now points out the manner of coming, which is that we must approach, not with the feet, but by faith; or rather, to come is nothing else than to believe—at least, if you define accurately the word believe; as we have already said that we believe in Christ, when we embrace him as he is held out to us in the Gospel, full of power, wisdom, righteousness, purity, life, and all the gifts of the Holy Spirit. Besides, he now confirms more plainly and fully the promise which we lately mentioned, for he shows that he has a rich abundance to satisfy us to the full.

The metaphor appears, no doubt, to be somewhat harsh, when he says that rivers of living water shall flow out of the belly of believers; but there can be no doubt as to the meaning, that they who believe shall suffer no want of spiritual blessings. He calls it living water, the fountain of which never grows

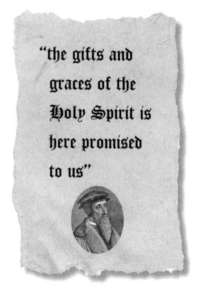

"the gifts and graces of the Holy Spirit is here promised to us"

dry, nor ceases to flow continually. As to the word "rivers" being in the plural number, I interpret it as denoting the diversified graces of the Spirit, which are necessary for the spiritual life of the soul. In short, the perpetuity, as well as the abundance, of the gifts and graces of the Holy Spirit is here promised to us.

HANDLING PEACEFUL TIMES

Then the church throughout Judea, Galilee and Samaria enjoyed a time of peace. It was strengthened; and encouraged by the Holy Spirit, it grew in numbers, living in the fear of the Lord. As Peter traveled about the country, he went to visit the saints in Lydda. There he found a man named Aeneas, a paralytic who had been bedridden for eight years. "Aeneas," Peter said to him, "Jesus Christ heals you. Get up and take care of your mat." Immediately Aeneas got up. All those who lived in Lydda and Sharon saw him and turned to the Lord.
—Acts 9:31–35, NIV

the Churches were edified, they walked in the fear of God, and they were filled with the consolation of the Holy Spirit. For as we are more likely to riot and behave excessively in times of peace, the Churches are better off, for the most part, amidst the tumult of war, than if they should enjoy the rest they so desire. But if holy conversation with others and the consolation of the Spirit, which allows the state of the church to flourish, is taken away, the Church loses not only its happiness, but it finally comes to nothing.

Therefore, let us learn not to abuse external peace in partying and satisfied laziness; but the more rest we are given from our enemies, let us encourage ourselves to go even farther in godliness while we may. And if

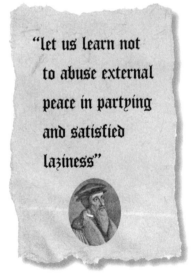

"let us learn not to abuse external peace in partying and satisfied laziness"

at any time the Lord lets loose the bridle of the wicked to trouble us, let the inward consolation of the Spirit be sufficient for us. Finally, as well in peace as in war, let us always joyfully go forward toward him who has a reward for us.

TRUE HAPPINESS

The world and its desires pass away, but the man who does the will of God lives forever. —1 John 2:17, NIV

Since there is nothing in the world but what is fading and momentary, John hence concludes that they who seek their happiness from the world make a wretched and miserable provision for themselves, especially when God calls us to the unspeakable glory of eternal life. It is as though John had said, "The true happiness which God offers to his children is eternal; it is then a shameful thing for us to be entangled with the world, which with all its benefits will soon vanish away."

I take "desire" here as meaning whatever is desired or coveted, or what captivates the desires of men. The meaning is that what is most precious in the world and deemed especially desirable is nothing but a shadowy phantom.

By saying that they who do the will of God shall live forever, or perpetually, John means that they who seek God shall be perpetually blessed. Were anyone to object and say that no one does what God commands, the obvious answer is that what is spo-

"they who seek God shall be perpetually blessed"

ken of here is not the perfect keeping of the Law, but the obedience of faith—which, however imperfect it may be, is yet approved by God. The will of God is first made known to us in the Law; but as no one satisfies the Law, no happiness can be hoped from it. But Christ comes to meet the despairing with new aid; and Christ not only regenerates us by his Spirit so that we may obey God but also makes it so that our attempts, such as they are, should obtain the praise of perfect righteousnes.

THE LAST TIME

Dear children, this is the last hour; and as you have heard that the antichrist is coming, even now many antichrists have come. This is how we know it is the last hour. —1 John 2:18, NIV

In this verse John strengthens the faithful against attacks by which they might have been disturbed. Already many sects had risen up, which rent the unity of faith and caused disorder in the churches. But John not only fortifies the faithful, in case they should falter, but turns the whole to a contrary purpose. For John reminds them that the last time had already come, and therefore he exhorts them to a greater carefulness. It is as though he had said, "While various errors arise, it is good for you to be alert rather than to be overwhelmed; for we ought from this to conclude that Christ is not far distant. Let us then attentively look for him, lest he should come upon us suddenly." In the same way, it is good for us to comfort ourselves at this day and to see by faith the coming advent of Christ— while Satan is causing confusion for the sake of disturbing the Church—for these are the signs of the last time.

But so many ages have passed since the death of John as to seem to prove that this prophecy is not true. To this I answer that John, according to the common mode adopted in the Scripture, declares to the faithful that nothing more now remained but that Christ should appear for the redemption of the world. But as he fixes no time, he did not beguile the people of that age by a vain hope, nor did he intend to cut short in future the course of the Church and the many successions of years during which the Church has hitherto remained in the world. And doubtless, if the eternity of God's kingdom is kept in mind, so long a time will appear to us as a moment. We must understand the meaning of the Apostle: He calls "the last time" the time during which all things shall be so completed, that nothing will remain except the last revelation of Christ.

SUBMITTING THE INTELLECT TO GOD

Then Joshua, together with all Israel, took Achan son of Zerah, the silver, the robe, the gold wedge, his sons and daughters, his cattle, donkeys and sheep, his tent and all that he had, to the Valley of Achor. Joshua said, "Why have you brought this trouble on us? The LORD will bring trouble on you today." Then all Israel stoned him, and after they had stoned the rest, they burned them. —Joshua 7:24–25, NIV

If we are disturbed and offended by the severity of Achan's punishment, we must always be brought back to this point: that though our reason dissents from the judgments of God, we must check our presumption by a pious modesty and soberness, and not condemn whatever does not please us. It seems harsh—no, it seems barbarous and inhuman—that young children, without fault, should be hurried off to cruel execution, to be stoned and burned. That dumb animals should be treated in the same manner is not so strange, as they were created for the sake of men, and thus deservedly follow the fate of their owners. Everything, therefore, which Achan possessed including his children perished with him as an accessory. But still it seems a cruel vengeance to stone and burn children for the crime of their father, and here God publicly inflicts punishment on children for the sake of their parents.

But if we consider how much more deeply divine knowledge penetrates than human intellect can possibly do, we will rather acquiesce in God's decree than hurry ourselves to a precipice by giving way to presumption and extravagant pride. It was certainly not owing to some reckless hatred on God's part that the sons of Achan were pitilessly slain. Not only were they the creatures of God's hand, but circumcision, the infallible symbol of God's adoption, was engraved on their flesh; and yet he adjudges them to death. What here remains for us, but to acknowledge our weakness and submit to God's incomprehensible counsel?

CHRIST OUR MEDIATOR

Jacob left Beersheba and set out for Haran. When he reached a certain place, he stopped for the night because the sun had set. Taking one of the stones there, he put it under his head and lay down to sleep. He had a dream in which he saw a stairway resting on the earth, with its top reaching to heaven, and the angels of God were ascending and descending on it. —Genesis 28:10–12, NIV

The author of Genesis here teaches how opportunely, and (as we may say) in the critical moment, the Lord aided his servant. For who would not have said that holy Jacob was neglected by God, since he was exposed to wild beasts and to every kind of injury from earth and sky, and found nowhere any help or solace? But with Jacob reduced to the last necessity, the Lord suddenly stretches out his hand to him, and wonderfully takes care of his trouble with a remarkable oracle. So, now, the Lord gives a memorable example of his paternal care towards the faithful.

The form of the vision is related, which is very pertinent to the subject of it: that God manifested himself as seated upon a ladder, the extremities of which touched heaven and earth, and which was the vehicle of angels descending from heaven to earth. But to us, who hold to the principle that the covenant of God was founded in Christ and that Christ himself was the eternal image of the Father, there is nothing in this vision that is difficult or ambiguous. For since men are alienated from God by sin, though he fills and sustains all things by his power, yet we do not perceive the communication by which he wants to draw us to him; but, on the other hand, so greatly are we at variance with him, that we, in our turn, flee from him, regarding him as against us. It is Christ alone, therefore, who connects heaven and earth. He is the only Mediator who reaches from heaven down to earth. He is the medium through which the fullness of all celestial blessings flows down to us and through which we, in turn, ascend to God.

STRENGTH THROUGH WEAKNESS

So Jacob was left alone, and a man wrestled with him till daybreak. When the man saw that he could not overpower him, he touched the socket of Jacob's hip so that his hip was wrenched as he wrestled with the man. Then the man said, "Let me go, for it is daybreak." But Jacob replied, "I will not let you go unless you bless me." —Genesis 32:24–25, NIV

here is described the victory of Jacob, which, however, was not gained without a wound. In saying that the wrestling angel, or God, wished to quit the contest because he saw he would lose, the author of Genesis speaks in the way of people. For we know that God, when he descends from his majesty to us, often transfers the properties of human nature to himself.

Though Jacob gains the victory, yet the angel strikes him on the thigh, making Jacob lame even to the end of his life. And although the vision was by night, yet the Lord designed this reminder of it that would continue through all his days, so that it would not appear to have been a vain dream. Moreover, by this sign it is made manifest to all the faithful that they can conquer in their temptations only by being injured and wounded in the conflict. For we know that the strength of God is made perfect in our weakness, in order that our exaltation may be joined with humility. If our own strength remained complete and there were no injury or dislocation produced in us, immediately the flesh would become proud; and we would forget that we had conquered only by the help of God. But the wound received, and the weakness which follows it, compel us to be modest.

Moreover, this passage teaches us always to expect the blessing of God, even if we may have experienced his presence to be harsh and painful, even to the breaking of our bones. For it is far better for the children of God to be blessed, though mutilated and half destroyed, than for them to desire that peace in which they shall fall asleep, or for them to withdraw themselves from the presence of God so as to turn away from his command, that they may rebel with the wicked.

CONSTANCY IN FAITH

I look for your deliverance, O LORD. —*Genesis 49:18, NIV*

It may be asked, in the first place, why Jacob interrupts this blessing upon his sons and suddenly bursts forth in this expression. I think, indeed, that when he saw, as if from a high tower, the way his children would live continually among change, being even buffeted by storms which would threaten to overwhelm them, he was moved with concern and fear. He, therefore, foreseeing many troubles, many dangers, many assaults, and even many slaughters which threatened his children with as many destructions, could not help but sympathize with them and, as a man, be troubled at the sight. When this sad confusion of things presented itself to him—which was not only violent enough to shake his faith, but was more sufficient to overwhelm his mind—his best remedy was to oppose it with this shield. Moreover, because he could not be the maker of his own salvation, it was necessary for him to rest upon the promise of God.

In the same manner also, must we, at this day, hope for the salvation of the Church. For although it seems to be tossed on a turbulent sea, and almost sunk in the waves, and though still greater storms are to be feared in future; yet amidst many destructions, salvation is to be hoped for in that deliverance which the Lord has promised. It is even possible that Jacob, foreseeing through the Spirit the greatness of his children's ingratitude, treachery, and wickedness—by which the grace of God might be smothered—was fighting against these temptations. But although he expected salvation not for himself alone, but for all his children, this, however, deserves to be specially noted: that he exhibits the life-giving covenant of God to many generations, so as to show his own confidence that, after his death, God would be faithful to his promise. Whence also it follows that, with his last breath and in the midst of death, he laid hold on eternal life. But if he—amidst obscure shadows, relying on a redemption seen afar off—boldly went forth to meet death, what can we do, we on whom the clear day has shined?

TRUSTING GOD, NOT FLESH

This is what the LORD says: "Cursed is the one who trusts in man, who depends on flesh for his strength and whose heart turns away from the LORD." —Jeremiah 17:5, NIV

We shall understand the Prophet's meaning if we bear in mind the condition of the Jews and the difficulties the Prophet had to contend with as he daily threatened them and labored to restore them to God. But no progress was made, and why? Because all God's promises were coldly received, for they thought themselves ever safe and secure. Jeremiah's threats also were coldly received because the Jews believed the aid they expected from the Egyptians would be their shield and strongest fortress. Hence the Prophet was forced to cry out, not only once, or ten times, but a hundred times, "Cursed is the one who trusts in man, who depends on flesh for his strength."

This is however a general truth. We also, even today, talk of general truths which we apply to individual cases. The spirit declares here, generally, that all are cursed who trust in humans. We indeed know that the human race is in various ways deceived when humans trust themselves. They begin with themselves and seek security in this thing or that thing. For all are inflated with vain and false confidence in their own prudence or dexterity or power. There is then no one who does not trust in himself before he trusts in others; I speak even of the most wretched. It is indeed what we ought to be ashamed of; but there is no one so contemptible that he won't swell with some secret pride, esteeming something in himself, and even ascribing to himself some high dignity. But when people look behind and before themselves, they gather help to themselves from all parts of the world. However, their goings-around are useless, and even turn out to be their own destruction; for God not only mocks the folly of those who trust in flesh, but declares that they are accursed. This curse of God ought to strike us with terror, for we hence learn that God is highly displeased with all those who seek their own salvation in the world and in creatures.

PROGRESS

For we are made partakers of Christ, if we hold the beginning of our confidence steadfast unto the end. —Hebrews 3:14

e commends them for having begun well; but lest, under the pretext of the grace which they had obtained, they should indulge themselves in carnal security, he says that there was need of perseverance. For many, having only tasted the Gospel, do not think of any progress as though they had reached the summit. Thus it is that they not only stop in the middle of their race, yea, nigh the starting-posts, but turn another way.

Plausible indeed is this objection, "What can we wish more after having found Christ?" But if he is possessed by faith, we must persevere in it, so that he may be our perpetual possession. Christ then has given himself to be enjoyed by us on this condition: that by the same faith by which we have been admitted into a participation of him, we are to

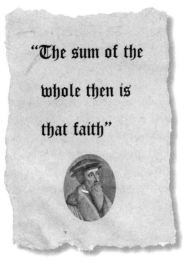

"The sum of the whole then is that faith"

preserve so great a blessing even to death. Hence he says "beginning," intimating that their faith was only begun.

We shall be firmly fixed and beyond the danger of vacillating, provided faith be our foundation. The sum of the whole then is that faith, whose beginnings only appear in us, is to make constant and steady progress to the end.

SPIRITUAL EXERCISE

The Lord is near to all who call on him, to all who call on him in truth. —Psalm 145:18, NIV

The end for which the Lord taught us to pray is not so much for his sake as for ours. He wills, indeed, that due honor be paid him by acknowledging that everything people desire or feel to be useful, and pray to obtain, is derived from God. But even the benefit of the homage which we thus pay him returns to ourselves.

Although it is true that while we are listless or insensible to our wretchedness, he wakes and watches for use and sometimes even assists us unasked; it is very much for our interest to be constantly supplicating him; first, that our heart may always be inflamed with a serious and ardent desire of seeking, loving, and serving him, while we accustom ourselves to have recourse to him as a sacred anchor in every necessity; secondly, that no desires of which we are ashamed to make him the witness may enter our minds, while we learn to place all our wishes in his sight, and thus pour out our heart before him; and, lastly, that we may be prepared to receive all his benefits with true gratitude and thanksgiving, while our prayers remind us that they proceed from his hand. Moreover, having obtained what we asked, being persuaded that he has answered our prayers, we are led to long more earnestly for his favor, and at the same time have greater pleasure in welcoming the blessings obtained by our prayers.

Lastly, use and experience confirm the thought of his providence in our minds in a manner adapted to our weakness, when we understand that he not only promises that he will never fail us, and spontaneously gives us access to approach him in every time of need, but has his hand always stretched out to assist his people, not amusing them with words, but proving himself to be a present aid. Though our most merciful Father never slumbers nor sleeps, he very often seems to do so, that thus he may exercise us, when we might otherwise be listless and slothful, in asking, entreating, and earnestly beseeching him to our great good.

KNOWING YOURSELF

To fear the LORD is to hate evil; I hate pride and arrogance, evil behavior and perverse speech. —*Proverbs 8:13, NIV*

t was not without reason that the ancient proverb so strongly recommended to man the knowledge of himself. For if it is deemed disgraceful to be ignorant of things pertaining to the business of life, much more disgraceful is self-ignorance, in consequence of which we miserably deceive ourselves in matters of the highest moment, and so walk blindfold. But the more useful the precept is, the more careful we must be not to use it preposterously, as we see certain philosophers have done. For they, when exhorting man to know himself, state the motive to be that he may not be ignorant of his own excellence and dignity. They wish him to see nothing in himself but what will fill him with vain confidence and inflate him with pride.

But self-knowledge consists in this: First, when reflecting on what God gave us at our creation, and still continues graciously to give, we perceive how great the excellence of our nature would have been had its integrity remained, and, at the same time, remember that we have nothing of our own, but depend entirely on God, from whom we hold at pleasure whatever he has seen it necessary to bestow. Secondly, when viewing our miserable condition since Adam's fall, all confidence and boasting are overthrown, we blush for shame, and feel truly humble.

For as God at first formed us in his own image, that he might elevate our minds to the pursuit of virtue, and the contemplation of eternal life, so to prevent us from heartlessly burying those noble qualities which distinguish us from the lower animals, it is of importance to know that we were endued with reason and intelligence, in order that we might cultivate a holy and honorable life, and regard a blessed immortality as our destined aim. At the same time, it is impossible to think of our primeval dignity without being immediately reminded of the sad spectacle of our disgrace and corruption, ever since we fell from our original position in the person of our first parent.

NO ROOM TO BOAST

Where, then, is boasting? It is excluded. On what principle? On that of observing the law? No, but on that of faith. —Romans 3:27, NIV

In examining ourselves—the search which divine truth enjoins and the knowledge which it demands—we are left of all means of boasting, and so inclined to submission. This is the course which we must follow if we would attain to the true goal, both in speculation and practice.

Know how much more plausible the view is which invites us rather to ponder on our good qualities than to contemplate what must overwhelm us with shame—our miserable destitution and ignominy. There is nothing more acceptable to the human mind than flattery, and, accordingly, when told that its endowments are of a high order, it is apt to be excessively credulous. Hence it is not strange that the greater part of mankind have erred so blatantly bad in this matter. Owing to the innate self-love by which all are blinded, we most willingly persuade ourselves that we do not possess a single quality which is deserving of hatred; and hence, independent of any countenance from without, general credit is given to the very foolish idea that man is perfectly sufficient of himself for all the purposes of a good and happy life.

If any are disposed to think more modestly and concede somewhat to God, still, in making the division, they apportion matters so that the chief ground of confidence and boasting always remains with themselves. Then, if a discourse is pronounced which flatters the pride spontaneously springing up in man's inmost heart, nothing seems more delightful. Accordingly, in every age, he who is most forward in praising the excellence of human nature is received with the loudest applause.

But be this heralding of human excellence what it may, by teaching man to rest in himself, it does nothing more than fascinate by its sweetness, and, at the same time, so delude as to drown in perdition all who assent to it. Whosoever, therefore, gives heed to those teachers, who merely employ us in contemplating our good qualities, so far from making progress in self-knowledge, will be plunged into the most harmful and destructive ignorance.

A BEACON TO THE DISTANT SHORE

Then spake Jesus again unto them, saying, I am the light of the world:
he that followeth me shall not walk in darkness, but shall have
the light of life. —John 8:12

It is a beautiful commendation of Christ, when he is called the light of the world; for, since we are all blind by nature, a remedy is offered, by which we may be freed and rescued from darkness and made partakers of the true light. Nor is it only to one person or to another that this benefit is offered, for Christ declares that he is the light of the whole world; for by this universal statement he intended to remove the distinction, not only between Jews and Gentiles, but between the learned and ignorant, between persons of distinction and the common people.

It must also be observed that the power and office of illuminating is not confined to the personal presence of Christ; for though he is far removed from us with respect

"yet he daily sheds his light upon us"

to his body, yet he daily sheds his light upon us—by the doctrine of the Gospel, and by the secret power of his Spirit. Yet we have not a full definition of this light, unless we learn that we are illuminated by the Gospel and by the Spirit of Christ, that we may know that the fountain of all knowledge and wisdom is hidden in him.

175

THE ADMIRATION OF GOD'S POWER

Marvel not that I said unto thee, Ye must be born again. The wind bloweth where it listeth, and thou hearest the sound thereof, but canst not tell whence it cometh, and whither it goeth: so is every one that is born of the Spirit. —John 3:7–8

Nicodemus reckoned that what he had heard about regeneration and a new life was incredible, because the manner of this regeneration exceeded his capacity. To prevent him from entertaining any scruple of this sort, Christ shows that even in the bodily life there is displayed an amazing power of God, the reason of which is concealed. For all draw from the air their vital breath; we perceive the agitation of the air, but know not whence it comes to us or whither it departs. If in this frail and transitory life God acts so powerfully that we are constrained to admire his power, what folly is it to attempt to measure by the perception of our own mind his secret work in the heavenly and supernatural life, so as to believe no more than what we see?

When Christ says to Nicodemus that he ought not to wonder, we must not understand it in such a manner as if he intended that we should despise a work of God, which

> "for many reject as fabulous what they think too lofty and difficult"

is so illustrious, and which is worthy of the highest admiration. He means that we ought not to wonder with that kind of admiration which hinders our faith; for many reject as fabulous what they think too lofty and difficult. In a word, let us not doubt that by the Spirit of God we are formed again and made new men, though his manner of doing this be concealed from us.

CHRIST PROPOSES A REMEDY

And no man hath ascended up to heaven, but he that came down from heaven, even the Son of man which is in heaven. —John 3:13

We must attend to the words that Christ alone, who is heavenly, ascends to heaven, but that the entrance is closed against all others. For, in the former clause, he humbles us when he excludes the whole world from heaven. Paul enjoins those who are desirous to be wise with God to be fools with themselves (1 Cor. 3:18). There is nothing which we do with greater reluctance. For this purpose we ought to remember that all our senses fail and give way when we come to God; but, after having shut us out from heaven, Christ quickly proposes a remedy when he adds that what was denied to all others is granted to the Son of God.

"we have an entrance into heaven in common with him who clothed himself with our flesh"

And this too is the reason why he calls himself the Son of man, so we may not doubt that we have an entrance into heaven in common with him who clothed himself with our flesh, that he might make us partakers of all blessings. Since, therefore, he is the Father's only Counselor (Isa. 9:6), he admits us into those secrets which otherwise would have remained in concealment. Christ, therefore, who is in heaven, hath clothed himself with our flesh, so, by stretching out his brotherly hand to us, he may raise us to heaven along with him.

OUR WICKED NATURE

For God so loved the world, that he gave his only begotten Son, that whosoever believeth in him should not perish, but have everlasting life.
—John 3:16

hrist opens up the first cause and, as it were, the source of our salvation, which he does so that no doubt may remain; for our minds cannot find calm repose until we arrive at the unmerited love of God. As the whole matter of our salvation must not be sought anywhere else than in Christ, so we must see whence Christ came to us, and why he was offered to be our Savior.

Both points are distinctly stated to us; namely, that faith in Christ brings life to all, and that Christ brought life, because the Heavenly Father loves the human race and wishes that they should not perish. And this order ought to be carefully observed; for such is the wicked ambition which belongs to our nature, so when the question relates to the origin of our salvation, we quickly form diabolical imaginations about our own merits. Accordingly, we imagine that God is reconciled to us, because he has reckoned us worthy that he should look upon us.

But Scripture everywhere extols his pure and unmingled

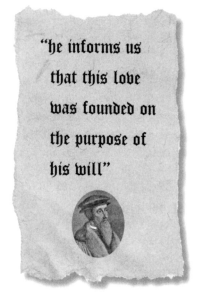

"he informs us that this love was founded on the purpose of his will"

mercy, which sets aside all merits. And the words of Christ mean nothing else, when he declares the cause to be in the love of God. For if we wish to ascend higher, the Spirit shuts the door by the mouth of Paul when he informs us that this love was founded on the purpose of his will (Eph. 1:5). And, indeed, it is very evident that Christ spoke in this manner, in order to draw away men from the contemplation of themselves to look at the mercy of God alone.

THE WONDER OF SALVATION

Meanwhile, Saul was still breathing out murderous threats against the Lord's disciples. He went to the high priest and asked him for letters to the synagogues in Damascus, so that if he found any there who belonged to the Way, whether men or women, he might take them as prisoners to Jerusalem. As he neared Damascus on his journey, suddenly a light from heaven flashed around him. He fell to the ground and heard a voice say to him, "Saul, Saul, why do you persecute me?" "Who are you, Lord?" Saul asked. "I am Jesus, whom you are persecuting," he replied.
—Acts 9:1–5, NIV

In this history we have a universal figure of that grace which the Lord shows forth daily in calling us all. All people do not set themselves so violently against the Gospel; yet, nevertheless, both pride and also rebellion against God are naturally engendered in all. We are all wicked and cruel naturally; therefore, in that we are turned to God, that happens by the wonderful and secret power of God, contrary to nature.

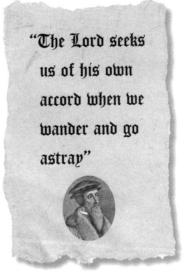

"The Lord seeks us of his own accord when we wander and go astray"

Therefore, such is the beginning of our conversion: The Lord seeks us of his own accord when we wander and go astray, though he is not called and sought, and he changes the stubborn affections of our heart, so that he may have us ready to be taught. When as a deadly enemy to Christ, rebellious against the Gospel, puffed up with the confidence which he rested on his wisdom, inflamed with hatred of the true faith, blinded with hypocrisy, wholly set upon the overthrowing of the truth, he is suddenly changed into a new man—in a way that no one looked for—and from a wolf is not only turned into a sheep but does also become a shepherd, it is as if Christ should bring forth with his hand some angel sent from heaven.

INGRATITUDE AND GOD'S JUDGMENT

But if the wicked will turn from all his sins that he hath committed, and keep all my statutes, and do that which is lawful and right, he shall surely live, he shall not die. All his transgressions that he hath committed, they shall not be mentioned unto him: in his righteousness that he hath done he shall live. —Ezekiel 18:21–22

To some it seems harsh, and at variance with the divine mercy, utterly to deny forgiveness to any who redirect themselves to it. This is easily disposed of. It is not said that pardon will be refused if they turn to the Lord, but it is altogether denied that they can turn to repentance—inasmuch as for their ingratitude they are struck by the just judgment of God with eternal blindness. There is nothing contrary to this in the application which is afterwards made of the example of Esau, who tried in vain, by crying and tears, to recover his lost birthright; nor in the denunciation of the Prophet, "They cried, and I would not hear." Such modes of expression do not denote true conversion or calling upon God, but that anxiety with which the wicked are compelled to see what they before securely disregarded; that is, nothing can avail but the assistance of the Lord. This, however, they do not so much implore as lament the loss of. Hence all that the Prophet means by crying, and the apostle by tears, is the dreadful torment which stings and excruciates the wicked in despair.

It is of consequence carefully to observe this: for otherwise God would be inconsistent with himself when he proclaims through the Prophet that "If the wicked will turn from all his sins that he has committed…he shall surely live, he shall not die" (Ezek. 18:21–22). And (as I have already said) it is certain that the mind of man cannot be changed for the better unless by his preventing grace. The promise as to those who call upon him will never fail; but the names of conversion and prayer are improperly given to that blind torment by which the degenerate are distracted when they see that they must seek God if they would find a remedy for their calamities, and yet shun to approach him.

CONFESSION OF SINS

I will give you the keys of the kingdom of heaven; whatever you bind on earth will be bound in heaven, and whatever you loose on earth will be loosed in heaven. —Matthew 16:19, NIV

One form of confession is made on our own account, and to it reference is made in the passage in James, "Confess your sins one to another" (James 5:16); for the meaning is that by disclosing our infirmities to each other, we are to obtain the aid of mutual counsel and consolation. Although James, by not specifying any particular individual into whose bosom we are to disburden our feelings, leaves us the free choice of confessing to any member of the church who may seem fittest; yet as for the most part pastors are to be supposed better qualified than others, our choice ought chiefly to fall upon them. And the ground of preference is that the Lord, by calling them to the ministry, points them out as the persons by whose lips we are to be taught to subdue and correct our sins and derive consolation from the hope of pardon.

For as the duty of mutual admonition and correction is committed to all Christians, but is specially enjoined on ministers, so while we ought all to console each other mutually and confirm each other in confidence in the divine mercy, we see that ministers, to assure our consciences of the forgiveness of sins, are appointed to be the witnesses and sponsors of it, so that they are themselves said to forgive sins (Matt. 16:19; 18:18). When you hear this attributed to them, reflect that it is for your use. Let every believer, therefore, remember that if in private he is so agonized and afflicted by a sense of his sins that he cannot obtain relief without the aid of others, it is his duty not to neglect the remedy which God provides for him—that is, to have recourse for relief to a private confession to his own pastor, and for consolation privately implore the assistance of him whose business it is, both in public and private, to comfort the people of God with Gospel doctrine.

CONFESSION AND THE CHURCH

The punishment inflicted on him by the majority is sufficient for him.
—2 Corinthians 2:6, NIV

Of another form of confession, our Savior speaks in Matthew. "If thou bring thy gift to the altar, and there remember that thy brother has ought against thee; leave there thy gift before the altar; first be reconciled to thy brother, and then come and offer thy gift" (Matt. 5:23–24). Thus love, which has been interrupted by our fault, must be restored by acknowledging and asking pardon for the fault.

Under this head is included the confession of those who by their sin have given offense to the whole Church. For if Christ attaches so much importance to the offense of one individual that he forbids the sacrifice of all who have sinned in any respect against their brethren, until by due satisfaction they have regained their favor, how much greater reason is there that he who by some evil example has offended the Church should be reconciled to it by the acknowledgment of his fault? Thus the member of the Church of Corinth was restored to communion after

he had humbly submitted to correction (2 Cor. 2:6). This form of confession existed in the ancient Christian Church, as Cyprian relates: "They practice repentance," says he, "for a proper time, then they come to confession, and by the laying on of the hands of the bishop and clergy, are admitted to communion."

Scripture knows nothing of any other form or method of confessing, and it belongs not to us to bind new chains upon consciences which Christ most strictly prohibits from being brought into bondage. Meanwhile, that the flock present themselves before the pastor whenever they would partake of the Holy Supper, I am so far from disapproving that I am most desirous it should be everywhere observed. For both those whose conscience is hindered may obtain singular benefit, and those who require admonition thus afford an opportunity for it, provided always no countenance is given to tyranny and superstition.

SUCCESS COMES FROM GOD

Not that I speak in respect of want: for I have learned, in whatsoever state I am, therewith to be content. —Philippians 4:11

If we believe that all prosperous and desirable success depends entirely on the blessing of God, and that when it is wanting all kinds of misery and calamity await us, it follows that we should not eagerly contend for riches and honors, trusting to our own dexterity and assiduity, or leaning on the favor of men, or confiding in any empty imagination of fortune, but instead we should always have respect to the Lord that under his support we may be conducted to whatever lot he has provided for us.

First, the result will be that instead of rushing on regardless of right and wrong, by wiles and wicked arts, and with injury to our neighbors, to catch at wealth and seize upon honors, we will only follow such fortune as we may enjoy with innocence. As this blessing attends him only who thinks purely and acts uprightly, so it calls off all who long for it from sinister designs and evil actions. Secondly, a curb will be laid upon us, restraining a too eager desire of becoming rich, or an ambitious striving after honor. What God with his own lips pronounces cursed, never can be prosecuted with his blessing. Lastly, if our success is not equal to our wish and hope, we shall, however, be kept from impatience and detestation of our condition, whatever it be, knowing that so to feel were to murmur against God—at whose pleasure riches and poverty, contempt and honors, are dispensed.

In short he who leans on the divine blessing in the way which has been described, will not, in the pursuit of those things which men are wont most eagerly to desire, employ wicked arts which he knows would avail him nothing; nor when anything prosperous befalls him will he impute it to himself and his own diligence, or industry, or fortune, instead of ascribing it to God as its author.

GOD'S PROVIDENCE

When the day of Pentecost came, they were all together in one place.
Suddenly a sound like the blowing of a violent wind came from heaven
and filled the whole house where they were sitting. They saw what
seemed to be tongues of fire that separated and came to rest on each of
them. All of them were filled with the Holy Spirit and began to speak
in other tongues as the Spirit enabled them. —Acts 2:1–4, *NIIV*

The diversity of languages hindered the Gospel from being spread abroad any farther, so that if the preachers of the Gospel had spoken one language only, all the world would have thought that Christ had been shut up in the small corner of Jewry. But God invented a way for it to break out when he divided and clove the tongues of the Apostles, so that they might spread among all people what had been delivered to them.

"Thus emerges the manifold goodness of God"

Thus emerges the manifold goodness of God, because a plague and punishment of man's pride was turned into matter of blessing. For whence came the diversity of languages, except so that God could bring the wicked and ungodly counsels of humans to nothing. But God furnishes the Apostles with the diversity of tongues now, that he may bring and call home, into a blessed unity, people who wander here and there.

I said that this was done for our sake, not only because the fruit of it came to us, but because we know that the Gospel became ours not by chance, but by the appointment of God, who for this very purpose gave the Apostles tongues of fire, lest any nation should lack that doctrine which was committed unto them.

THE GIFT OF SALVATION

And I will shew wonders in heaven above, and signs in the
earth beneath; blood, and fire, and vapor of smoke; The sun shall be
turned into darkness, and the moon into blood, before that great
and notable day of the Lord come: And it shall come to pass,
that whosoever shall call on the name of the Lord shall be saved.
—Acts 2:19–21

s God pricks us forward, as if we were sluggish asses, with threats and terrors to seek salvation, see that after that he has brought darkness upon the face of heaven and earth, he shows us a means whereby salvation may shine before our eyes: if we shall call upon him. For we must diligently note this circumstance. If God simply promises salvation, that is a great matter; but it is far greater that he promises the same amidst manifold dungeons of death. "When," he says, "all things shall be out of order, and the fear of destruction shall possess all things, only call upon me, and you shall be saved." Therefore, however we may be swallowed up in the gulf of miseries, yet is there set before us a way to escape.

We must also note the universal word "anyone." For God admits all people to himself without exception, and by this means he invites them to salvation. Therefore, as much as no one is excluded from calling upon God, the gate of salvation is set open to all—neither is there any other thing which keeps us back from entering in, save only our own unbelief.

God was called upon in all ages but since he showed himself to be a Father in Christ, we have all the more easy access to him. This ought both to embolden us the more, and to take from us all sluggishness. As Jesus himself also says, by this privilege our willingness to pray is doubled to us: "Until now you have not asked for anything in my name. Ask and you will receive, and your joy will be complete" (John 16:24). It is as if he says, "Although I did not yet appear to be a mediator and interceder in the faith, still you prayed; but now, when you shall have me to be your father, with how much more courage should you pray?"

185

REPENTANCE

And Peter said to them, "Repent, and be baptized every one of you in the name of Jesus Christ for the forgiveness of your sins; and you shall receive the gift of the Holy Spirit." —Acts 2:38, NIV

There is greater force in the Greek word which is translated "repent," for it signifies the conversion of the mind, that the whole person may be renewed and made another person. Let us know that this is the true repentance: when people are renewed in the spirit of their minds, as Paul teaches (Rom. 12:2). We have in these few words almost the whole sum of Christianity, namely, how by renouncing themselves and taking their farewell of the world, people may addict themselves wholly to God. This sermon must continually sound in the Church: "Repent!" (Mark 1:15)—not so that those who have already been counted faithful and have a place in the Church may begin to repent, but that they may go forward in doing so.

Thus we must observe this order in teaching, so that those who yet live unto the world and the flesh can begin to crucify the old man, so that they

> "the inward conversion of the heart ought to bring forth fruits in the life"

may rise unto newness of life; and so that those who are already entered the course of repentance may continually go forward towards the mark. Furthermore, because the inward conversion of the heart ought to bring forth fruits in the life, repentance cannot be rightly taught unless works be required, but such works as are sound testimonies of innocence and holiness.

FREEDOM IN FAITH

And ye shall know the truth, and the truth shall make you free.
—John 8:32

e commends the knowledge of the Gospel from the fruit which we derive from it, or—which is the same thing—from its effect, namely, that it restores us to freedom. This is an invaluable blessing. Hence it follows that nothing is more excellent or desirable than the knowledge of the Gospel. All men feel and acknowledge that slavery is a very wretched state; and since the Gospel delivers us from it, it follows that we derive from the Gospel the treasure of a blessed life.

We must now ascertain what kind of liberty is here described by Christ; namely, that which sets us free from the tyranny of Satan, sin, and death. And if we obtain it by means of the Gospel, it is evident from this that we are by nature the slaves of sin. Next, we must ascertain what is the method of our deliverance. For

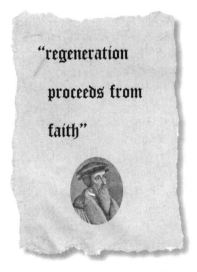

"regeneration proceeds from faith"

so long as we are governed by our sense and by our natural disposition, we are in bondage to sin. But when the Lord regenerates us by his Spirit, he likewise makes us free, so that, loosed from the snares of Satan, we willingly obey righteousness. But regeneration proceeds from faith, and hence it is evident that freedom proceeds from the Gospel.

WISE TEACHING

Brothers, I could not address you as spiritual but as worldly—mere
infants in Christ. I gave you milk, not solid food, for you were not yet
ready for it. Indeed you are still not ready.
—*1 Corinthians 3:1–2, NIV*

Christ is at once milk to babes, and strong meat to those that are of full age (Heb. 5:13–14). The same truth of the Gospel is administered to both, but so as to suit their capacity. Hence it is the part of a wise teacher to accommodate the capacity of those under instruction, so that in dealing with the weak and ignorant, he begins with first principles, and does not go higher than they are able to follow (Mark 4:33). He drops in his instructions little by little, lest it should run over, if poured in more abundantly. At the same time, those first principles will contain everything necessary to be known, no less than the advanced lessons those who are stronger.

Some, while they do but mutter out, from fear of danger, something of the Gospel in an indistinct manner, pretend to have Paul's example here. Meanwhile, they present Christ at such a distance, and with so many disguises, that they constantly keep their followers in destructive ignorance. I shall say nothing of their mixing up many corruptions, their presenting Christ not simply in half, but torn to fragments, their not merely concealing such gross idolatry, but confirming it also by their own example. How unlike they are to Paul is sufficiently manifest; for milk is nourishment and not poison, and nourishment that is suitable and useful for bringing up children until they are farther advanced.

That they may not flatter themselves too much on their own discernment, he first of all tells them what he had found among them at the beginning, and then adds, what is still more severe, that the same faults remain among them to this day. For they ought at least, in putting on Christ, to have put off the flesh; thus we see that Paul complains that the success which his doctrine ought to have had was impeded. For if the hearer does not occasion delay by his slowness, it is the part of a good teacher to be always going up higher, till perfection has been attained.

LONGING FOR HEAVEN

*Meanwhile we groan, longing to be clothed with our heavenly dwelling,
because when we are clothed, we will not be found naked. For while we
are in this tent, we groan and are burdened, because we do not wish
to be unclothed but to be clothed with our heavenly dwelling,
so that what is mortal may be swallowed up by life.*
—2 Corinthians 5:2–4, NIV

The wicked groan because they are not content with their present condition; but afterwards an opposite disposition prevails, that is, a clinging to life, so that they view death with horror, and do not feel the long continuance of this mortal life to be a burden. The groaning of believers, on the other hand, arises from this—they know that they are here in a state of exile from their native land; they know that they are shut up in the body as in a prison. Hence they feel this life to be a burden, because in it they cannot enjoy true and perfect blessedness, because they cannot escape from the bondage of sin otherwise than by death, and hence they aspire to be elsewhere.

As, however, it is natural for all animals to desire existence, how can it be, that believers are willing to cease to exist? The Apostle solves this question when he says that believers do not desire death for the sake of losing any thing, but as having regard to a better life. At the same time, the words express more than this. For he admits that we naturally have an aversion to the quitting of this life, considered in itself, as no one willingly allows himself to be stripped of his garments. Afterwards, however, he adds that the natural horror of death is overcome by confidence; just as an individual will, without any reluctance, throw away a coarse, dirty, threadbare, and tattered garment, with the view of his being arrayed in an elegant, handsome, new, and durable one.

Further, he explains the metaphor by saying that what is mortal may be destroyed by life. For as flesh and blood cannot inherit the kingdom of God (1 Cor. 15:50), it is necessary that what is corruptible in our nature should perish, in order that we may be thoroughly renewed and restored to a state of perfection. On this account, our body is called a prison, in which we are confined.

THE FOUNTAIN OF LIFE

For with you is the fountain of life; in your light we see light.
—Psalm 36:9, NIV

We clearly see how completely destitute man is of all good, how devoid of every means of procuring his own salvation. Hence, if he would obtain relief in his necessity, he must go beyond himself and obtain it in some other quarter. It has further been shown that the Lord kindly and spontaneously manifests himself in Christ, in whom he offers all happiness for our misery, all abundance for our want, opening up the treasures of heaven to us, so that we may turn with full faith to his beloved Son, depend upon him with full expectation, rest in him, and cleave to him with full hope. This, indeed, is that secret and hidden philosophy which cannot be learned by syllogisms: a philosophy thoroughly understood by those whose eyes God has so opened as to see light in his light (Ps. 36:9).

But after we have learned by faith to know that whatever is necessary for us or defective in us is supplied in God and in our Lord Jesus Christ—in whom it has pleased the Father that all fullness should dwell, that we may then draw as from an inexhaustible fountain—it remains for us to seek and in prayer beg of him what we have learned to be in him. To know God as the sovereign giver of all good, inviting us to present our requests, and yet not to approach or ask of him, would be like a person told of a treasure who allowed it to remain buried in the ground. Hence the Apostle, to show that a faith unaccompanied with prayer to God cannot be genuine, states this to be the order: As faith springs from the Gospel, so by faith our hearts are framed to call upon the name of God (Rom. 10:14). And this is the very thing which he had expressed some time before, that the Spirit of adoption, which seals the testimony of the Gospel on our hearts, gives us courage to make our requests known unto God, calls forth groanings which cannot be uttered, and enables us to cry, "Abba, Father" (Rom. 8:26).

JOY TELLS US, IT'S TRUE!

Your father Abraham rejoiced to see my day: and he saw it, and was glad. —John 8:56

faith has its degrees in beholding Christ. Thus the ancient prophets beheld Christ at a distance, as he had been promised to them, and yet were not permitted to behold him present—as he made himself familiarly and completely visible, when he came down from heaven to men.

Again, we are taught by these words that, as God did not disappoint the desire of Abraham, so he will not now permit any one to breathe after Christ without obtaining some good fruit which shall correspond to his holy desire. The reason why he does not grant the enjoyment of himself to many is—the wickedness of men for few desire him. Abraham's joy testifies that he regarded the knowledge of the kingdom of Christ as an incomparable treasure and the reason why we are told that he rejoiced to see the day of Christ is that we may know that there

"their consciences are calm and cheerful."

was nothing which he valued more highly.

But all believers receive this fruit from their faith, that, being satisfied with Christ alone, in whom they are fully and completely happy and blessed, their consciences are calm and cheerful. And indeed no man knows Christ aright, unless he gives him this honor of relying entirely upon him.

ASKING GOOD QUESTIONS

And as Jesus passed by, he saw a man which was blind from his birth.
And his disciples asked him, saying, Master, who did sin, this man, or
his parents, that he was born blind? —John 9:1–2

first, while every man is ready to censure others with extreme bitterness, there are few who apply to themselves, as they ought to do, the same severity. If my brother meets with adversity, I instantly acknowledge the judgment of God; but if God chastises me with a heavier stroke, I wink at my sins. But in considering punishments, every man ought to begin with himself, and to spare himself as little as any other person. Wherefore, if we wish to be candid judges in this matter, let us learn to be quick in discerning our own evils rather than those of others.

The second error lies in excessive severity; for no sooner is any man touched by the hand of God, than we conclude that this shows deadly hatred, and we turn small offenses into crimes, and almost despair of his salvation. On the contrary, by extenuating our sins, we scarcely think that we have committed very small offenses, when we have committed a

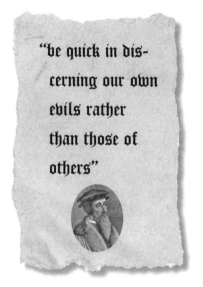

"be quick in discerning our own evils rather than those of others"

very aggravated crime.

Thirdly, we do wrong in this respect, that we pronounce condemnation on all, without exception, whom God visits with the cross or with tribulation. What we have lately said is undoubtedly true, that all our distresses arise from sin; but God afflicts his own people for various reasons. Sometimes he does not look at their sins, but only tries their obedience, or trains them to patience—as we see that holy Job.

DON'T TRUST MONEY

When Simon saw that the Spirit was given at the laying on of the apostles' hands, he offered them money and said, "Give me also this ability so that everyone on whom I lay my hands may receive the Holy Spirit." Peter answered: "May your money perish with you, because you thought you could buy the gift of God with money! You have no part or share in this ministry, because your heart is not right before God. Repent of this wickedness and pray to the Lord. Perhaps he will forgive you for having such a thought in your heart. For I see that you are full of bitterness and captive to sin." —Acts 8:18–23, NIV

Let us remember, first, so that we may be free from the infection of Simon, that the gifts of the Spirit are not gotten with money, but that they are given of the free and mere goodness of God, for the edifying of the Church. That is they are given, so that all may study to help their siblings in Christ according to the measure of their ability; so that all may distribute about the common good of the Church what they have received; and that the excellency of no one may hinder, but that Christ may excel all.

Whereas Peter exhorts Simon to repentance and prayer, he puts him in some hope of pardon thereby. For no one shall ever be touched with any desire of repentance save only he who shall believe that God will have mercy upon him; on the other side, despair will always carry us headlong unto boldness. Therefore, we see how Peter raises up Simon now unto hope of salvation— whom he had thrown down before with the cruel lightning and thunderbolt of words— and yet Simon's sin was no small sin. But, if it could be, we ought to pluck people even out of hell.

Therefore, until such time as even the most wicked do by manifest signs betray themselves to be lost, no one of them is to be handled so sharply that the remission of sins cannot be set before him or her. Yea, we must deal with those who, because of their hardness and stubbornness, need sharp chiding, in such a way that we throw them down with one hand, and set them on foot with the other.

FULL ASSURANCE OF FAITH

"The words of the LORD are pure words: as silver tried in a furnace of earth, purified seven times." —Psalm 12:6

s faith is not contented with a dubious and fickle opinion, so neither is it contented with an obscure and ill-defined conception. The certainty which it requires must be full and decisive, as is usual in regard to matters ascertained and proved. So deeply rooted in our hearts is unbelief, so prone are we to it, that while all confess with the lips that God is faithful, no man ever believes it without an arduous struggle. Especially when brought to the test, we by our wavering betray the vice which lurked within. Nor is it without cause that the Holy Spirit bears such distinguished testimony to the authority of God, in order that it may cure the disease of which I have spoken and induce us to give full credit to the divine promises: "The words of the LORD are pure words, as silver tried in a furnace of earth purified seven times" (Ps.12:6). "The word of the LORD is tried: he is a buckler to all those that trust in him" (Ps. 18:30). Certainly, whenever God thus recommends his Word, he indirectly rebukes our unbelief—the purport of all that is said being to eradicate perverse doubt from our hearts.

There are very many also who are harassed by miserable anxiety while they doubt whether God will be merciful to them. They think, indeed, that they are most fully persuaded of the divine mercy, but they confine it within too narrow limits. The idea they entertain is that this mercy is great and abundant, is shed upon many, is offered and ready to be bestowed upon all; but that it is uncertain whether it will reach to them individually, or rather whether they can reach to it. Thus their knowledge stopping short leaves them only mid-way, not so much confirming and tranquilizing the mind as harassing it with doubt and unease. Very different is that feeling of full assurance (pleroforiva) which the Scriptures uniformly attribute to faith—an assurance which leaves no doubt that the goodness of God is clearly offered to us. This assurance we cannot have without truly perceiving its sweetness, and experiencing it in ourselves.

IMPLICIT FAITH

For it is with your heart that you believe and are justified, and it is
with your mouth that you confess and are saved.
—Romans 10:10, NIV

We grant, indeed, that so long as we are pilgrims in the world faith is implicit—not only because as yet many things are hidden from us, but because, involved in the mists of error, we attain not to all. The highest wisdom, even of him who has attained the greatest perfection, is to go forward, and endeavor in a calm and teachable spirit to make further progress. Hence Paul exhorts believers to wait for further illumination in any matter in which they differ from each other (Phil. 3:15). And certainly experience teaches that so long as we are in the flesh, our attainments are less than is to be desired. In our daily reading we fall in with many obscure passages which convict us of ignorance. With this curb God keeps us modest, assigning to each a measure of faith that every teacher, however excellent, may still be disposed to learn.

Striking examples of this implicit faith may be observed in the disciples of Christ before they were fully illuminated. We see with what difficulty they take in the first rudiments, how they hesitate in the minutest matters, how, though hanging on the lips of their Master, they make no great progress. As Christ previously bore testimony to their faith, we cannot say that they were altogether devoid of it; nay, had they not been persuaded that Christ would rise again, all their zeal would have been extinguished. Nor was it superstition that led the women to prepare spices to embalm a dead body of whose revival they had no expectation; but, although they gave credit to the words of one whom they knew to be true, yet the ignorance which still possessed their minds involved their faith in darkness and left them in amazement. Hence they are said to have believed only when, by the reality, they perceive the truth of what Christ had spoken; not that they then began to believe, but the seed of a hidden faith, which lay as it were dead in their hearts, then burst forth in vigor. They had, therefore, a true but implicit faith, having reverently embraced Christ as the only teacher.

THE ONLY WAY

Verily, verily, I say unto you, He that entereth not by the door into the sheepfold, but climbeth up some other way, the same is a thief and a robber. —John 10:1

I t is useless, I think, to scrutinize too closely every part of this parable. Let us rest satisfied with this general view: As Christ states a resemblance between the Church and a sheepfold, in which God assembles all his people, so he compares himself to a door, because there is no other entrance into the Church but by himself. Hence it follows that they alone are good shepherds who lead men straight to Christ, and that they are truly gathered into the fold of Christ (so as to belong to his flock) who devote themselves to Christ alone. But all this relates to doctrine; for, since all the treasures of wisdom and knowledge are hidden in Christ (Col. 2:3), he who turns aside from him to go elsewhere neither keeps the road nor enters by the door.

Now, whoever shall not despise Christ or his instructor will easily rid himself of that hesitation which keeps so many in a state of perplexity regarding what is the Church, and who are they to whom we ought to listen as shepherds. For if they who are called shepherds attempt to lead

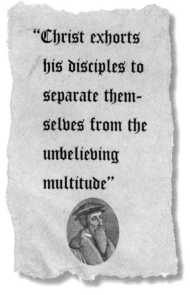

"**Christ exhorts his disciples to separate themselves from the unbelieving multitude**"

us away from Christ, we ought to flee from them, at the command of Christ, as we would flee from wolves or thieves; and we ought not to form or maintain intercourse with any society but that which is agreed in the pure faith of the Gospel. For this reason Christ exhorts his disciples to separate themselves from the unbelieving multitude of the whole nation, not to suffer themselves to be governed by wicked priests, and not to allow themselves to be imposed upon by proud and empty names.

THE DESIGN OF CHRIST

Jesus answered, Verily, verily, I say unto thee, Except a man be born of water and of the Spirit, he cannot enter into the kingdom of God.
—John 3:5

We must always keep in remembrance the design of Christ; namely, that he intended to exhort Nicodemus to newness of life, because he was not capable of receiving the Gospel until he began to be a new man. Christ added, by way of explanation, that it is not in a natural way that men are born a second time, and that it is not necessary for them to be clothed with a new body, but that they are born when they are renewed in mind and heart by the grace of the Spirit. Accordingly, he employed the words Spirit and water to mean the same thing, and this ought not to be regarded as a harsh or forced interpretation; for it is a frequent and common way of speaking in Scripture when the Spirit is mentioned to add the word "water" or "fire," expressing his power.

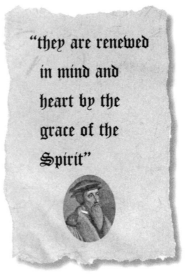

"they are renewed in mind and heart by the grace of the Spirit"

We sometimes meet with the statement that it is Christ who baptizes with the Holy Ghost and with fire (Matt. 3:11; Luke 3:16)—where fire means nothing different from the Spirit, but only shows what is his efficacy in us. As to the word "water" being placed first, it is of little consequence; or rather, this mode of speaking flows more naturally than the other, because the metaphor is followed by a plain and direct statement, as if Christ had said that no man is a son of God until he has been renewed by water, and that this water is the Spirit who cleanses us anew and who, by spreading his energy over us, imparts to us the rigor of the heavenly life, though by nature we are utterly dry.

197

A Striking Faith

So the men set out in pursuit of the spies on the road that leads to the fords of the Jordan, and as soon as the pursuers had gone out, the gate was shut. —Joshua 2:7, NIV

Although Rahab helped much by deluding the men pursuing the Israelite spies, a new cause of anxiety arises; for once the gates had been shut, the city, like a prison, excluded the hope of escape. The Israelites were therefore aroused once again, by a serious trial, to call upon God. It is impossible that they could have been ignorant of what was then going on, especially since God, for the purpose of magnifying his grace, purposely exposed them to a series of dangers. And now, when they knew that they were being pursued, we infer that they were anxious and alarmed. Their fear must have been more than slightly increased when they were told that their exit was precluded by the shutting of the gates.

It appears, however, that Rahab was not at all dismayed, since she displays so much presence of mind, and so calmly, for her own safety and that of her family. And in this composure and firmness, her faith, which the Bible in other places praises, is striking. Thinking on human principles, she never would have braved the fury of the king and her people, and asked a favor from guests who were half dead with terror. Anyone who will carefully weigh all the circumstances will easily perceive that she had a lively faith.

If the tree is known by its fruits, we see in Rahab some extraordinary fruit—which itself is evidence of faith. Secondly, a principle of piety must have given birth to her feeling that the neighboring nations were already conquered, in a way, and ready to be finished off. Rahab declares in the sincerity of her heart that God has destined the land for the children of Israel, because all the inhabitants have fainted away before them, and believes that God claims a supreme rule over the hearts of people—a rule which the pride of the world denies.

FREE RIGHTEOUSNESS

Christ is the end of the law so that there may be righteousness for everyone who believes. —Romans 10:4, NIV

The Apostle here deals with an objection that might have been made against him, for the Jews might have appeared to have kept the right way by depending on the righteousness of the Law. It was necessary for Paul to disprove this false opinion, and this is what he does here. He shows that anyone is a false interpreter of the Law who seeks to be justified by her or his own works, because the Law has been given for this end: to lead us by the hand to another righteousness. Whatever the Law teaches, whatever it commands, whatever it promises, always has a reference to Christ as its main object, and hence all its parts ought to be applied to him. But this cannot be done, unless we, being stripped of all righteousness and confounded with the knowledge of our sin, seek free righteousness from Christ alone.

It hence follows that Paul is right to reprehend the evil abuse of the Law by the Jews, who absurdly made an obstacle of that which was to be their help. It appears that they shamefully mutilated the Law of God for they rejected its soul and seized on the dead body of the letter. For though the Law promises reward to those who observe its righteousness, it substitutes, after having proved all guilty, another righteousness in Christ—which is not attained by works, but is received by faith as a free gift. Thus the righteousness of faith receives a testimony from the Law. We have then here a remarkable passage that proves that the Law in all its parts had a reference to Christ; and hence no one can rightly understand it, who does not continually level at this mark.

PROCLAIMING THE GOSPEL

How, then, can they call on the one they have not believed in? And how can they believe in the one of whom they have not heard? And how can they hear without someone preaching to them? And how can they preach unless they are sent? As it is written, "How beautiful are the feet of those who bring good news." —Romans 10:14–15, NIV

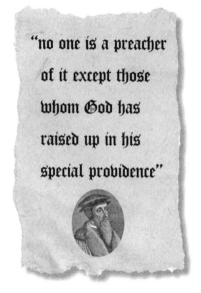

"no one is a preacher of it except those whom God has raised up in his special providence"

he meaning of these verses is that we are, in a way, mute until God's promise opens our mouth to pray. And this is the order which God shows us through the prophet Zechariah, when God says, "I will say, 'They are my people,' and they will say, 'The LORD is our God'" (Zech. 13:9). It is not our job to imagine a God according to whatever we may desire; we ought to possess a right knowledge of God, such as is set forth in the Bible. And when we form an idea of God as good, according to our own understanding, it is not a sure nor a solid faith which we have, but an uncertain and evanescent dream. It is therefore necessary to have the Word, so that we may have a right knowledge of God. But if anyone were to say, because of these verses, that God cannot reveal himself to us except through preaching, I deny that to teach this idea was Paul's intention; for Paul was only thinking of God's ordinary ways, and did not intend to prescribe a law for the distribution of God's grace.

Paul suggests that it is a proof and a pledge of divine love when any nation is favored with the preaching of the Gospel, and that no one is a preacher of it except those whom God has raised up in his special providence. Thus there is no doubt that God visits all nations to whom the Gospel is proclaimed. The Gospel does not fall like rain from the clouds, but is brought by the hands of people wherever it is sent from above.

CHRIST OUR INTERCESSOR

My dear children, I write this to you so that you will not sin. But if anybody does sin, we have one who speaks to the father in our defense—Jesus Christ, the Righteous One. —1 John 2:1, NIV

We are to depart from sin; and yet, though we are always exposed to God's judgment, we are certain that Christ intercedes for us by the sacrifice of his death, so that the Father is gracious to us. In the meantime, John here also anticipates an objection, in case any reader should think that John gave us a license to sin when he spoke of God's mercy and showed that it is presented to us all. He then joins together the two parts of the Gospel which unthinking people separate, and thus lacerate and mutilate. Besides, the doctrine of grace has always been put down by the ungodly. When Christ's expiation of our sin is mentioned, the ungodly arrogantly say that a license is thus given to sin. To prevent these insults, John testifies first that the idea behind his doctrine was to keep us from sinning; for when he says "so that you will not sin," he means only that his readers, as far as they are able, should abstain from sins. And for the same reason John says what he says about fellowship with God, that we should conform to God. John is not, however, silent about the gratuitous remission of sins. For though heaven should fall and all things be confused, yet this part of truth ought never to be omitted; but, on the contrary, what Christ is ought to be preached clearly and distinctly.

For this reason John immediately adds the second clause, that when we sin we have an advocate. By these words he confirms that we are very far from being perfectly righteous, that we contract new guilt daily, and that yet there is a remedy for reconciling us to God, if we flee to Christ. In short, John means that we are not only called away from sin by the Gospel, because God invites us to himself and offers to us the Spirit of regeneration, but that a provision is made for miserable sinners.

VAIN LOVE

Do not love the world or anything in the world. If anyone loves the world, the love of the Father is not in him. —1 John 2:15, NIV

ohn said before that the only rule for living religiously is to love God. But since when we are occupied with the vain love of the world, we turn away all our thoughts and affections another way, this vanity must first be torn away from us in order that the love of God may reign within us. Until our minds are cleansed, the former doctrine of loving God may be said a hundred times, but with no effect. It would be like pouring water on a ball; you can't gather a drop, because there is no empty place to retain water.

By "the world," John means everything connected with the present life, apart from the kingdom of God and the hope of eternal life. So John includes in it corruptions of every kind, and the abyss of all evils. In the world are pleasures, delights, and all those allurements by which we are captivated, so that we withdraw ourselves from

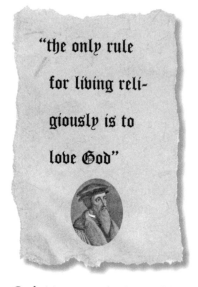

"the only rule for living religiously is to love God"

God. Moreover, the love of the world is severely condemned, because we must forget God and ourselves when we regard nothing as much as the earth; and when a corrupt lust of this kind rules in someone and holds him or her so entangled that she or he thinks not of the heavenly life, that person is possessed by a beastly stupidity.

NO ROOM FOR SIN

But you know that he appeared so that he might take away our sins.
And in him is no sin. —1 John 3:5, NIV

hen he says, "And in him is no sin," John does not speak of Christ personally, but of Christ's whole body. Wherever Christ diffuses his powerful grace, John denies that there is any more room for sin. John therefore immediately draws this inference: that those who remain in Christ do not sin. For if Christ dwells in us by faith, he performs his own work; that is, he cleanses us from sins. It hence appears what it is to sin. For Christ by his Spirit does not perfectly renew us at once, or in an instant, but he continues our renovation throughout life. It must, therefore, be that the faithful are exposed to sin as long as they live in the world; but as far as the kingdom of Christ prevails in them, sin is abolished.

In the meantime, they are designated according to the prevailing principle; that is, they are said to be righteous and to live righteously because they sin-

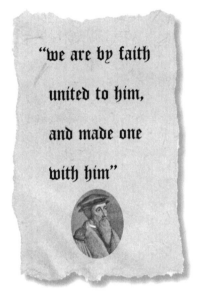

"we are by faith united to him, and made one with him"

cerely aspire to righteousness. They are said not to sin, because they consent not to sin though they labor under the infirmity of their flesh. But, on the contrary, they struggle, groaning, so that they can truly testify with Paul that they do the evil they would not. John says that the faithful abide in Christ, because we are by faith united to him, and made one with him.

SHOWING MERCY

Joshua had his family come forward man by man, and Achan son of Carmi, the son of Zimri, the son of Zerah, of the tribe of Judah, was taken. Then Joshua said to Achan, "My son, give glory to the LORD, the God of Israel, and give him the praise. Tell me what you have done; do not hide it from me." —Joshua 7:18–19, NIV

Joshua interrogates Achan without having any doubt, and when the discovery is made, urges Achan to confess to stealing condemned goods from the city of Jericho. Joshua calls Achan "son," neither ironically nor hypocritically, but truly and sincerely declaring that he felt like a father toward Achan whom he had already doomed to death.

By this example, judges are taught that, while they punish crimes, they ought to temper their harshness so as not to lay aside the feelings of humanity and, on the other hand, that they ought to be merciful without being reckless and remiss. In other words, they ought to be like parents toward those they condemn, without substituting undue mildness for the sternness of justice. Many use flattering kindness to throw wretched criminals off guard; they pretend that they mean to pardon them and then, after a

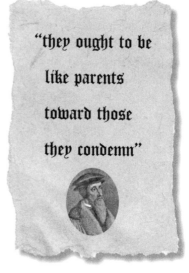

"they ought to be like parents toward those they condemn"

confession has been extracted, suddenly hand them over to the executioner, when the guilty were hoping to be saved.

But Joshua, satisfied with having found the criminal before the tribunal of God, does not at all flatter him with a vain hope of pardon, and is thus more at liberty to pronounce the sentence which God has dictated.

REMEDY FOR FEAR

Let us therefore come boldly unto the throne of grace, that we may obtain mercy, and find grace to help in time of need. —Hebrews 4:16

the ground of this assurance is that the throne of God is not arrayed in naked majesty to confound us, but is adorned with a new name—even that of grace—which ought ever to be remembered whenever we shun the presence of God. For the glory of God, when we contemplate it alone, can produce no other effect than to fill us with despair; so awful is his throne.

The Apostle, then, that he might remedy our insecurity and free our minds from all fear and trembling, adorns it with "grace," and gives it a name which can allure us by its sweetness. It is as though he had said, "Since God has affirmed to his throne as it were the banner of 'grace' and of his paternal love towards us, there are no reasons why his majesty should drive us away."

The import of the whole is that we are to call upon God without fear, since we know

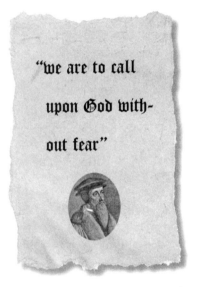

"we are to call upon God without fear"

that he is eager to help us, and that this may be done is owing to the benefit conferred on us by Christ (as we find from Eph. 3:12). For when Christ receives us under his protection and patronage, he covers with his goodness the majesty of God, which would otherwise be terrible to us, so that nothing appears there but grace and paternal favor.

PROMISE OF PARDON

For this is the covenant that I will make with the house of Israel after those days, saith the LORD; I will put my laws into their mind, and write them in their hearts: and I will be to them a God, and they shall be to me a people. —Hebrews 8:10

Whatever desire then there may be in us to live righteously, we are still guilty of eternal death before God, because our life is ever very far from the perfection which the Law requires. There would then be no stability in the covenant, except God gratuitously forgave our sins. But it is the peculiar privilege of the faithful who have once embraced the covenant offered to them in Christ, that they feel assured that God is propitious to them; nor is the sin to which they are liable a hindrance to them, for they have the promise of pardon.

And it must be observed that this pardon is promised to them, not for one day only, but to the very end of life, so that they have a daily reconciliation with God. For this favor is extended to the whole of Christ's kingdom, as Paul

"by fleeing to God's mercy, which alone can pardon us"

abundantly proves in the fifth chapter of his second Epistle to the Corinthians. And doubtless this is the only true asylum of our faith, to which if we flee not, constant despair must be our lot. For we are all of us guilty; nor can we be otherwise released than by fleeing to God's mercy, which alone can pardon us.

SECURE IN HIS HANDS

And I give unto them eternal life; and they shall never perish, neither shall any man pluck them out of my hand. —John 10:28

It is an inestimable fruit of faith that Christ bids us be convinced of our security when we are brought by faith into his fold. But we must also observe on what foundation this certainty rests. It is because he will be a faithful guardian of our salvation, for he testifies that our salvation is in his hand.

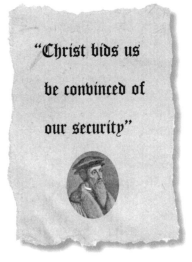

"Christ bids us be convinced of our security"

And if this were not enough, he says that they will be safely guarded by the power of his Father. This is a remarkable passage, by which we are taught that the salvation of all the elect is not less certain than the power of God is invincible. Besides, Christ did not intend to throw this word foolishly into the air, but to give a promise which should remain deeply axed in their minds; and, therefore, we infer that the statement of Christ is intended to show that the elect are absolutely certain of their salvation.

We are surrounded, indeed, by powerful adversaries, and so great is our weakness, that we are every moment in imminent danger of death; but as he who keeps what we have committed to him (2 Tim. 1:12) is greater or more powerful than all, we have no reason to tremble as if our life were in danger. In short our salvation is certain because it is in the hand of God; for our faith is weak, and we are too prone to waver. But God, who has taken us under his protection, is sufficiently powerful to scatter, with his breath alone, all the forces of our adversaries.

THE INVITATION TO ALL

And looking upon Jesus as he walked, he saith, Behold the Lamb of God! —John 1:36

ere we see also how small and low the beginning of the Church was. John, indeed, prepared disciples for Christ, but it is only now that Christ begins to collect a Church. He has no more than two men who are mean and unknown, but even this contributes to illustrate his glory: that within a short period, without human aid, and without a strong hand, he spreads his kingdom in a wonderful and incredible manner.

We ought also to observe what is the chief object to which John directs the attention of men; it is to find in Christ the forgiveness of sins. And as Christ had presented himself to the disciples for the express purpose that they might come to him, so now when they come, he gently encourages them. For he does not wait until they first address him, but asks, "What do you seek?" This kind and gracious invitation belongs to all.

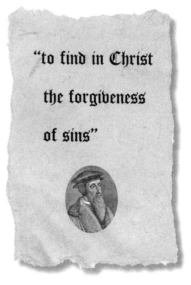

"to find in Christ the forgiveness of sins"

We ought not therefore to fear that Christ will withdraw from us or refuse to us easy access, provided that he sees us desirous to come to him; but on the contrary, he will stretch out his hand to assist our endeavors. And how will not he meet those who come to him, who seeks at a distance those who are wandering and astray, so he may bring them back to the right road?

FAITH UNDEFEATED BY FEAR

Now is my soul troubled; and what shall I say? Father, save me from this hour: but for this cause came I unto this hour. Father, glorify thy name. Then came there a voice from heaven, saying, I have both glorified it, and will glorify it again. —John 12:27–28

It is of consequence to understand aright how much our salvation cost the Son of God. If any one now ask, "Did Christ descend to hell at the time when he deprecated death?" I answer that this was the commencement, and that from it we may infer how dire and dreadful were the tortures which he endured when he felt himself standing at the bar of God as a criminal in our stead. And although the divine power of the Spirit veiled itself for a moment that it might give place to the infirmity of the flesh, we must understand that the trial arising from feelings of grief and fear was such as not to be at variance with faith. And in this was fulfilled what is said in Peter's sermon as to having been loosed from the pains of death, because "it was not possible he could behold of it" (Acts 2:24).

Though feeling forsaken of God, he did not cease in the slightest degree to confide in his goodness. This appears from the celebrated prayer in which, in the depth of his agony, he exclaimed, "My God, my God, why hast thou forsaken me?" (Matt. 27:46). Amid all his agony he ceases not to call upon his God, while exclaiming that he is forsaken by him. Where does the feeling or desire of obedience reside but in the soul? And we know that his soul was troubled in order that ours, being free from anxious uneasiness, might obtain peace and quiet. Moreover, we see that in his human nature he felt a repugnance to what he willed in his divine nature. I say nothing of his subduing the fear of which we have spoken by a contrary affection. This appearance of repugnance is obvious in the words, "Father, save me from this hour: but for this cause came I unto this hour. Father, glorify thy name" (John 12:27–28). Still, in this perplexity, there was no violent emotion, such as we exhibit while making the strongest endeavors to subdue our own feelings.

VICTORY IN THIS RESURRECTION

Who was delivered for our offences, and was raised again for our justification. —Romans 4:25

necessarily, we must know the resurrection from the dead, without which all that has hitherto been said would be defective. For seeing that in the cross, death, and burial of Christ, nothing but weakness appears, faith must go beyond all these, in order that it may be provided with full strength. Hence, although in his death we have an effectual completion of salvation, because by it we are reconciled to God, satisfaction is given to his justice, the curse is removed, and the penalty paid; still it is not by his death but by his resurrection that we are said to be begotten again to a living hope (1 Pet. 1:3). This is because, by rising again, as he became victorious over death, so the victory of our faith consists only in his resurrection. The nature of it is better expressed in the words of Paul, "Christ was delivered for our offences, and was raised again for our justification" (Rom. 4:25); as if he had said, by his death sin was taken away, by his resurrection righteousness was renewed and restored. For how could he by dying have freed us from death, if he had yielded to its power? How could he have obtained the victory for us, if he had fallen in the contest?

Our salvation may be thus divided between the death and the resurrection of Christ: By the former, sin was abolished and death annihilated; and by the latter, righteousness was restored and life revived, the power and efficacy of the former being still bestowed upon us by means of the latter. Paul accordingly affirms that he was declared to be the Son of God by his resurrection (Rom. 1:4), because he then fully displayed that heavenly power which is both a bright mirror of his divinity and a sure support of our faith—as he also elsewhere teaches that "though he was crucified through weakness, yet he lives by the power of God" (2 Cor. 13:4). In the same sense, in another passage, treating of perfection, he says, "That I may know him and the power of his resurrection" (Phil. 3:10). In perfect accordance with this is the passage in Peter that God "raised him up from the dead and gave him glory that your faith and hope might be in God" (1 Pet. 1:21).

DEATH AND RESURRECTION

And if Christ be not raised, your faith is vain; ye are yet in your sins.
—1 Corinthians 15:17

Let us remember that when death only is mentioned, everything peculiar to the resurrection is at the same time included. And let us remember that there is a like representation in the term resurrection, as often as it is used apart from death, everything peculiar to death being included. But as, by rising again, he obtained the victory and became the resurrection and the life, Paul justly argues, "If Christ be not raised, your faith is vain; ye are yet in your sins" (1 Cor. 15:17). Accordingly, in another passage, after exulting in the death of Christ in opposition to the terrors of condemnation, he thus enlarges, "Christ that died, yea rather, that is risen again, who is even at the right hand of God, who also makes intercession for us" (Rom. 8:34).

Then, as we have already explained that the mortification of our flesh depends on communion with the cross, so we must also understand that a corresponding benefit is derived from his resurrection. For as the Apostle says, "Like as Christ was raised up from the dead by the glory of the Father, even so we also should walk in newness of life" (Rom. 6:4).

Accordingly, as in another passage, from our being dead with Christ, he inculcates, "Mortify therefore your members which are upon the earth" (Col. 3:5); so from our being risen with Christ he infers, "seek those things which are above, where Christ sits at the right hand of God" (Col. 3:1). In these words we are not only urged by the example of a risen Savior to follow newness of life, but are taught that by his power we are renewed unto righteousness.

A third benefit derived from it is that it assures us of our own resurrection, of which it is certain that his is the surest representation. But it is to be observed that when he is said to have "risen from the dead," these terms express the reality both of his death and resurrection, as if it had been said that he died the same death as other men naturally die and received immortality in the same mortal flesh which he had assumed.

A BEAUTIFUL HARMONY

He that descended is the same also that ascended up far above all heavens, that he might fill all things. —Ephesians 4:10

Christ's resurrection is naturally followed by his ascension into heaven. For although Christ, by rising again, began fully to display his glory and virtue, having laid aside the abject and ignoble condition of a mortal life and the dishonor of the cross; yet it was only by his ascension to heaven that his reign truly commenced. This the Apostle shows when he says he ascended "that he might fill all things" (Eph. 4:10), thus reminding us that under the appearance of contradiction there is a beautiful harmony—inasmuch as though he departed from us, it was that his departure might be more useful to us than that presence which was confined in a humble tabernacle of flesh during his abode on the earth. Hence John, after repeating the celebrated invitation, "If any man thirst, let him come unto me and drink," immediately adds, "The Holy Ghost was not yet given; because that Jesus was not yet glorified" (John 7:37, 39). This our Lord himself also declared to his Disciples, "It is expedient for you that I go away: for if I go not away the Comforter will not come unto you" (John 16:7).

To console them for his bodily absence, he tells them that he will not leave them comfortless, but will come again to them. Indeed, it will be in a manner invisible, but more to be desired, because they were then taught by a surer experience that the government which he had obtained and the power which he exercises would enable his faithful followers not only to live well but also to die happily. And, indeed we see how much more abundantly his Spirit was poured out, how much more gloriously his kingdom was advanced, how much greater power was employed in aiding his followers and discomfiting his enemies. Being raised to heaven, he withdrew his bodily presence from our sight—not that he might cease to be with his followers, who are still pilgrims on the earth, but that he might rule both heaven and earth more immediately by his power.

ADVANTAGES OF FAITH

But unto every one of us is given grace according to the measure of the gift of Christ. Wherefore he saith, When he ascended up on high, he led captivity captive, and gave gifts unto men. —Ephesians 4:7–8

It is evident that faith derives manifold advantages. First, it perceives that the Lord, by his ascension to heaven, has opened up the access to the heavenly kingdom which Adam had shut. For having entered it in our flesh, as it were in our name, it follows that we are in a manner now seated in heavenly places—not entertaining a mere hope of heaven, but possessing it in our head.

Secondly, faith perceives that Christ's seat beside the Father is not without great advantage to us. Having entered the temple not made with hands, he constantly appears as our advocate and intercessor in the presence of the Father; directs attention to his own righteousness, so as to turn it away from our sins; so reconciles him to us, as by his intercession to pave for us a way of access to his throne, presenting it to miserable sinners (to whom it would otherwise be an object of dread) as filled with grace and mercy.

Thirdly, it discerns his power, on which depend our strength, might, resources, and triumph over hell: "When he ascended up on high, he led captivity captive" (Eph. 4:8). Spoiling his foes, he gave gifts to his people, and daily loads them with spiritual riches. He thus occupies his exalted seat that through transferring his virtue unto us, he may quicken us to spiritual life, sanctify us by his Spirit, and adorn his Church with various graces, by his protection preserve it safe from all harm, and by the strength of his hand curb the enemies raging against his cross and our salvation; in fine, that he may possess all power in heaven and earth, until he has utterly routed all his foes, who are also ours, and completed the structure of his Church. Such is the true nature of the kingdom, such the power which the Father has conferred upon him, until he arrive to complete the last act by judging the quick and the dead.

THE REDEEMER'S RETURN

But now he has appeared once for all at the end of the ages to do away with sin by the sacrifice of himself. Just as man is destined to die once, and after that to face judgment, so Christ was sacrificed once to take away the sins of many people; and he will appear a second time, not to bear sin, but to bring salvation to those who are waiting for him.
—Hebrews 9:26–28, NIV

Christ's kingdom in the world is in a manner veiled by the humiliation of a carnal condition, faith is most properly invited to meditate on the visible presence which he will exhibit on the last day. For he will descend from heaven in visible form, in like manner as he was seen to ascend, and appear to all with the inexpressible majesty of his kingdom, the splendor of immortality, the boundless power of divinity, and an attending company of angels. Hence we are told to wait for the Redeemer against that day on which he will separate the sheep from the goats and the elect from the degenerate, and when not one individual either of the living or the dead shall escape his judgment. From the extremities of the universe shall be heard the clang of the trumpet summoning all to his tribunal—both those whom that day shall find alive and those whom death shall previously have removed from the society of the living.

Our meaning being plain and clear is accordant with the Creed which was certainly written for popular use. There is nothing contrary to it in the Apostle's declaration that it is appointed unto all men once to die. For though those who are surviving at the last day shall not die after a natural manner, yet the change which they are to undergo, as it shall resemble, is not improperly called death (Heb. 9:27). "We shall not all sleep, but we shall all be changed" (1 Cor. 15:51). What does this mean? Their mortal life shall perish and be swallowed up in one moment, and be transformed into an entirely new nature. Though no one can deny that that destruction of the flesh will be death, it still remains true that the quick and the dead shall be summoned to judgment (1 Thess. 4:16); for "the dead in Christ shall rise first; then we which are alive and remain shall be caught up together with them in the clouds to meet the lord in the air."

SECURELY SEATED

Jesus said to them, "I tell you the truth, at the renewal of all things, when the Son of Man sits on his glorious throne, you who have followed me will also sit on twelve thrones, judging the twelve tribes of Israel." —Matthew 19:28, NIV

It is most comforting to think that judgment is vested in him who has already destined us to share with him in the honor of judgment (Matt. 19:28)—so far is it from being true that he will ascend the judgment-seat for our condemnation. How could a most merciful prince destroy his own people? How could the head disperse its own members? How could the advocate condemn his clients? For if the Apostle, when contemplating the interposition of Christ, is bold to exclaim, "Who is he that condemns?" (Rom. 8:33), much more certain is it that Christ, the intercessor, will not condemn those whom he has admitted to his protection. It certainly gives no small security that we shall be seated at no other tribunal than that of our Redeemer, from whom salvation is to be expected; and that he who in the Gospel now promises eternal blessedness, will then as Judge ratify his promise. The end for which the Father has honored the Son by committing all judgment to him (John 5:22) was to pacify the consciences of his people when alarmed at the thought of judgment.

Hitherto I have followed the order of the Apostles' Creed, because it states the leading articles of redemption in a few words, and may thus serve as a tablet in which the points of Christian doctrine, most deserving of attention, are brought separately and distinctly before us. I call it the Apostles' Creed, though I am by no means solicitous as to its authorship. I have no doubt that, from the very commencement of the Church and, therefore, in the very days of the Apostles, it held the place of a public and universally received confession, whatever be the quarter from which it originally proceeded. It is not probable that it was written by some private individual, since it is certain that, from time immemorial, it was deemed of sacred authority by all Christians.

215

THE SECRET CLEANSING OF THE SPIRIT

And that is what some of you were. But you were washed, you were sanctified, you were justified in the name of the Lord Jesus Christ and by the Spirit of our God. —1 Corinthians 6:11, NIV

We must see in what way we become possessed of the blessings which God has bestowed on his only-begotten Son, not for private use, but to enrich the poor and needy. And the first thing to be attended to is that so long as we are without Christ and separated from him, nothing which he suffered and did for the salvation of the human race is of the least benefit to us. To communicate to us the blessings which he received from the Father, he must become ours and dwell in us. Accordingly, he is called our Head and the first-born among many brethren, while, on the other hand, we are said to be fused into him and clothed with him. And although it is true that we obtain this by faith, yet since we see that all do not indiscriminately embrace the offer of Christ which is made by the Gospel, the very nature of the case teaches us to ascend higher and inquire into the secret efficacy of the Spirit, to which it is owing that we enjoy Christ and all his blessings.

Christ came by water and blood, as the Spirit testifies concerning him, that we might not lose the benefits of the salvation which he has purchased. For as there are said to be three witnesses in heaven—the Father, the Word, and the Spirit—so there are also three on the earth—water, blood, and Spirit. It is not without cause that the testimony of the Spirit is twice mentioned, a testimony which is engraved on our hearts by way of seal, and thus seals the cleansing and sacrifice of Christ. For which reason, also, Peter says that believers are "elect through sanctification of the Spirit, unto obedience and sprinkling of the blood of Jesus Christ" (1 Pet. 1:2). By these words he reminds us that, if the shedding of his sacred blood is not to be in vain, our souls must be washed in it by the secret cleansing of the Holy Spirit.

THE SPIRIT OF SANCTIFICATION

But ye are not in the flesh, but in the Spirit, if so be that the Spirit of God dwell in you. Now if any man have not the Spirit of Christ, he is none of his. —Romans 8:9

We must remember that Christ came provided with the Holy Spirit after a peculiar manner; namely, that he might separate us from the world and unite us in the hope of an eternal inheritance. Hence the Spirit is called the Spirit of sanctification, because he quickens and cherishes us—not merely by the general energy which is seen in the human race, as well as other animals, but because he is the seed and root of heavenly life in us.

Accordingly, one of the highest commendations which the prophets give to the kingdom of Christ is that under it the Spirit would be poured out in richer abundance. One of the most remarkable passages is that of Joel, "It shall come to pass afterward, that I will pour out my Spirit upon all flesh," (Joel 2:28). For although the prophet seems to confine the gifts of the Spirit to the office of prophesying, he yet intimates under a figure that God will, by the illumination of his Spirit, provide himself with Disciples who had previously been altogether ignorant of heavenly doctrine.

Moreover, as it is for the sake of his Son that God bestows the Holy Spirit upon us, and yet has deposited him in all his fullness with the Son, to be the minister and dispenser of his liberality, he is called at one time the Spirit of the Father, at another the Spirit of the Son: "You are not in the flesh but in the Spirit, if so be that the Spirit of God dwell in you. Now, if any man have not the Spirit of Christ, he is none of his" (Rom. 8:9). And hence he encourages us to hope for complete renovation: "If the Spirit of him that raised up Jesus from the dead dwell in you, he that raised up Christ from the dead shall also quicken your mortal bodies by his Spirit that dwells in you" (Rom. 8:11). There is no inconsistency in ascribing the glory of those gifts to the Father, inasmuch as he is the author of them, and, at the same time, ascribing them to Christ, with whom they have been deposited, that he may bestow them on his people.

INTENT ON THE SPIRIT

Jesus answered and said unto her, Whosoever drinketh of this water shall thirst again. —John 4:13

ere it will be proper to point out the titles which the Scripture bestows on the Spirit, when it treats of the commencement and entire renewal of our salvation. First, he is called the "Spirit of adoption" because he is witness to us of the free favor with which God the Father embraced us in his well-beloved and only-begotten Son, so as to become our Father's and give us boldness of access to him; in fact he dictates the very words, so that we can boldly cry, "Abba, Father." For the same reason, he is said to have "sealed us, and given the earnest of the Spirit in our hearts" because, as pilgrims in the world and persons in a manner dead, he so quickens us from above as to assure us that our salvation is safe in the keeping of a faithful God. Hence, also, the Spirit is said to be "life because of righteousness."

But since it is his secret irrigation that makes us bud forth and produce the fruits of righteousness, he is repeatedly described as water. Corresponding to this are the words of our Savior, to which I lately referred, "If any man thirst, let him come unto me and drink." On the other hand, as he is constantly employed in subduing and destroying the vices of our concupiscence and inflaming our hearts with the love of God and piety, he hence receives the name of Fire. In fine, he is described to us as a Fountain, whence all heavenly riches flow to us. Or he is described as the Hand by which God exerts his power, because by his divine inspiration he so breathes divine life into us that we are no longer acted upon by ourselves, but are ruled by his motion and agency, so that everything good in us is the fruit of his grace, while our own endowments without him are mere darkness of mind and perverseness of heart.

Already, indeed, it has been clearly shown that until our minds are intent on the Spirit, Christ is in a manner unemployed because we view him coldly without us, and so at a distance from us.

APPREHENDING FAITH

Now I commit you to God and to the word of his grace, which can build you up and give you an inheritance among all those who are sanctified. —Acts 20:32, NIV

necessarily, we must give a clearer definition of faith, so as to enable the readers to apprehend its nature and power. Here it is of importance to call to mind what was formerly taught: First, since God by his Law prescribes what we ought to do, failure in any one respect subjects us to the dreadful judgment of eternal death, which it denounces. Secondly, because it is not only difficult but altogether beyond our strength and ability to fulfill the demands of the Law, if we look only to ourselves and consider what is due to our merits, no ground of hope remains; but we lie forsaken of God under eternal death. Thirdly, there is only one method of deliverance which can rescue us from this miserable calamity—that is, when Christ the Redeemer appears (by whose hand our heavenly Father, out of his infinite goodness and mercy, has been pleased to succor us) if we with true faith embrace this mercy and with firm hope rest in it.

It is now proper to consider the nature of this faith, by means of which those who are adopted into the family of God obtain possession of the heavenly kingdom. For the accomplishment of so great an end, it is obvious that no mere opinion or persuasion is adequate. Seeing that God dwells in light that is inaccessible, Christ must intervene. Hence he calls himself "the light of the world" and, in another passage, "the way, the truth, and the life." None cometh to the Father (who is the fountain of life) except by him; for "no man knows who the Father is but the Son, and he to whom the Son will reveal him." It is true, indeed, that faith has respect to God only, but to this we should add that it acknowledges Jesus Christ whom he has sent. God would remain far off, concealed from us, were we not irradiated by the brightness of Christ. All that the Father had, he deposited with his only begotten Son, in order that he might manifest himself in him and thus, by the communication of blessings, express the true image of his glory.

TREASURES OF GRACE

But ye have not so learned Christ; If so be that ye have heard him, and have been taught by him, as the truth is in Jesus. —Ephesians 4:20–21

he true knowledge of Christ consists in receiving him as he is offered by the Father; namely, as invested with his Gospel. For, as he is appointed as the end of our faith, so we cannot directly tend towards him except under the guidance of the Gospel. Therein are certainly unfolded to us treasures of grace. Paul makes faith the inseparable attendant of doctrine (Eph. 4:20–21).

Still I do not confine faith to the Gospel in such a sense as not to admit that enough was delivered to Moses and the Prophets to form a foundation of faith; but as the Gospel exhibits a fuller manifestation of Christ, Paul justly terms it the doctrine of faith (1 Tim. 4:6). For which reason he says that by the coming of faith the Law was abolished (Rom. 10:4), including under the expression a new and unwonted mode of teaching, by which Christ, from the period of his appearance as the great Master, gave a fuller illustration of the Father's mercy and testified more surely of our salvation.

We must remember that there is an inseparable relation between faith and the Word, and that these can no more be disconnected from each other than rays of light from the sun. Hence in Isaiah the Lord exclaims, "Hear, and your soul shall live" (Isa. 4:3). If faith declines in the least degree from the mark at which it ought to aim, it does not retain its nature, but becomes uncertain credulity and vague wandering of mind. Take away the Word, therefore, and no faith will remain. Whether God uses the agency of man, or works immediately by his own power, it is always by his word that he manifests himself to those whom he designs to draw to himself.

Faith includes not merely the knowledge that God is, but also a perception of his will toward us. It concerns us to know not only what he is in himself, but also in what character he is pleased to manifest himself to us. We now see, therefore, that faith is the knowledge of the divine will in regard to us, as ascertained from his word. And the foundation of it is a previous persuasion of the truth of God.

MERCY AND TRUTH

I have not hid thy righteousness within my heart; I have declared thy faithfulness and thy salvation: I have not concealed thy lovingkindness and thy truth from the great congregation. Withhold not thou thy tender mercies from me, O LORD: let thy lovingkindness and thy truth continually preserve me. —Psalm 40:10–11

Since the heart of man is not brought to faith by every word of God, we must still consider what it is that faith properly has respect to in the Word. The declaration of God to Adam was, "Thou shall surely die" (Gen. 2:17), and to Cain, "The voice of thy brother's blood cries unto me from the ground" (Gen. 4:10); but these, so far from being fitted to establish faith, tend only to shake it. At the same time, we deny not that it is the office of faith to assent to the truth of God whenever, whatever, and in whatever way he speaks; we are only inquiring what faith can find in the Word of God to lean and rest upon. When conscience sees only wrath and indignation, how can it but tremble and be afraid? And how can it avoid shunning the God whom it thus dreads? But faith ought to seek God, not shun him.

We are allured to seek God when told that our safety is treasured up in him; and we are confirmed in this when he declares that he studies and takes an interest in our welfare. Hence there is need of the gracious promise, in which he testifies that he is a propitious Father, since there is no other way in which we can approach to him—the promise being the only thing on which the heart of man can recline. For this reason, the two things, mercy and truth, are uniformly conjoined in the Psalms as having a mutual connection with each other. For it were of no avail to us to know that God is true, did he not in mercy allure us to himself; nor could we of ourselves embrace his mercy did not he expressly offer it. "I have declared thy faithfulness and thy salvation: I have not concealed thy lovingkindness and thy truth. Withhold not thy tender mercies from me, O LORD: let thy lovingkindness and thy truth continually preserve me" (Ps. 40:10–11). We shall now have a full definition of faith if we say that it is a firm and sure knowledge of the divine favor toward us, founded on the truth of a free promise in Christ, and revealed to our minds and sealed on our hearts by the Holy Spirit.

CONFIDENT TRUST

Therefore, since we have been justified through faith, we have peace with God through our Lord Jesus Christ, through whom we have gained access by faith into this grace in which we now stand. And we rejoice in the hope of the glory of God. —Romans 5:1–2, NIV

The principal hinge on which faith turns is this: We must not suppose that any promises of mercy which the Lord offers are only true out of us, and not at all in us; we should rather make them ours by inwardly embracing them. In this way only is engendered that confidence which he elsewhere terms peace (Rom. 5:1), though perhaps he rather means to make peace follow from it. This is the security which quiets and calms the conscience in the view of the judgment of God, and without which it is necessarily irritated and almost torn with tumultuous dread—unless when it happens to slumber for a moment, forgetful both of God and of itself. And verily it is but for a moment. It never long enjoys that miserable obliviousness, for the memory of the divine judgment, ever and anon recurring, stings it to the quick.

In one word, he only is a true believer who, firmly persuaded that God is reconciled and is a kind Father to him, hopes everything from his kindness, and who, trusting to the promises of the divine favor with undoubting confidence, anticipates salvation; as the Apostle shows in these words, "We are made partakers of Christ, if we hold the beginning of our confidence steadfast unto the end" (Heb. 3:14). He thus holds that none hope well in the Lord save those who confidently glory in being the heirs of the heavenly kingdom. No man, I say, is a believer but he who, trusting to the security of his salvation, confidently triumphs over the devil and death, as we are taught by the noble exclamation of Paul: "I am persuaded, that neither death, nor life, nor angels, nor principalities, nor powers, nor things present, nor things to come, nor height, nor depth, nor any other creature, shall be able to separate us from the love of God, which is in Christ Jesus our Lord" (Rom. 8:38). In like manner, the same Apostle does not consider that the eyes of our understanding are enlightened unless we know what is the hope of the eternal inheritance to which we are called (Eph. 1:18). Thus he uniformly intimates throughout his writings that the goodness of God is not properly comprehended when security does not follow as its fruit.

A PERPETUAL STRUGGLE

My soul is downcast within me; therefore I will remember you from the
land of the Jordan, the heights of Hermon—from Mount Mizar.
—Psalm 42:6, NIV

hen we say that faith must be certain and secure, we certainly speak not of an assurance which is never affected by doubt, nor a security which anxiety never assails. We rather maintain that believers have a perpetual struggle with their own distrust, and are thus far from thinking that their consciences possess a placid quiet, uninterrupted by anxiety. On the other hand, whatever be the mode in which they are assailed, we deny that they fall off and abandon that sure confidence which they have formed in the mercy of God.

Scripture does not set before us a brighter or more memorable example of faith than in David, especially if regard be had to the constant tenor of his life. And yet how far his mind was from being always at peace is declared by innumerable complaints, of which it will be sufficient to select a few. When he rebukes the turbulent movements of his soul, what else is it but a censure of his unbelief? "Why art thou cast down, my soul?

And why art thou disquieted in me? hope thou in God" (Ps. 42:5). His alarm was undoubtedly a manifest sign of distrust, as if he thought that the Lord had forsaken him. In another passage we have a fuller confession: "I said in my haste, I am cut off from before thine eyes" (Ps. 31:22). In another passage, in anxious and wretched perplexity, he debates with himself, nay, raises a question as to the nature of God: "Has God forgotten to be gracious? has he in anger shut up his tender mercies?" (Ps. 77:9). What follows is still harsher: "I said this is my infirmity; but I will remember the years of the right hand of the Most High." As if desperate, he adjudges himself to destruction. He not only confesses that he is agitated by doubt, but, as if he had fallen in the contest, leaves himself nothing in reserve—God having deserted him, and made the hand which was wont to help him the instrument of his destruction. Thus David, when he seemed to be overwhelmed, ceased not by urging himself forward to ascend to God.

FAITH OVERCOMES

Your wrath has swept over me; your terrors have destroyed me.
—Psalm 88:16, NIV

The believer finds within himself two principles: the one filling him with delight in recognizing the divine goodness, the other filling him with bitterness under a sense of his fallen state; the one leading him to recline on the promise of the Gospel, the other alarming him by the conviction of his iniquity; the one making him exult with the anticipation of life, the other making him tremble with the fear of death. This diversity is owing to imperfection of faith, since we are never so well in the course of the present life as to be entirely cured of the disease of distrust and completely replenished and engrossed by faith. Hence those conflicts: the distrust cleaving to the remains of the flesh rising up to assail the faith enlisting in our hearts. But if in the believer's mind certainty is mingled with doubt, must we not always be carried back to the conclusion that faith consists not of a sure and clear, but only of an obscure and confused, understanding of the divine will in regard to us? By no means. Though we are distracted by various thoughts, it does not follow that we are immediately divested of faith. Though we are agitated and carried to and fro by distrust, we are not immediately plunged into the abyss; though we are shaken, we are not therefore driven from our place. The invariable issue of the contest is that faith in the long run surmounts the difficulties by which it was beset and seemed to be endangered.

The whole, then, comes to this: As soon as the minutest particle of faith is instilled into our minds, we begin to behold the face of God—placid, serene, and propitious—far off, indeed, but still so distinctly as to assure us that there is no delusion in it. In proportion to the progress we afterwards make (and the progress ought to be uninterrupted), we obtain a nearer and surer view, the very continuance making it more familiar to us. Thus we see that a mind illumined with the knowledge of God is at first involved in much ignorance—ignorance, however, which is gradually removed. Still this partial ignorance or obscure discernment does not prevent that clear knowledge of the divine favor which holds the first and principal part in faith.

SHIELDED BY FAITH

In addition to all this, take up the shield of faith, with which you can
extinguish all the flaming arrows of the evil one.
—Ephesians 6:16, NIV

to withstand assaults, faith arms and fortifies itself with the Word of God. When the temptation suggested is that God is an enemy because he afflicts, faith replies that while he afflicts he is merciful, his chastening proceeding more from love than anger. To the thought that God is the avenger of wickedness, it opposes the pardon ready to be bestowed on all offences whenever the sinner retakes himself to the divine mercy. Thus the pious mind, how much soever it may be agitated and torn, at length rises superior to all difficulties and allows not its confidence in the divine mercy to be destroyed. Nay, rather, the disputes which exercise and disturb it tend to establish this confidence.

A proof of this is that the saints, when the hand of God lies heaviest upon them, still lodge their complaints with him, and continue to invoke him when to all appearance he is least disposed to hear. But of what use were it to lament before him if they had no hope of solace? They never would invoke him did they not believe that he is ready to assist them. Thus the disciples, while reprimanded by their Master for the weakness of their faith in crying out that they were perishing, still implored his aid (Matt. 8:25). And he, in rebuking them for their want of faith, does not disown them or class them with unbelievers, but urges them to shake off the vice.

Therefore, as we have already said, we again maintain that faith remaining fixed in the believer's breast never can be eradicated from it. However it may seem shaken and bent in this direction or in that, its flame is never so completely quenched as not at least to lurk under the embers. In this way, it appears that the Word, which is an incorruptible seed, produces fruit similar to itself. Its germ never withers away utterly and perishes. Faith, as Paul declares (Eph. 6:16), is our shield which, receiving these darts, either wards them off entirely, or at least breaks their force, and prevents them from reaching the vitals.

REPENTANCE AND FAITH

I have declared to both Jews and Greeks that they must turn to God in repentance and have faith in our Lord Jesus. —Acts 20:21, NIV

When we attribute the origin of repentance to faith, we do not dream of some period of time in which faith is to give birth to it; we only wish to show that a man cannot seriously engage in repentance unless he knows that he is of God. But no man is truly persuaded that he is of God until he has embraced his offered favor. Some are perhaps misled that not a few are subdued by terror of conscience, or disposed to obedience before they have been imbued with a knowledge, nay, before they have had any taste of the divine favor (see Acts 20:21). This is that initial fear which some writers class among the virtues, because they think it approximates to true and genuine obedience.

But we are not here considering the various modes in which Christ draws us to himself, or prepares us for the study of piety. All I say is that no righteousness can be found where the Spirit, whom Christ received in order to communicate it to his members, does not reign. Then, according to the passage in the Psalms, "There is forgiveness with thee, that thou may be feared" (Ps. 130:4). No man will ever reverence God who does not trust that God is propitious to him; no man will ever willingly set himself to observe the Law who is not persuaded that his services are pleasing to God. The indulgence of God in tolerating and pardoning our iniquities is a sign of paternal favor. This is also clear from the exhortation in Hosea, "Come, and let us return unto the LORD: for he has torn, and he will heal us; he has smitten, and he will bind us up" (Hos. 6:1). The hope of pardon is employed as a stimulus to prevent us from becoming reckless in sin.

PARTAKERS OF GRACE

One of the two which heard John speak, and followed him, was Andrew, Simon Peter's brother. He first findeth his own brother Simon, and saith unto him, We have found the Messias, which is, being interpreted, the Christ. And he brought him to Jesus. And when Jesus beheld him, he said, Thou art Simon the son of Jona: thou shalt be called Cephas, which is by interpretation, A stone. —John 1:40–42

The design of the Evangelist is to inform us how gradually the Disciples were brought to Christ. Here he relates about Peter, and afterwards he will mention Philip and Nathaniel. The circumstance of Andrew immediately bringing his brother expresses the nature of faith, which does not conceal or quench the light, but rather spreads it in every direction. Andrew has scarcely a spark, and yet, by means of it, he enlightens his brother. Woe to our sluggishness, therefore, if we do not, after having been fully enlightened, endeavor to make others partakers of the same grace.

We may observe in Andrew two things which Isaiah requires from the children of God; namely, that each should take his neighbor by the hand, and next, that he should say, "Come, let us go up into the mountain of the LORD, and he will teach us" (Isa. 2:3). For Andrew stretches out the hand to his brother, but at the same time desires that he may become a fellow-disciple with him in the school of Christ.

We ought also to observe the purpose of God, which determined that Peter, who was to be far more eminent, was brought to the knowledge of Christ by the agency and ministry of Andrew. None of us, however excellent, may refuse to be taught by an inferior; for that man will be severely punished for his peevishness, or rather for his pride, who, through his contempt of a man, will not deign to come to Christ.

DILIGENT AND CONSTANT

And his disciples remembered that it was written, The zeal of thine house hath eaten me up. —John 2:17

he Evangelist says that Christ's zeal was one of the marks by which the Disciples knew that it was Jesus who protected and restored the kingdom of God. Now observe that they followed the guidance of Scripture in order to form such an opinion concerning Christ as they ought to entertain; and, indeed, no man will ever learn what Christ is, or the object of what he did and suffered, unless he has been taught and guided by Scripture. So far, then, as each of us shall desire to make progress in the knowledge of Christ, it will be necessary that Scripture shall be the subject of our diligent and constant meditation.

Nor is it without a good reason that David mentions the house of God when the divine glory is concerned; for though God is sufficient for himself, and needs not the services of any, yet he wishes that his glory should be displayed in the

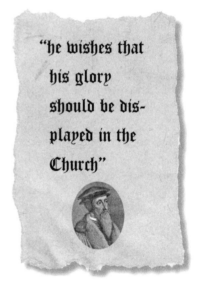

"he wishes that his glory should be displayed in the Church"

Church. In this way he gives a remarkable proof of his love towards us, because he unites his glory by an indissoluble link with our salvation. Now as Paul informs us that a general doctrine is presented to the whole body (Rom. 15:3), let each of us apply to the invitation of Christ; for, so far as lies in our power, we may not permit the temple of God to be in any way polluted.

CHRIST'S APPROVAL

But Jesus did not commit himself unto them, because he knew all men.
—John 2:24

nothing is more dangerous than hypocrisy, for it is this reason among others that it is an exceedingly common fault. There is scarcely any man who is not pleased with himself; and while we deceive ourselves by empty flatteries, we imagine that God is blind like ourselves.

But here we are reminded how widely his judgment differs from ours. For he sees clearly those things which we cannot perceive, because they are concealed by some disguise; and he estimates according to their hidden source—that is, according to the most secret feeling of the heart—those things which dazzle our eyes by false luster. This is why Solomon says that God weighs in his balance the hearts

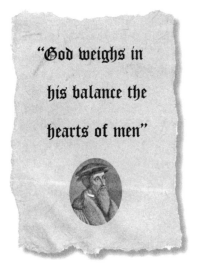

"God weighs in his balance the hearts of men"

of men, while they flatter themselves in their ways (Prov. 21:2).

Let us remember, therefore, that none are the true disciples of Christ but those whom he approves, because in such a matter he alone is competent to decide and to judge.

THE PAINS OF DEATH

Whom God hath raised up, having loosed the pains of death: because it was not possible that he should be holden of it. —Acts 2:24

We must seek for a surer exposition of Christ's descent to hell. Nothing had been done if Christ had only endured corporeal death. In order to interpose between us and God's anger and to satisfy his righteous judgment, it was necessary that he should feel the weight of divine vengeance. Whence also it was necessary that he should engage, as it were, at close quarters with the powers of hell and the horrors of eternal death. There is nothing strange in its being said that he descended to hell, seeing he endured the death which is inflicted on the wicked by an angry God. It is frivolous and ridiculous to object that in this way the order is perverted, it being absurd that an event which preceded burial should be placed after it. But after explaining what Christ endured in the sight of man, the Apostles' Creed appropriately adds the invisible and incomprehensible judgment which he endured before God to teach us that not only was the body of Christ given up as the price of redemption, but that there was a greater and more excellent price—that he bore in his soul the tortures of condemned and ruined man.

In this sense, Peter says that God raised up Christ, "having loosed the pains of death: because it was not possible he should behold of it" (Acts 2:24). He does not mention death simply, but says that the Son of God endured the pains produced by the curse and wrath of God, the source of death. How small a matter had it been to come forth securely, and as it were in sport to undergo death. Herein was a true proof of boundless mercy that he shunned not the death he so greatly dreaded. Christ then, praying in a loud voice and with tears, is heard in that he feared, not so as to be exempted from death, but so as not to be swallowed up of it like a sinner, though standing as our representative. Thus by engaging with the power of the devil, the fear of death, and the pains of hell, he gained the victory and achieved a triumph, so that we now fear not in death those things which our Prince has destroyed.

230

BEARING INFIRMITIES

For we have not an high priest which cannot be touched with the feeling of our infirmities; but was in all points tempted like as we are, yet without sin. —Hebrews 4:15

It becomes us boldly to profess the agony of Christ, if we are not ashamed of the cross. And certainly had not his soul shared in the punishment, he would have been a Redeemer of bodies only. The object of his struggle was to raise up those who were lying prostrate. So far is this from detracting from his heavenly glory that his goodness, which can never be sufficiently celebrated, becomes more conspicuous in this: He declined not to bear our infirmities. Hence also that consolation to our anxiety and grief which the Apostle sets before us (Heb. 4:15). There is no reason to take alarm at infirmity in Christ, infirmity to which he submitted not under the constraint of violence and necessity, but merely because he loved and pitied us. Whatever he spontaneously suffered detracts in no degree from his majesty. In Christ was an infirmity which was pure and free from every species of taint, inasmuch as it was kept within the limits of obedience. No moderation can be seen in the depravity of our nature; but as Christ was upright, all his affections were under such restraint as prevented everything like excess. Hence he could resemble us in grief, fear, and dread, but still with this mark of distinction.

Let the pious reader consider how far it is honorable to Christ to make him more effeminate and timid than the generality of men. Robbers and other malefactors rebelliously hasten to death, many men magnanimously despise it, others meet it calmly. If the Son of God was amazed and terror-struck at the prospect of it, where was his firmness or magnanimity? We are even told, which in a common death would have been deemed most extraordinary, that in the depth of his agony his sweat was like great drops of blood falling to the ground. Nor was this a spectacle exhibited to the eyes of others, since it was from a secluded spot that he uttered his groans to his Father. And that no doubt may remain, it was necessary that angels should come down from heaven to strengthen him with miraculous consolation.

THE RENOVATED SOUL

If thou wilt return, O Israel, saith the LORD, return unto me: and if thou wilt put away thine abominations out of my sight, then shalt thou not remove. And thou shalt swear, The LORD liveth, in truth, in judgment, and in righteousness; and the nations shall bless themselves in him, and in him shall they glory. —Jeremiah 4:1–2

In the conversion of the life to God, we require a transformation not only in external works, but in the soul itself, which is able only after it has put off its old habits to bring forth fruits conformable to its renovation. The prophet, intending to express this, enjoins those whom he calls to repentance to make them "a new heart and a new spirit" (Ezek. 18:31). Hence Moses, on several occasions, when he would show how the Israelites were to repent and turn to the Lord, tells them that it must be done with the whole heart and the whole soul (a mode of expression of frequent recurrence in the prophets), and by terming it the liberation of the heart, points to the internal affections.

But there is no passage better fitted to teach us the genuine nature of repentance than the following: "If thou wilt return, O Israel, says the Lord, return unto me...Break up your fallow ground, and sow not among thorns. Circumcise yourselves to the LORD, and take away the foreskins of your heart" (Jer. 4:1-4). See how he declares to them that it will be of no avail to commence the study of righteousness unless impiety shall first have been eradicated from their inmost heart. And to malice the deeper impression, he reminds them that they have to do with God, and can gain nothing by deceit, because he hates a double heart. For this reason Isaiah derides the preposterous attempts of hypocrites, who zealously aimed at an external repentance by the observance of ceremonies, but in the meanwhile cared not "to loose the bands of wickedness, to undo the heavy burdens, and to let the oppressed go free" (Isa. 58:6). In these words he admirably shows wherein the acts of unfeigned repentance consist.

A SINCERE FEAR

Godly sorrow brings repentance that leads to salvation and leaves no regret, but worldly sorrow brings death. —2 Corinthians 7:10, NIV

repentance must necessarily proceed from a sincere fear of God. Before the mind of the sinner can be inclined to repentance, he must be aroused by the thought of divine judgment; but when the thought that God will one day ascend his tribunal to take an account of all words and actions has taken possession of his mind, it will not allow him to rest or have one moment's peace, but will perpetually urge him to adopt a different plan of life so that he may be able to stand securely at that judgment-seat.

Hence the Scripture, when insisting on repentance, often introduces the subject of judgment, as in Jeremiah, "Lest my fury come forth like fire, and burn that none can quench it, because of the evil of your doings" (Jer. 4:4). Paul, in his discourse to the Athenians says, "The times of this ignorance God winked at; but now commands all men every where to repent: because he has appointed a day in the which he will judge the world in righteousness" (Acts 17:30–31). Sometimes God is declared to be a judge from the punishments already inflicted, thus leading sinners to reflect that worse awaits them if they do not quickly repent.

As repentance begins with dread and hatred of sin, the Apostle sets down godly sorrow as one of its causes (2 Cor. 7:10). By godly sorrow he means when we not only tremble at the punishment, but hate and despise the sin, because we know it is displeasing to God.

There is, moreover, a rebellious spirit which must be broken as with hammers. The stern threatening which God employs is extorted from him by our depraved dispositions, for while we are asleep it would be in vain to allure us by soothing measures.

And there is another reason why the fear of God lies at the root of repentance: Though the life of men were possessed of all kinds of virtue, still if they do not bear reverence to God, no matter how much they may be lauded in the world, they are mere abomination in heaven— inasmuch as it is the principal part of righteousness to render to God that service and honor of which he is impiously defrauded, whenever it is not our express purpose to submit to his authority.

MORTIFICATION

Depart from evil, and do good; seek peace, and pursue it.
—Psalm 34:14

We must now show what is meant when we say that repentance consists of two parts: mortification of the flesh, and the quickening of the Spirit. In accommodation to a carnal people, the Prophets express this in simple and homely terms, but clearly, when they say, "Depart from evil, and do good," (Ps. 34:14), and, "Wash you, make you clean, put away the evil of your doings from before mine eyes; cease to do evil; learn to do well; seek judgment; relieve the oppressed" (Isa. 1:16–17). In dissuading us from wickedness they demand the entire destruction of the flesh, which is full of perverseness and malice. It is a most difficult and arduous achievement to renounce ourselves and lay aside our natural disposition. For the flesh must not be thought to be destroyed unless everything that we have of our own is abolished. But seeing that all the desires of the flesh are enmity against God (Rom. 8:7), the first step to the obedience of his Law is the renouncement of our own nature.

Renovation is afterwards manifested by the fruits produced by it: justice, judgment, and mercy. Since it were not sufficient duly to perform such acts—were not the mind and heart previously endued with sentiments of justice, judgment, and mercy—this is done when the Holy Spirit, instilling his holiness into our souls, so inspired them with new thoughts and affections that they may justly be regarded as new. And, indeed, as we are naturally opposed to God, unless self-denial precede, we shall never tend to that which is right.

Hence we are so often enjoined to put off the old man, to renounce the world and the flesh, to forsake our lusts, and be renewed in the spirit of our mind. Moreover, the very name mortification reminds us how difficult it is to forget our former nature, because we hence infer that we cannot be trained to the fear of God and learn the first principles of piety unless we are violently smitten with the sword of the Spirit and annihilated, as if God were declaring that to be ranked among his sons there must be a destruction of our ordinary nature.

REND YOUR HEART

Rend your heart, and not your garments. —Joel 2:13, NIV

he fruits of repentance are offices of piety towards God, and love towards men, general holiness and purity of life. In short, the more a man studies to conform his life to the standard of the divine Law, the surer signs he gives of his repentance. Accordingly, in inciting us to repentance, the Spirit brings before us at one time each separate precept of the Law and at another the duties of the second table; although there are also passages in which, after condemning impurity in its fountain in the heart, he afterwards descends to external marks, by which repentance is proved to be sincere.

Anyone moderately versant in Scripture will understand by himself, without being reminded by others, that when he has to do with God, nothing is gained without beginning with the internal affections of the heart. There is a passage of Joel which will avail not a little for the understanding of others: "Rend your heart, and not your garments" (Joel 2:13). Both are also briefly expressed by James in these words: "Cleanse your hands, ye sinners; and purify your hearts, ye double-minded" (James 4:8). Here, indeed, the accessory is set down first, but the source and principle is afterwards pointed out: hidden defilements must be wiped away, and an altar erected to God in the very heart.

There are, moreover, certain external exercises which we employ in private as remedies to humble us and tame our flesh, and in public, to testify our repentance. These have their origin in that revenge of which Paul speaks (2 Cor. 7:2), for when the mind is distressed, it naturally expresses itself in sackcloth, groans, and tears, shuns ornament and every kind of show, and abandons all delights. Then he who feels how great an evil the rebellion of the flesh is, tries every means of curbing it. Besides, he who considers aright how grievous a thing it is to have offended the justice of God, cannot rest until, in his humility, he has given glory to God.

REPENTANCE

*But of him are ye in Christ Jesus, who of God is made unto us wisdom,
and righteousness, and sanctification, and redemption.*
—1 Corinthians 1:30

As hatred of sin, which is the beginning of repentance, first gives us access to the knowledge of Christ—who manifests himself to none but miserable and afflicted sinners, groaning, laboring, burdened, hungry, and thirsty, pining away with grief and wretchedness—so if we would stand in Christ, we must aim at repentance, cultivate it during our whole lives, and continue it to the last. Christ came to call sinners, but to call them to repentance. He was sent to bless the unworthy, but by "turning away every one" "from his iniquities." When God offers forgiveness of sins, he in return usually stipulates for repentance, intimating that his mercy should induce men to repent. "Keep ye judgment," says he, "and do justice: for my salvation is near to come." Again, "The Redeemer shall come to Zion, and unto them that turn from transgression in Jacob." Again, "Repent, therefore, and be converted, that your sins may be blotted out." However, it is to be observed that repentance is not made a condition in such a sense as to be a foundation for meriting pardon; nay, it rather indicates the end at which they must aim if they would obtain favor, God having resolved to take pity on men for the express purpose of leading them to repent.

Therefore, so long as we dwell in the prison of the body, we must constantly struggle with the vices of our corrupt nature, and so with our natural disposition. Truly we may say that the life of a Christian man is constant study and exercise in mortifying the flesh, until it is certainly slain and the Spirit of God obtains dominion in us. Wherefore, he seems to me to have made most progress who has learned to be most dissatisfied with himself. He does not, however, remain in the miry clay without going forward; but rather hastens and sighs after God that, intertwined both into the death and the life of Christ, he may constantly meditate on repentance. Unquestionably those who have a genuine hatred of sin cannot do otherwise, for no man ever hated sin without being previously enamored of righteousness.

OUR ONLY HOPE IS HEAVEN

*When they heard this, they were furious and gnashed their teeth at
him. But Stephen, full of the Holy Spirit, looked up to heaven and saw
the glory of God, and Jesus standing at the right hand of God.*
—Acts 7:54–55, NIV

We cannot express the straits the servant of Christ was brought into, when he saw himself beset all around with raging enemies. His good cause was oppressed, partly with false accusations and malice, partly with violence and outrageous outcries. He was environed with stern faces on every side. He himself was beckoned to a cruel and horrible kind of death. He found succor and ease nowhere. Therefore, destitute of human help, he turns himself toward God.

We must first note this that Stephen looked to God, who is the judge of life and death, turning his eyes from the world, at a time when he was brought into extreme despair of all things, when there is nothing but death before his eyes. This done, we must also add that his expectation was not in vain, because Christ appeared to him by and by. Luke shows that Stephen was now armed with a power of the Spirit that could not be overcome, so that nothing could hinder him from beholding the heavens. Therefore Stephen looks to heaven, that he may gather courage by beholding Christ that dying he may triumph gloriously—having overcome death.

But as for us, it is no marvel if Christ does not show himself to us, because we are so set and tied to the earth. Hereby it comes to pass, that our hearts fail us at every light rumor of danger, and even at the falling of a leaf. And that for good reason: Where is our strength but in Christ? But we pass over the heavens, as if we had no help anywhere else but in the world. Therefore, Luke gives this reason why Stephen looked up steadfastly toward heaven—because he was full of the Spirit. We must also ascend into heaven, having this Spirit to be our director and guide, whenever we are oppressed with troubles. And, surely, until such time as the Spirit illuminates us, our eyes are not so quick of sight that they can come unto heaven. Yea, the eyes of the flesh are so dull, that they cannot ascend into heaven.

LORD, QUICKEN OUR SIGHT

"Look," he said, "I see heaven open and the Son of Man standing at the right hand of God." —Acts 7:54–56, NIV

Stephen courageously triumphs over his enemies, when he affirms plainly that he saw a miracle. Here the question can be asked: How were the heavens opened? For my part, I think that there was nothing changed in the nature of the heavens; but Stephen had new quickness of sight granted him, which pierced all barriers, even into the invisible glory of the kingdom of heaven. For even if there were some opening or parting made in heaven, yet human eyes could never reach so far. Again, Stephen alone did see the glory of God. For that spectacle was not only hidden from the wicked, who stood in the same place, but they were also so blinded within themselves, that they did not see the manifest truth. Therefore, he says that the heavens are opened to him in this respect, because nothing keeps him from beholding the glory of God. Whereupon it follows that the miracle was not wrought in heaven, but in his eyes.

It is certain that Christ appeared unto him not after some natural manner, but after a new and singular sort. I ask you, of what color was the glory of God, that it could be seen naturally with the eyes of the flesh? Therefore, we must imagine nothing in this vision but that which is divine. Moreover, this is worth noting: The glory of God did not appear unto Stephen wholly as it was, but according to his human capacity. For that infiniteness cannot be comprehended with the ability measured out to any creature. Therefore, if we desire to feel Jesus present by the working of his grace, we must seek him in heaven, as he revealed himself to Stephen there.

LOVING IN ADVERSITY

While they were stoning him, Stephen prayed, "Lord Jesus, receive my spirit." Then he fell on his knees and cried out, "Lord, do not hold this sin against them." When he had said this, he fell asleep.
—*Acts 7:59–60, NIV*

When Stephen prays, "Lord, do not hold this against them," he joins the love of humans with faith in Christ; and surely if we desire to be gathered to Christ for our salvation, we must put on this love. Whereas Stephen prays for his enemies, and those enemies most deadly— and even in the very instant when their cruelty might provoke him to desire revenge—he declares sufficiently what feeling he bears toward all people.

And we know that we are all commanded to do the same thing which Stephen did. Because there is nothing more hard than to forgive injuries, so that we wish well to those who would have us undone (Matt. 5:43-44), therefore we must always set Stephen before our eyes for an example. He cries indeed with a loud voice, but he shows no disposition before his audience which was not spoken sincerely and from the heart, as God himself witness-

"he joins the love of humans with faith in Christ"

es. Yet he cries aloud, so as to leave out nothing which might serve to alleviate the cruelty of the enemies.

Undoubtedly Stephen prayed not in vain and Paul is a sufficient testimony that this sin was not laid to all their the Jews' charges. Now, because he made this prayer when he was at the point of death, he was not moved with any hope of obtaining pardon, to be so careful to appease his enemies, but only that they might repent.

CONVERSION OF ALL

Jesus answered and said unto her, If thou knewest the gift of God, and who it is that saith to thee, Give me to drink; thou wouldest have asked of him, and he would have given thee living water. —John 4:10

availing himself of the opportunity, Christ now begins to preach about the grace and power of his Spirit, and that to a woman who did not at all deserve that he should speak a word to her. This is certainly an astonishing instance of his goodness. For what was there in this wretched woman that, from being a prostitute, she suddenly became a disciple of the Son of God? (Though in all of us he has displayed a similar instance of his compassion.) All the women, indeed, are not prostitutes, nor are all the men stained by some heinous crime; but what excellence can any of us plead as a reason why he deigned to bestow on us the heavenly doctrine and the honor of being admitted into his family?

Nor was it by accident that the conversation with such a person occurred; for the Lord showed us, as in a model, that those to whom he imparts the doctrine of salvation are not selected on the ground of merit.

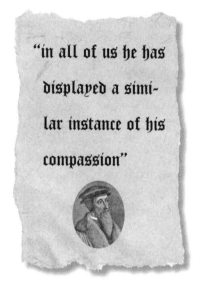

"in all of us he has displayed a similar instance of his compassion"

And it appears at first sight a wonderful arrangement that he passed by so many great men in Judea, and yet held familiar discourse with this woman. But it was necessary that, in his person, it should be explained how true is that saying of the Prophet, I was found by them that sought me not; "I was made manifest to them that asked not after me. I said to those who sought me not, 'Behold, here I am'" (Isa. 65:1).

FURTHER PROGRESS FROM THE LAW

The woman saith unto him, I know that Messias cometh, which is called Christ: when he is come, he will tell us all things. —John 4:25

his, at least, is beyond all controversy: The woman prefers Christ to Moses and to all the Prophets in the office of teaching, for she comprehends three things in a few words.

First, she comprehends that the doctrine of the Law was not absolutely perfect, and that nothing more than first principles was delivered in it; if there had not been some further progress to be made, she would not have said that the Messiah will tell us all things. There is an implied contrast between him and the Prophets that it is his peculiar office to conduct his Disciples to the goal, while the Prophets had only given them the earliest instructions and, as it were, led them into the course.

Secondly, the woman declares that she expects such a Christ as will be the interpreter of his Father, and the teacher and instructor of all the godly.

Lastly, she expresses her belief that we ought not to desire anything better or more

"we ought not to desire anything better or more perfect than his doctrine"

perfect than his doctrine, but that, on the contrary, this is the farthest object of wisdom, beyond which it is unlawful to proceed. I wish that those who now boast of being the pillars of the Christian Church would at least imitate this poor woman, so as to be satisfied with the simple doctrine of Christ, rather than claim I know not what power of superintendence for putting forth their inventions.

SMALL MEASURES OF FAITH

Jesus saith unto him, Go thy way; thy son liveth. And the man believed the word that Jesus had spoken unto him, and he went his way.
—John 4:50

The first thing that strikes us here is the astonishing kindness and disdain of Christ that he bears with the man's ignorance, and stretches his power beyond what had been expected. He requested that Christ would come to the place and cure his son. He thought it possible that his son could be freed from sickness and disease, but not that he could be raised up after he was dead. Therefore he urges Christ to make haste, so his son's recovery may not be prevented by his death. Accordingly, when Christ pardons both, we may conclude from it how highly he values even a small measure of faith. It is worthy of observation that Christ, while he does not comply with his desire, grants much more than he had requested; for he testifies as to the present health of his son.

Thus it frequently happens that our Heavenly Father, while he does not comply with our wishes in every particular, proceeds to relieve us by unexpected methods, so we may learn

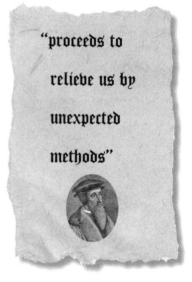

"proceeds to relieve us by unexpected methods"

not to prescribe to him in anything. When he says, "Thy son lives," he means that he has been rescued from the danger of death. For how many will you find that profit as much by many sermons as this man, who was half a heathen, profited by hearing a single word? So much the more ought we to labor with zeal to arouse our sluggishness and, above all, to pray that God would touch our hearts in such a manner, so we may not be less willing to believe than he is ready and gracious to promise.

242

HELP IN OUR WEAKNESS

Likewise the Spirit also helpeth our infirmities: for we know not what we should pray for as we ought: but the Spirit itself maketh intercession for us with groanings which cannot be uttered. —Romans 8:26

As our faculties are far from being able to attain to such high perfection, we must seek for some means to assist them. As the eye of our mind should be intent upon God, so the affection of our heart ought to follow in the same course. But both fall far beneath this, or rather, they faint and fail and are carried in a contrary direction.

To assist this weakness, God gives us the guidance of the Spirit in our prayers to dictate what is right and regulate our affections. For seeing "we know not what we should pray for as we ought, the Spirit itself makes intercession for us with groans which cannot be uttered" (Rom. 8:26), not that he actually prays or groans, but he excites in us sighs, and wishes, and confidence, which our natural powers are not at all able to conceive. Nor is it without cause Paul gives the name of groans which cannot be uttered to the prayers which believers send forth under the guidance of the Spirit. For those who are truly exercised in prayer are not unaware that blind anxieties so restrain and perplex them, that they can scarcely find what it becomes them to utter; nay, in attempting to lisp they halt and hesitate.

Hence it appears that to pray aright is a special gift. We do not here speak of laziness, as if we were to leave the office of prayer to the Holy Spirit, and give way to that carelessness to which we are too prone. Thus we sometimes hear the impious expression, that we are to wait in suspense until he take possession of our minds while otherwise occupied. Our meaning is that, weary of our own heartlessness and sloth, we are to long for the aid of the Spirit. Nor, indeed, does Paul, when he enjoins us to pray in the Spirit (1 Cor. 14:15) cease to exhort us to vigilance, intimating that while the inspiration of the Spirit is effectual to the formation of prayer, it by no means impedes or retards our own endeavors; since in this matter God is pleased to try how efficiently faith influences our hearts.

CLARIFYING FREE WILL

For all have sinned and fall short of the glory of God, and are justified freely by his grace through the redemption that came by Christ Jesus."
—Romans 3:23–24, NIV

t will be beyond dispute that free will does not enable any man to perform good works, unless he is assisted by grace; indeed, it is the special grace which the elect alone receive through regeneration. For I stay not to consider the extravagance of those who say that grace is offered equally and superfluously to all. But it has not yet been shown whether man is entirely deprived of the power of well-doing, or whether he still possesses it in some, though in a very feeble and limited degree—a degree so feeble and limited, that it can do nothing of itself, but when assisted by grace, is able also to perform its part.

Man is said to have free will, not because he has a free choice of good and evil, but because he acts voluntarily, and not by compulsion. This is perfectly true; but why should so small a matter have been dignified with so proud a title?

It is an admirable freedom that man is not forced to be the servant of sin, while he is, however, a voluntary slave; his will is bound by the fetters of sin. I loathe mere verbal disputes, by which the Church is hurried to no purpose; but I think we ought religiously to avoid terms which imply some absurdity, especially in subjects where error is of deadly consequence. How few are there who, when they hear free will attributed to man, do not immediately imagine that he is the master of his mind and will and that he can incline himself either to good or evil? It may be said that such dangers are removed by carefully clarifying the meaning to the people. But such is the inclination of the human mind to go astray, that it will more quickly draw error from one little word, than truth from a lengthy discourse.

NO POSSESSIONS

He giveth power to the faint; and to them that have no might he increaseth strength. Even the youths shall faint and be weary, and the young men shall utterly fall: But they that wait upon the LORD shall renew their strength; they shall mount up with wings as eagles; they shall run, and not be weary; and they shall walk, and not faint.
—Isaiah 40: 29–31

He who is most deeply belittled and alarmed by the consciousness of his disgrace, nakedness, want, and misery, has made the greatest progress in the knowledge of himself. Man is in no danger of taking too much from himself, provided he learns that whatever he wants is to be recovered in God. But he cannot assign to himself one particle beyond his due, without losing himself in vain confidence, and, by transferring divine honor to himself, becoming guilty of the greatest impiety. Assuredly, whenever our minds are seized with a longing to possess something of our own, which may reside in us rather than in God, we may rest assured that the thought is suggested by no other counselor than he who enticed our first parents to aspire to be like gods, knowing good and evil.

It is sweet, indeed, to have so much virtue of our own as to be able to rest in ourselves. But let the many solemn passages deter us from indulging this vain confidence: "Cursed be the man that trusts in man, and makes flesh his arm" (Jer. 17:5). "He delights not in the strength of the horse; he takes not pleasure in the legs of a man. The LORD takes pleasure in those that fear him, in those that hope in his mercy" (Ps. 147:10–11). The scope of all these passages is that we must not entertain any opinion of our own strength if we would enjoy the favor of God, who "resists the proud, but gives grace unto the humble" (James 4:6). None are admitted to enjoy the blessings of God save those who are yearning under a sense of their own poverty. The Lord certainly does not deprive his servants of the light of the sun or moon, but he dissuades them from confidence even in those objects which they deem most excellent.

HUMILITY, HUMILITY, AND HUMILITY

They close up their callous hearts, and their mouths speak
with arrogance. —Psalm 17:10, NIV

I have always been exceedingly delighted with the words of Chrysostom, "The foundation of our philosophy is humility;" and still more with those of Augustine who said, "Orator, when asked, 'What is the first precept in eloquence?' answered, 'Delivery.' 'What is the second?' 'Delivery' 'What the third?' 'Delivery.' So, if you ask me in regard to the precepts of the Christian Religion, I will answer: first, second, and third, Humility." By humility he means not when a man, with a consciousness of some virtue, refrains from pride, but when he truly feels that he has no refuge but in humility.

This is clear from another passage, "Let no man flatter himself: of himself he is a devil: his happiness he owes entirely to God. What have you of your own but sin? Take your sin which is your own; for righteousness is of God." Again, "Why presume so much on the capability of nature? It is wounded, maimed, vexed, lost. The thing wanted is genuine confession, not false defiance," and "When any one knows that he is nothing in himself, and has no help from himself, the weapons within himself are broken, and the war is ended." All the weapons of impiety must be bruised, broken and burnt in the fire; you must remain unarmed, having no help in yourself. The more dependent you are, the more the Lord will sustain you.

In expounding the seventieth Psalm, he forbids us to remember our own righteousness, in order that we may recognize the righteousness of God, and shows that God bestows his grace upon us, so we may know that we are nothing—that we stand only by the mercy of God—seeing that in ourselves we are altogether wicked. Let us not contend with God for our right, as if anything attributed to him were lost to our salvation. As our insignificance is his exaltation, so the confession of our insignificance has its remedy in his mercy.

CORRUPTED GIFTS

Through him all things were made; without him nothing was made that had been made. In him was life, and that life was the light of men. The light shines in the darkness, but the darkness has not understood it. —John 1:3–5, NIV

I feel pleased with the well-known saying that has been borrowed from the writings of Augustine, which says that man's natural gifts were corrupted by sin and his supernatural gifts withdrawn; supernatural gifts meaning the light of faith and righteousness, which would have been sufficient for the attainment of heavenly life and everlasting happiness. When he withdrew his allegiance to God, man was deprived of the spiritual gifts by which he had been raised to the hope of eternal salvation. Hence it follows that he is now in exile from the kingdom of God, so that all things which pertain to the blessed life of the soul are extinguished in him until he recovers them by the grace of regeneration. Among these are faith, love to God, charity towards our neighbor, the study of righteousness and holiness. All these, when Christ restores them to us, are to be regarded as from outside ourselves and above nature. If so, we infer that they were previously abolished.

On the other hand, soundness of mind and integrity of heart were at the same time withdrawn, and it is this which constitutes the corruption of natural gifts. For although there is still some residue of intelligence and judgment as well as will, we cannot call a mind sound and entire that is both weak and immersed in darkness. As to the will, its depravity is but too well known. Therefore—since reason, by which man discerns between good and evil and by which he understands and judges—is a natural gift, it could not be entirely destroyed; but being partly weakened and partly corrupted, a shapeless ruin is all that remains. In this sense it is said that "The light shines in darkness, and the darkness comprehended it not" (John 1:5); these words clearly express both points: In the perverted and degenerate nature of man there are still some sparks which show that he is a rational animal and differs from the brutes, inasmuch as he is endued with intelligence; yet this light is so smothered by clouds of darkness that it cannot shine forth to any good effect. Similarly, the will, because inseparable from the nature of man, did not perish but was so enslaved by depraved lusts as to be incapable of one righteous desire.

OUR INTELLIGENCE

Then I applied myself to the understanding of wisdom and also of madness and folly, but I learned that this, too, is a chasing after the wind. For with much wisdom comes much sorrow; the more knowledge, the more grief. —Ecclesiastes 1:17–18, NIV

To charge the intellect with perpetual blindness, leaving it no intelligence of any description whatever, is disgusting not only to the Word of God but also to common experience. We see that there has been implanted in the human mind a certain desire of investigating truth, to which it never would aspire unless some delight in truth existed previously. There is, therefore, to this extent, discernment in the human mind; it is naturally influenced by the love of truth, the neglect of which in the lower animals is a proof of their gross and irrational nature. Still it is true that this love of truth fails before it reaches the goal, thereby falling away into vanity. As the human mind is unable—from dullness—to pursue the right path of investigation, and—after various wanderings—stumbling every now and then like one groping in darkness, at length gets completely bewildered, so its whole procedure proves how unfit it is to search the truth and find it. Hence Solomon, throughout the Book of Ecclesiastes, after enumerating all the studies in which men think they attain the highest wisdom, pronounces them vain and frivolous.

However, man's efforts are not always so utterly fruitless as not to lead to some result, especially when his attention is directed to inferior objects. Nay, even with regard to superior objects, though he is more careless in investigating them, he makes some progress. Here, however, his ability is more limited, and he is never made more sensible of his weakness than when he attempts to soar above the sphere of the present life. We have one kind of intelligence of earthly things, and another of heavenly things. By earthly things, I mean those which relate not to God and his kingdom, to true righteousness and future blessedness, but have some connection with the present life and are in a manner confined within its boundaries. By heavenly things, I mean the pure knowledge of God, the method of true righteousness, and the mysteries of the heavenly kingdom.

CIVIL ORDER

Those who forsake the law praise the wicked, but those who keep the law resist them. Evil men do not understand justice, but those who seek the Lord understand it fully. —Proverbs 28:4–5, NIV

Since man is by nature a social animal, he is disposed, from natural instinct, to cherish and preserve society. Accordingly, we see that the minds of all men have impressions of civil order and honesty. Hence, every individual understands how human societies must be regulated by laws—and is also able to comprehend the principles of those laws. Thus the universal agreement in regard to such subjects, both among nations and individuals, the seeds of them being implanted in the breasts of all without a teacher or lawgiver.

The truth of this fact is not affected by the wars and dissensions which immediately arise. While some—such as thieves and robbers—would invert the rules of justice, loosen the bonds of law, and give free scope to their lust, others (a vice of most frequent occurrence) deem that to be unjust which is elsewhere regarded as just, and, hold that to be praiseworthy which is elsewhere forbidden. For such persons do not hate the laws from not knowing that they are good and sacred, but, inflamed with headlong passion, quarrel with what is clearly reasonable, and licentiously hate what their mind and understanding approve.

Quarrels of this latter kind do not destroy the primary idea of justice. For while men dispute with each other about particular enactments, their ideas of equity agree in substance. This, no doubt, proves the weakness of the human mind, which—even when it seems on the right path—halts and hesitates. Still, however, it is true that some principle of civil order is impressed on all. And this is ample proof that, in regard to the constitution of the present life, no man is devoid of the light of reason.

RECOGNIZING GOD'S TRUTH

There are different kinds of gifts, but the same Spirit. There are different kinds of service, but the same Lord. There are different kinds of working, but the same God works all of them in all men.
—*1 Corinthians 12:4–6, NIV*

In reading profane authors, the recognizable light of truth displayed in them should remind us that the human mind, however much fallen and perverted from its original integrity, is still decorated and invested with admirable gifts from its Creator. If we reflect that the Spirit of God is the only fountain of truth, we will be careful, as we would avoid offering insult to him, not to reject or condemn truth wherever it appears. In despising the gifts, we insult the Giver.

How, then, can we deny that truth must have beamed on those ancient lawgivers who arranged civil order and discipline with so much equity? Shall we say that the philosophers, in their exquisite researches and skilful description of nature, were blind? Shall we deny the possession of intellect to those who drew up rules for discourse, and taught us to speak in accordance with reason? Shall we say that those who, by the cultivation of the medical art, expended their industry on our behalf were only raving? What shall we say of the mathematical sciences? Shall we deem them to be the dreams of madmen? Nay, we cannot read the writings of the ancients on these subjects without the highest admiration—an admiration which their excellence will not allow us to withhold. But shall we deem anything to be noble and praiseworthy, without tracing it to the hand of God? Far from us is such ingratitude—an ingratitude not chargeable even on heathen poets, who acknowledged that philosophy and laws, and all useful arts were the inventions of the gods.

Therefore, since it is manifest that men whom the Scriptures call carnal are so acute and clear-sighted in the investigation of inferior things, their example should teach us how many gifts the Lord has left in possession of human nature, notwithstanding its having been robbed of the true good.

WEAKNESS OF MIND

The LORD knoweth the thoughts of man, that they are vanity.
—Psalm 94:11

We must refute the opinion of those who hold that all sins proceed from preconceived severity and malice. We know too well from experience how often we fall, even when our intention is good. Our reason is exposed to so many forms of delusion, is liable to so many errors, stumbles on so many obstacles, and is entangled by so many snares that it is ever wandering from the right direction.

Is it indeed true that all thought, intelligence, discernment, and industry are so defective that, in the sight of the Lord, we cannot think or aim at any thing that is right? To us, who can scarcely bear to part with acuteness of intellect (in our estimation a most precious endowment), it seems hard to admit this, whereas it is regarded as most just by the Holy Spirit, who "knows the thoughts of man, that they are vanity" (Ps. 94:11), and distinctly declares that "every imagination of the thoughts of his heart was only evil continually" (Gen. 6:5; 8:21).

If everything which our mind conceives, meditates, plans and resolves is always evil, how can it ever think of doing what is pleasing to God, to whom righteousness and holiness alone are acceptable? It is thus plain that our mind, in whatever direction it turns, is miserably exposed to vanity. David was conscious of its weakness when he prayed, "Give me understanding, and I shall keep thy law" (Ps. 119:34). This he does not proclaim once only, but in one psalm repeats the same prayer almost ten times, the repetition intimating how strong the necessity which urged him to pray.

What he thus asked for himself alone, Paul prays for the churches in general. "For this cause," he says, "we also, since the day we heard it, do not cease to pray for you, and to desire that you might be filled with the knowledge of his will, in all wisdom and spiritual understanding; that you might walk worthy of the Lord" (Col. 1:9–10). Whenever he represents this as a blessing from God, we should remember that he at the same time testifies that it is not in the power of man.

GOD'S RESTRAINT

The LORD looks down from heaven on the sons of men to see if there are any who understand, any who seek God. All have turned aside, they have together become corrupt; there is no one who does good, not even one. —Psalm 14:2–3, NIV

In every age there have been some who, under the guidance of nature, were all their lives devoted to virtue. It is of no consequence that many blots may be detected in their conduct; by the mere study of virtue, they evinced that there was somewhat of purity in their nature. Such examples, then, seem to warn us against supposing that the nature of man is utterly vicious, since, under its guidance, some have not only excelled in illustrious deeds but also conducted themselves most honorably through the whole course of their lives.

But we ought to consider that, notwithstanding the corruption of our nature, there is some room for divine grace—such grace that, without purifying it, may lay it under internal restraint. For, did the Lord let every mind loose to act without restraint in its lusts, doubtless there is not a man who would not show that his nature is capable of all the crimes with which Paul charges it (Rom. 3 compared with Ps. 14:3). Can you exempt yourself from the number of those whose feet are swift to shed blood, whose hands are foul with robbery and murder, whose throats are like open tombs, whose tongues are deceitful, whose lips are venomous, whose actions are useless, unjust, rotten, deadly, whose soul is without God, whose inward parts are full of wickedness, whose eyes are watching for deception, whose minds are prepared for insult, whose every part, in short, is framed for endless deeds of wickedness?

If every soul is capable of such abominations (and the Apostle declares this boldly), it is surely easy to see what the result would be if the Lord were to permit human passion to follow its bent. No ravenous beast would rush so furiously, no stream, however rapid and violent, so spontaneously burst its banks. In the elect, God cures these; in others, he only lays them under such restraint as may prevent them from breaking forth to a degree incompatible with the established order of things.

CHRIST FORGIVES THE WEAKEST

The impotent man answered him, Sir, I have no man, when the water is troubled, to put me into the pool: but while I am coming, another steppeth down before me. —John 5:7

This diseased man does what almost all of us are wont to do; for he limits the assistance of God according to his own thought, and does not venture to promise to himself anything more than he conceives in his mind. Christ forgives his weakness, and in this we have a mirror of that forbearance of which every one of us has daily experience: when, on the one hand, we keep our attention fixed on the means which are within our reach, and when, on the other hand, contrary to expectation, he displays his hand from hidden places and thus shows how far his goodness goes beyond the narrow limits of our faith.

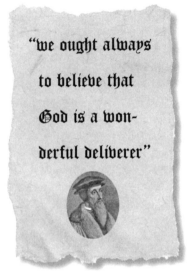

"we ought always to believe that God is a wonderful deliverer"

Besides, this example ought to teach us patience. Thirty-eight years were a long period, during which God had delayed to render to this poor man that favor which, from the beginning, he had determined to confer upon him. However long, therefore, we may be held in suspense, though we groan under our distresses, let us never be discouraged by the tediousness of the lengthened period. For, when our afflictions are long continued, though we discover no termination of them, still we ought always to believe that God is a wonderful deliverer who, by his power, easily removes every obstacle out of the way.

REAL FAITH

After three days the officers went throughout the camp, giving orders to the people: "When you see the ark of the covenant of the LORD your God, and the priests, who are Levites, carrying it, you are to move out from your positions and follow it. Then you will know which way to go, since you have never been this way before. But keep a distance of about a thousand yards between you and the ark; do not go near it."
—Joshua 3:2–4, NIV

Although the way the miracle will happen hasn't been explained when the ark of the covenant is brought forward like a banner to guide the way, it was natural for the Israelites to infer that the Lord was preparing something unusual. And while they are kept in suspense, their faith is again proved by a serious trial. For it was an example of rare virtue to give implicit obedience to the command, and thus follow the ark, while they were obviously uninformed as to the result. This, indeed, is the special characteristic of faith, not to inquire curiously what the Lord is to do, nor to dispute subtlety as to how that which he declares can possibly be done, but to cast all our anxious cares upon his providence—and knowing that his power, on which we may rest, is boundless—to raise our thoughts above the world and embrace by faith that which we cannot comprehend by reason.

Since the younger Levites, who had the job of carrying the ark, were strictly forbidden to touch it, or even to look at it when it was uncovered, it is normal that the common people were not allowed to come within a considerable distance of it. The dignity of the ark, therefore, is shown, when the people are ordered to prove their veneration of it by leaving a long space between themselves and it. For although God intimately invites us to himself, truly faithful trust in God does not beget self-assurance and boldness but, on the contrary, is always coupled with fear. In this way the ark of the covenant was, indeed, a strong and pleasant pledge of God's favor but, at the same time, had an awful majesty, fit to subdue worldly pride. This humility and modesty, moreover, had the effect of developing the Israelites' faith by preventing them from confining the grace of God within narrow limits and reminding them that, though they were far distant from the ark, the divine power was ever near.

TRUE RELIGION AND RIGHTEOUSNESS

Brothers, my heart's desire and prayer to God for the Israelites is that they may be saved. For I can testify about them that they are zealous for God, but their zeal is not based on knowledge. Since they did not know the righteousness that comes from God and sought to establish their own, they did not submit to God's righteousness.
—*Romans 10:1–3, NIV*

There was a good reason why Paul should regard the Jews with compassion rather than hatred; since he perceived that they had fallen only through ignorance, and not through malignancy of mind, and especially because he saw that they were led by some respect for God to persecute the kingdom of Christ. Let us hence learn where our good intentions may guide us if we yield to them. It is commonly thought a good and a very fit excuse when someone who is scolded says that he meant no harm. And this pretext is believed to be good by many at this day, so that we don't apply our minds to finding the truth of God, because we think that whatever we do wrong through ignorance is excusable. But no one of us would excuse the Jews for having crucified Christ, for having cruelly raged against the Apostles, and for having attempted to destroy and extinguish the Gospel; and yet they had the same defense as that in which we confidently excuse ourselves. Away, then, with these vain evasions about good intention.

See how the Jews went astray through unthinking zeal! For they sought to set up a righteousness of their own, and this foolish confidence proceeded from their ignorance of God's righteousness. Notice the contrast between the righteousness of God and people. They are opposed to one another, as things wholly contrary. It follows that God's righteousness is subverted as soon as people set up their own. And again, the righteousness of God is no doubt God's gift; and in like manner, the righteousness of people is that which they derive from themselves, or believe that they bring before God. Those who seek to be justified through themselves do not submit to God's righteousness, for the first step towards obtaining the righteousness of God is to renounce our own righteousness. Paul grievously dishonors the pride by which hypocrites are inflated when they cover righteousness with a hollow mask of zeal, for all such prideful people are adverse to and rebel against the righteousness of God.

RIGHTEOUSNESS BY FAITH

Moses describes in this way the righteousness that is by the law: "The man who does these things will live by them. But the righteousness that is by faith says: 'Do not say in your heart, "Who will ascend to Heaven?" (that is, to bring Christ down) or "Who will descend into the deep?"' (that is, to bring Christ up from the dead). First he said, "Sacrifices and offerings, burnt offerings and sin offerings you did not desire, nor were you pleased with them" (although the law required them to be made.) —Romans 10:5–8, NIV

To make it obvious how different is the righteousness of faith from that of works, Paul now compares them. But he refers not now to the Prophets, but to the testimony of Moses, and for this reason: that the Jews might understand that the Law was not given by Moses in order to detain them in a dependence on works but, on the contrary, to lead them to Christ. In order to instruct the people in the doctrine of repentance, it was necessary for Moses to teach what manner of life was acceptable to God; and this he taught in the precepts of the Law. That he might also instill into the minds of the people the love of righteousness and implant in them the hatred of sin, he added promises and threats—proposing rewards to the just and dreadful punishments on sinners. It was now the duty of the people to consider in how many ways they drew punishments on themselves, and how far they were from deserving anything at God's hands by their works, so that being thus led to despair of their own righteousness, they might flee to the haven of divine goodness, and so to Christ himself.

Paul quotes from a passage taken from Deut. 30:12, where Moses speaks of the doctrine of the Law, and Paul applies it to evangelic promises. Moses shows that the way to true life was made plain when the will of God was no longer hid from the Jews. Moses doesn't only mean the Law, but generally the whole of God's truth, which includes the Gospel; for the word of the Law by itself is never in our heart—no, not the least syllable of it—until it is implanted in us by the faith of the Gospel. And then, even after our regeneration, the word of the Law cannot properly be said to be in our heart for it demands perfection, which even the faithful are far distant from reaching.

A CLEAR VOICE

Saying, This is the blood of the testament which God hath enjoined unto you. —Hebrews 9:20

his passage reminds us that the promises of God are then only profitable to us when they are confirmed by the blood of Christ. For what Paul testifies in 2 Cor. 1:20—that all God's promises are yea and amen in Christ—this happens when his blood like a seal is engraven on our hearts, or when we not only hear God speaking, but also see Christ offering himself as a pledge for those things which are spoken. If this thought only came to our minds, that what we read is not written so much with ink as with the blood of Christ, that when the Gospel is preached, his sacred blood dis-

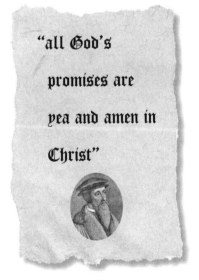

"all God's promises are yea and amen in Christ"

tills together with the voice, there would be far greater attention as well as reverence on our part.

CULTIVATE UNITY

Not forsaking the assembling of ourselves together, as the manner of some is; but exhorting one another: and so much the more, as ye see the day approaching. —Hebrews 10:25

It is an evil which prevails everywhere among mankind: that every one sets himself above others, and especially that those who seem in anything to excel cannot well endure their inferiors to be on an equality with themselves. And then there is so much gloom almost in all, that individuals would gladly make churches for themselves if they could; for they find it so difficult to accommodate themselves to the ways and habits of others. The rich envy one another, and hardly one in a hundred can be found among the rich who allows to the poor the name and rank of brethren. Unless similarity of habits or some allurements or advantages draw us together, it is very difficult even to maintain a continual concord among ourselves.

Extremely needed, therefore, by us all is the admonition to be stimulated to love and not to envy, and not to separate from those whom God has joined to us, but to embrace with brotherly kindness all

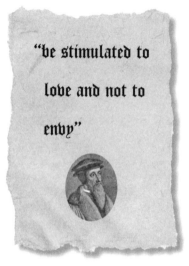

"be stimulated to love and not to envy"

those who are united to us in faith. And surely it behaves us the more earnestly to cultivate unity, as the more eagerly watchful Satan is either to tear us by any means from the Church or stealthily to seduce us from it. And such would be the happy effect, were no one to please himself too much, and were all of us to preserve this one object: mutually to provoke one another to love, and to allow no glorifying of ourselves, but that of doing "good works."

SUPPORTED BY HOPE

Now faith is the substance of things hoped for, the evidence of things not seen. —Hebrews 11:1

he Apostle here reminds us that faith regards not present things, but such as are waited for. Nor is this kind of contradiction without its force and beauty. Faith, he says, is the prop or foundation on which we plant our foot. The prop of what? Of things absent, which are so far from being really possessed by us, that they are far beyond the reach of our understanding.

The same view is to be taken of the second clause, when he calls faith the evidence or demonstration of things not seen. For demonstration makes things to appear or to be seen, and it is commonly applied to what is subject to our senses.

Then these two things, though apparently inconsistent, do yet perfectly harmonize when we speak of faith. For the Spirit of God shows to us hidden things, the knowledge of which cannot reach our senses. Promised to us is eternal life, but it is promised to the dead. We are assured of a happy resurrection, but we are as yet involved in corruption. We are pronounced just, as yet sin dwells in us. We hear that we are happy, but we are as yet in the midst of many miseries. An abundance of all good things is promised to us, but still we often hunger and thirst. God proclaims that he will come quickly, but he seems deaf when we cry to him.

What would become of us were we not supported by hope, and did not our minds emerge out of the midst of darkness above the world through the light of God's Word and of his Spirit? Faith, then, is rightly said to be the substance of things which are as yet the objects of hope and the evidence of things not seen.

ALL THE TREASURES

Jesus Christ the same yesterday, and to day, and for ever.
—Hebrews 13:8

he only way by which we can persevere in the right faith is to hold to the foundation, and not in the smallest degree to depart from it. For he who holds not to Christ knows nothing but mere vanity, though he may comprehend heaven and earth; for in Christ are included all the treasures of celestial wisdom. This then is a remarkable passage, from which we learn that there is no other way of being truly wise than by fixing all our thoughts on Christ alone.

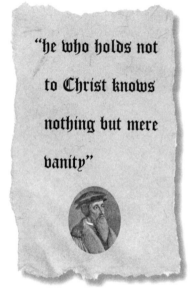

"he who holds not to Christ knows nothing but mere vanity"

Now as he is dealing with the Jews, he teaches them that Christ had ever possessed the same sovereignty which he holds at this day: "the same," he says, "yesterday, and today, and forever." By these words he intimates that Christ, who was then made known in the world, had reigned from the beginning of the world, and that it is not possible to advance farther when we come to him. Yesterday then comprehends the whole time of the Old Testament; and that no one might expect a sudden change after a short time, as the promulgation of the Gospel was then but recent, he declares that Christ had been lately revealed for this very end—that the knowledge of him might continue the same for ever.

THE SOURCE OF KNOWLEDGE

His divine power has given us everything we need for life and godliness through our knowledge of him who called us by his own glory and goodness. Through these he has given us his very great and precious promises, so that through them you may participate in the divine nature and escape the corruption in the world caused by evil desires.
—2 Peter 1:3–4, NIV

While revealed truth concurs with the general consent of mankind in teaching that the second part of wisdom consists in self-knowledge, they differ greatly as to the method by which this knowledge is to be acquired.

In the judgment of the flesh, man deems his self-knowledge complete when, with overweening confidence in his own intelligence and integrity, he takes courage and spurs himself on to virtuous deeds, and when, declaring war upon vice, he uses his utmost endeavor to attain to the honorable and the fair.

But he who tries himself by the standard of divine justice finds nothing to inspire him with confidence; hence, the more thorough his self-examination, the greater his despondency. Abandoning all dependence on himself, he feels that he is utterly incapable of duly regulating his conduct.

It is not the will of God, however, that we should forget the primeval dignity which he bestowed on our first parents. It is impossible for us to think of our first original, or the end for which we were created, without being urged to meditate on immortality and to seek the kingdom of God. But such meditation, so far from raising our spirits, rather casts them down and makes us humble.

Hence, in considering the knowledge which man ought to have of himself, it seems proper to divide it thus: first, to consider the end for which he was created, and the qualities—by no means contemptible qualities—with which he was endued, thus urging him to meditate on divine worship and the future life; and, secondly, to consider his faculties, or rather want of faculties—a want which, when perceived, will annihilate all his confidence, and cover him with confusion. The tendency of the former view is to teach him what his duty is, of the latter, to make him aware how far he is able to perform it.

RISING UPWARD

Unto thee, O LORD, do I lift up my soul. O my God, I trust in thee: let me not be ashamed, let not mine enemies triumph over me.
—*Psalm 25:1–2*

Let everyone in professing to pray turn to God all his thoughts and feelings, and be not (as is usual) distracted by wandering thoughts; because nothing is more contrary to the reverence due to God than that levity which bespeaks a mind too much given to license and devoid of fear. In this matter we ought to labor the more earnestly the more difficult we experience it to be; for no man is so intent on prayer as not to feel many thoughts creeping in, and either breaking off the tenor of his prayer, or retarding it by some turning or digression.

Here let us consider how unbecoming it is when God admits us to familiar intercourse to abuse his great condescension by mingling things sacred and profane, reverence for him not keeping our minds under restraint; but just as if in prayer we were conversing with one like ourselves, forgetting him and allowing our thoughts to run to and fro. Let us know, then, that none duly prepare themselves for prayer but those who are so impressed with the majesty of God that they engage in it free from all earthly cares and affections. The ceremony of lifting up our hands in prayer is designed to remind us that we are far removed from God, unless our thoughts rise upward. As it is said in the psalm, "Unto thee, O LORD, do I lift up my soul" (Ps. 25:1). And Scripture repeatedly uses the expression to raise our prayers, meaning that those who would be heard by God must not grovel in the mire.

The sum is that the more liberally God deals with us, condescendingly inviting us to unburden our cares into his bosom, the less excusable we are if this admirable and incomparable blessing does not in our estimation outweigh all other things and win our affection, that prayer may seriously engage our every thought and feeling. This cannot be unless our mind, strenuously exerting itself against all impediments, rises upward.

BUSINESS REPLY MAIL

FIRST-CLASS MAIL   PERMIT NO. 1381   BOULDER, CO

POSTAGE WILL BE PAID BY ADDRESSEE

The Nation.

PO BOX 55149
BOULDER CO 80323-5149

DAMAGE CONTROL

24 Issues
Only $21⁹⁷

BE CAREFUL WHAT YOU ASK

Trust in him at all times, O people; pour out your hearts to him, for God is our refuge. —Psalm 62:8, NIV

Let us have our heart and mind framed as becomes those who are entering into conversation with God. This we shall accomplish in regard to the mind if, laying aside carnal thoughts and cares which might interfere with the direct and pure contemplation of God, it not only be wholly intent on prayer but also, as far as possible, be borne and raised above itself. All foreign and extraneous cares must be dispelled by which the mind might be driven to and fro in vague suspense, be drawn down from heaven, and kept groveling on the earth. When I say it must be raised above itself, I mean that it must not bring into the presence of God any of those things which our blind and stupid reason is wont to devise, nor keep itself confined within the little measure of its own vanity, but rise to a purity worthy of God.

We are to ask only in so far as God permits. For though he bids us pour out our hearts (Ps. 62:8), he does not indiscriminately give loose reins to foolish and depraved affections; and when he promises that he will grant believers their wish, his indulgence does not proceed so far as to submit to their caprice. In both matters, grievous delinquencies are everywhere committed. For not only do many without modesty, without reverence, presume to invoke God concerning their frivolities, but impudently bring forward their dreams, whatever they may be, before the tribunal of God. Such is the folly or stupidity under which they labor, that they have the hardihood to feast upon what is so vile to God, and then blush exceedingly to impart them to their fellow men. Men in prayer give greater license to their unlawful desires than if they were telling jocular tales among their friends. God does not suffer his condescension to be thus mocked but—vindicating his own light—places our wishes under the restraint of his authority. We must, therefore, attend to the observation of John: "This is the confidence that we have in him, that if we ask anything according to his will, he hears us" (1 John 5:14).

GOD'S WISDOM

Where is the wise? where is the scribe? where is the disputer of this world? hath not God made foolish the wisdom of this world? For after that in the wisdom of God the world by wisdom knew not God, it pleased God by the foolishness of preaching to save them that believe.
—1 Corinthians 1:20–21

The whole human race having been undone in the person of Adam, the excellence and dignity of our origin is so far from availing us that it rather turns to our greater disgrace, until God (who does not acknowledge man when defiled and corrupted by sin as his own work) appears as a Redeemer in the person of his only begotten Son. Since our fall from life unto death all knowledge of God the Creator, would be useless were it not followed up by faith, holding forth God to us as a Father in Christ.

The natural course undoubtedly was that the fabric of the world should be a school in which we might learn piety, and from it pass to eternal life and perfect felicity. But after looking at the perfection beheld wherever we turn our eye, above and below, we are met by the divine incapacity, which (while it involves innocent creatures in our fault) of necessity fills our own souls with despair. For although God is still pleased in many ways to manifest his paternal favor towards us, we cannot, from a mere survey of the world, infer that he is a Father. Conscience urging us within, and showing that sin is a just ground for our being forsaken, will not allow us to think that God accounts or treats us as sons.

In addition to this are our sloth and ingratitude. Our minds are so blinded that they cannot perceive the truth, and all our senses are so corrupt that we wickedly rob God of his glory. Wherefore, we must conclude with Paul, "After that in the wisdom of God the world by wisdom knew not God, it pleased God by the foolishness of preaching to save them that believe" (1 Cor. 1:21). By the "wisdom of God" he designates this magnificent theater of heaven and earth replenished with numberless wonders, the wise contemplation of which should have enabled us to know God. But this we do with little profit. Therefore, he invites us to faith in Christ—faith which, by a semblance of foolishness, disgusts the unbeliever. Therefore, although the preaching of the cross is not in accordance with human wisdom, we must humbly embrace it if we would return to God our Maker, from whom we are estranged, that he may again become our Father.

ONLY THROUGH JESUS

And this is life eternal, that they might know thee the only true God, and Jesus Christ, whom thou hast sent. I have glorified thee on the earth: I have finished the work which thou gavest me to do.
—John 17:3–4

After the fall of our first parent, it is certain that no knowledge of God without a Mediator was effectual to salvation. Christ speaks not of his own age merely, but embraces all ages, when he says, "This is life eternal that they might know thee the only true God, and Jesus Christ, whom thou hast sent" (John 17:3).

The more shameful therefore is the presumption of those who throw heaven open to the unbelieving and profane, in the absence of that grace which Scripture uniformly describes as the only door by which we enter into life. On a ground common to all ages and nations, it is declared that those who are estranged from God—and as such are under the curse, the children of wrath—cannot be pleasing to God until they are reconciled. To this we may add the answer which our Savior gave to the Samaritan woman: "Ye worship ye know not what; we know what we worship: for salvation is of the Jews" (John 4:22). By these words, he both charges every Gentile religion with falsehood and assigns the reason that under the Law the Redeemer was promised to the chosen people only. Consequently, no worship was ever pleasing to God in which respect was not had to Christ. Hence, Paul also affirms that all the Gentiles were "without God" and deprived of the hope of life.

Now, since John teaches that there was life in Christ from the beginning, and that the whole world had lost it (John 1:4), it is necessary to return to that fountain. Accordingly, Christ declares that inasmuch as he is a propitiator, he is life. And, indeed, the inheritance of heaven belongs to none but the sons of God (John 15:6). Now, it were most incongruous to give the place and rank of sons to any who have not been engrafted into the body of the only begotten Son.

PUNISHED FOR ANOTHER'S CRIME

But he was wounded for our transgressions, he was bruised for our iniquities: the chastisement of our peace was upon him; and with his stripes we are healed. —Isaiah 53:5

One principal point in the Gospel narrative is Christ's condemnation before Pontius Pilate, the governor of Judea, to teach us that the punishment to which we were liable was inflicted on that Just One. We could not escape the fearful judgment of God; and Christ, that he might rescue us from it, submitted to be condemned by a mortal, nay, by a wicked and profane man. For the name of Governor is mentioned not only to support the credibility of the narrative, but to remind us of what Isaiah says: "The chastisement of our peace was upon him" and "with his stripes we are healed" (Isa. 53:5). For, in order to remove our condemnation, it was not sufficient to endure any kind of death. To satisfy our ransom, it was necessary to select a mode of death in which he might deliver us, both by giving himself up to condemnations and undertaking our expiation. Had he been cut off by assassins, or slain in a seditious tumult, there could have been no kind of satisfaction in such a death. But when he is placed as a criminal at the bar, where witnesses are brought to give evidence against him, and the mouth of the judge condemns him to die, we see him sustaining the character of an offender and evil-doer.

When we read that Christ was led away from the judgment-seat to execution and was crucified between thieves, we have a fulfillment of the prophecy which is quoted by the Evangelist, "He was numbered with the transgressors" (Isa. 53:12; Mark 15:28). When we read that he was acquitted by the same lips that condemned him (for Pilate was forced once and again to bear public testimony to his innocence), let us call to mind what is said by another prophet, "I restored that which I took not away" (Ps. 69:4). Thus we perceive Christ representing the character of a sinner and a criminal, while, at the same time, his innocence shines forth and it becomes manifest that he suffers for another's and not for his own crime.

FROM IGNOMINY TO TRIUMPH

Yet it was the LORD'S will to crush him and cause him to suffer, and though the LORD makes his life a guilt offering, he will see his off-spring and prolong his days, and the will of the LORD will prosper in his hand. —Isaiah 53:10, NIV

The cross was cursed not only in the opinion of men, but by the enactment of the divine Law. Hence Christ, while suspended on it, subjects himself to the curse. And thus it was rightly done, in order that the whole curse—which on account of our iniquities awaited us, or rather lay upon us—might be taken from us by being transferred to him. This was also shadowed in the Law, since the word by which sin itself is properly designated was applied to the sacrifices and expiations offered for sin. By this application of the term, the Spirit intended to intimate that they were a kind of purification, bearing (by substitutions) the curse due to sin.

But that which was represented figuratively in the Mosaic sacrifices is exhibited in Christ the archetype. Wherefore, in order to accomplish a full expiation, he made his soul a propitiatory victim for sin (as the prophet says in Isa. 53:5, 10), on which the guilt and penalty being in a manner laid, ceases to be imputed to us. The Apostle declares this more plainly when he says, "He made him to be sin for us, who knew no sin; that we might be made the righteousness of God in him" (2 Cor. 5:21). The Son of God, though spotlessly pure, took upon him the disgrace and ignominy of our iniquities, and in return clothed us with his purity. To the same thing he seems to refer when he says that he "condemned sin in the flesh" (Rom. 8:3), the Father having destroyed the power of sin when it was transferred to the flesh of Christ. Therefore, this term indicates that Christ, in his death, was offered to the Father as a propitiatory victim—that, expiation being made by his sacrifice, we might cease to tremble at the divine wrath. It is now clear what the Prophet means when he says that "the Lord has laid upon him the iniquity of us all" (Isa. 53:6); namely, that as he was to wash away the pollution of sins, they were transferred to him by imputation.

BE READY FOR OPPOSITION

And Saul was there, giving approval to his death. On that day a great persecution broke out against the church at Jerusalem, and all except the apostles were scattered throughout Judea and Samaria.
—Acts 8:1, NIV

The persecution began with Stephen. After that, when their madness was thereby set on fire, it waxed hot against all Christians. Undoubtedly the Church had but a small rest before, nor was it free from the anger of the wicked; but the Lord spared his own for a time, that they might have some liberty, and now they began to be more sorely attacked.

These things must be applied unto our time also. If the furiousness of our enemies seem at any time to be fallen asleep, so that it casts its flames not far, let us know that the Lord is providing for our weakness. Yet, let us not in the meantime imagine that we shall have a continual truce, but let us be in readiness to suffer sorer wounds, as often as they shall break out suddenly.

Let us also remember, that if at any time the constancy of one Christian whets the cruelty of our enemies, the blame for that evil is unjustly ascribed to him or her. For Luke does not defame Stephen when he says that by means of him the Church was more attacked than before; but he rather turns this to Stephen's praise, because he did valiantly, as the standard-bearer, encourage others with his example to fight courageously. There was but this one only body of the godly in all the world, and it was rent in pieces through flight; yet there sprung up more Churches by and by from those lame members which were dispersed here and there, and so the body of Christ was spread abroad far and wide, whereas it was before shut up within the walls of Jerusalem.

LEARNING IN HUMILITY

The Spirit told Philip, "Go to that chariot and stay near it." Then Philip ran up to the chariot and heard the man reading Isaiah the prophet. "Do you understand what you are reading?" Philip asked. "How can I," he said, "unless someone explains it to me?" So he invited Philip to come up and sit with him. —Acts 8:29–31, NIV

Most excellent modesty of the eunuch, who not only permits Philip, who was one of the common sort, to discuss with him, but also willingly confesses his ignorance. And surely we must never hope that anyone will ever prove ready to be taught who is puffed up with the confidence of her or his own wit.

Hereby it comes to pass that the reading of the Scriptures profits so few these days, because we can scarce find one in a hundred who submits willingly to learn. For while almost all people are ashamed to be ignorant of whatever it is they're ignorant of, everyone would rather proudly nourish their ignorance than seem to be the students of others. Yea, a great many take it upon themselves arrogantly to teach others.

Nevertheless, let us remember that the eunuch did so confess his ignorance, that yet, notwithstanding, he was one of God's students when he read the Scripture. This is the true reverence of the Scripture when we acknowledge that there is wisdom laid up there which surpasses all our senses; and yet notwithstanding, we do not resent it, but, reading diligently, we depend upon the revelation of the Spirit and desire to have an interpreter given us. Thus must we be minded if we desire to have God to be our teacher, whose Spirit rests upon the humble and meek (Isa. 66:2). And if anyone, mistrusting themselves, submits to be taught, the angels shall rather come down from heaven than the Lord would allow us to labor in vain—though as did the eunuch we must use all the help the Lord offers us for the understanding of Scripture.

FOUNDED ONLY IN CHRIST

But the Scripture declares that the whole world is a prisoner of sin, so that what was promised, being given through faith in Jesus Christ, might be given to those who believe. —Galatians 3:22, NIV

God never showed himself propitious to his ancient people, nor gave them any hope of grace without a Mediator. I say nothing of the sacrifices of the Law—by which believers were plainly and openly taught that salvation was not to be found anywhere but in the expiation which Christ alone completed—all I maintain is that the prosperous and happy state of the Church was always founded in the person of Christ.

For although God embraced the whole posterity of Abraham in his covenant, yet Paul properly argues (Gal. 3:16) that Christ was truly the seed in which all the nations of the earth were to be blessed, since we know that all who were born of Abraham, according to the flesh, were not accounted the seed. It is plain that the seed of Abraham is considered chiefly in one head, and that the promised salvation is not attained without coming to Christ. Thus the primary adoption of the chosen people depended on the grace of the Mediator.

Although it is not expressed in very distinct terms in Moses, it appears to have been commonly known to all the godly. For before a king was appointed over the Israelites, Hannah (the mother of Samuel), describing the happiness of the righteous, speaks thus in her song, "He shall give strength unto his king, and exalt the horn of his anointed"—meaning by these words that God would bless his Church. To this corresponds the prediction, which is afterwards added, "I will raise me up a faithful priest, and he shall walk before mine anointed for ever" (1 Sam. 2:10, 35).

And there can be no doubt that our heavenly Father intended that a living image of Christ should be seen in David and his posterity. Accordingly, exhorting the righteous to fear him, he bids them, "Kiss the Son" (Ps. 2:12). Therefore, though the kingdom was broken up by the revolt of the ten tribes, the covenant which God had made in David and his successors behaved to stand.

THE OBJECT OF FAITH

Let thy hand be upon the man of thy right hand, upon the son of man whom thou madest strong for thyself. —Psalm 80:17

David, all others being excluded, was chosen to be the person in whom the good pleasure of the Lord should dwell; as it is said elsewhere, "He forsook the tabernacle of Shiloh....Moreover, he refused the tabernacle of Joseph, and chose not the tribe of Ephraim...but chose the tribe of Judah, the mount Zion which he loved....He chose David also his servant, and took him from the sheep folds: from following the ewes great with young he brought him to feed Jacob his people, and Israel his inheritance" (Ps. 78:60, 67, 70–71).

In fine, God, in thus preserving his Church, intended that its security and salvation should depend on Christ as its head. Accordingly, David exclaims, "The LORD is their strength, and he is the saving strength of his anointed. He then prays, "Save thy people, and bless thy inheritance," intimating that the safety of the Church was indissolubly connected with the government of Christ. In the same sense he elsewhere says, "Save, LORD: let the king hear us when we call" (Ps. 20:9).

These words plainly teach that believers, in applying for the help of God, had their sole confidence in that they were under the unseen government of the King. This may be inferred from another psalm, "Save now, I beseech thee O LORD: Blessed be he that cometh in the name of the LORD" (Ps. 118:25–26). Here it is obvious that believers are invited to Christ, in the assurance that they will be safe when entirely in his hand.

To the same effect is another prayer, in which the whole Church implores the divine mercy, "Let thy hand be upon the Man of thy right hand, upon the Son of man, whom thou made strong [or best fitted] for thyself" (Ps. 80:17). For though the author of the Psalm laments the dispersion of the whole nation, he prays for its revival in him who is sole Head. From all this it is abundantly plain that, as the Lord cannot be gracious to the human race without a Mediator, Christ was always held forth to the holy Fathers under the Law as the object of their faith.

OUR REDEEMER

Surely he hath borne our griefs, and carried our sorrows: yet we did esteem him stricken, smitten of God, and afflicted. But he was wounded for our transgressions, he was bruised for our iniquities: the chastisement of our peace was upon him; and with his stripes we are healed.
—Isaiah 53:4–5

Since the whole Scripture proclaims that he was clothed with flesh in order to become a Redeemer, it is presumptuous to imagine any other cause or end. We know well why Christ was at first promised—that is, that he might renew a fallen world and aid lost man. Hence under the Law he was typified by sacrifices to inspire believers with the hope that God would be propitious to them after he was reconciled by the expiation of their sins. Since from the earliest age (even before the Law was promulgated) there was never any promise of a Mediator without blood, we justly infer that he was destined in the eternal counsel of God to purge the pollution of man—the shedding of blood being the symbol of expiation. Thus, too, the prophets, in discoursing of him, foretold that he would be the Mediator between God and man. It is sufficient to refer to the very remarkable prophecy of Isaiah (Isa. 53:4–5), in which he foretells that he was "smitten for our iniquities"; that "the chastisement of our peace was upon him"; that as a priest "he was made an offering for sin"; that "by his stripes we are healed"; that since all "like lost sheep have gone astray," "it pleased the LORD to bruise him, and put him to grief" so that he might "bear our iniquities." After hearing that Christ was divinely appointed to bring relief to miserable sinners, whose overleaps these limits gives too much indulgence to a foolish curiosity.

Then when he actually appeared, he declared the cause of his advent to be that by appeasing God he might bring us from death unto life. To the same effect was the testimony of the Apostles concerning him (John 1:9; 10:14). Thus John, before teaching that the Word was made flesh, narrates the fall of man. But above all, let us listen to our Savior himself when discoursing of his office: "The hour is coming, and now is, when the dead shall hear the voice of the Son of God: and they that hear shall live." And "I am the resurrection and the life: he that believeth in me, though he were dead, yet shall he live."

GOD'S DECLARATION

This grace was given us in Christ Jesus before the beginning of time, but it has now been revealed through the appearing or our Savior, Christ Jesus, who has destroyed death and has brought life and immortality to light through the gospel. —2 Timothy 1:9–10, NIV

When the Spirit declares that by the eternal decree of God the two things were connected together—that is, that Christ should be our Redeemer and, at the same time, a partaker of our nature—it is unlawful to inquire further. He who is tickled with a desire of knowing something more, not contented with the immutable ordination of God, shows also that he is not even contented with that Christ who has been given us as the price of redemption. And, indeed, Paul not only declares for what end he was sent, but seasonably represses all the wantonness and prurience of the human mind: "He has chosen us in him before the foundation of the world, that we should be holy and without blame before him in love: having predestinated us unto the adoption of children by Jesus Christ to himself, according to the good pleasure of his will, to the praise of the glory of his grace, wherein he has made us accepted in the Beloved: In whom we have redemption through his blood" (Eph. 1:4-7).

Here certainly the fall of Adam is not presupposed as anterior in point of time, but our attention is directed to what God predetermined before all ages, when he was pleased to provide a cure for the misery of the human race. If, again, it is objected that this counsel of God depended on the fall of man, which he foresaw, to me it is sufficient and more to reply that those who propose to inquire—or desire to know more of Christ than God predestinated by his secret decree—are presuming with impious audacity to invent a new Christ. When discoursing of the proper office of Christ, Paul justly prays for the Ephesians that God would strengthen them "by his Spirit in the inner man," that they might "be able to comprehend with all saints what is the breadth and length, and depth and height; and to know the love of Christ which passes knowledge" (Eph. 3:16, 18)—as if he intended of set purpose to set barriers around our minds, and prevent them from declining one iota from the gift of reconciliation whenever mention is made of Christ.

IN GOD'S IMAGE

So God created man in his own image, in the image of God created he him; male and female created he them. —Genesis 1:27

While I grant that Adam bore the image of God, inasmuch as he was united to God (this being the true and highest perfection of dignity), yet I maintain that the likeness of God is to be sought for only in those marks of superiority with which God has distinguished Adam above the other animals. And likewise, with one consent, I acknowledge that Christ was even then the image of God, and whatever excellence was engraved on Adam had its origin in this, that by means of the only begotten Son he approximated to the glory of his Maker. Therefore, man, was created in the image of God (Gen. 1:27), and in him the Creator was pleased to behold, as in a mirror, his own glory. To this degree of honor he was exalted by the kindness of the only begotten Son.

But I add that, as the Son was the common head both of men and angels, so the dignity which was conferred on man belonged to the angels also. For when we hear them called the sons of God (Ps. 82:6), it would be incongruous to deny that they were endued with some

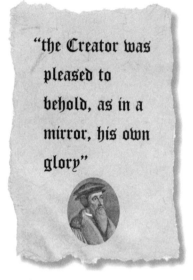

"the Creator was pleased to behold, as in a mirror, his own glory"

quality in which they resembled the Father. He was pleased that his glory should be represented in men and angels—and made manifest in both natures—so they could constantly enjoy the immediate presence of God because they are like him. Paul does not teach (Col. 3:10) that men are renewed in the image of God in any other way than by being associated with angels, that they may be united together under one head. In fine, if we believe Christ, our felicity will be perfected when we shall have been received into the heavens and made like the angels.

REAL FLESH

For what the law was powerless to do in that it was weakened by the sinful nature, God did by sending his own Son in the likeness of sinful man to be a sin offering. And so he condemned sin in sinful man, in order that the righteous requirements of the law might be fully met in us, who do not live according to the sinful nature but according to the Spirit. —Romans 8:3–4, NIV

We must see how, when clothed with our flesh, Christ fulfilled the office of Mediator. In ancient times, the reality of his human nature was impugned by the Manichees and Marcionites—the latter figuring to themselves a phantom instead of the body of Christ, and the former dreaming of his having been invested with celestial flesh. The passages of Scripture contradictory to both are numerous and strong.

The blessing is not promised in a heavenly seed, or the mask of a man, but the seed of Abraham and Jacob; nor is the everlasting throne promised to an aerial man, but to the Son of David, and the fruit of his loins. Hence, when manifested in the flesh, he is called the Son of David and Abraham—not because he was born of a virgin, and yet created in the air, but because, as Paul explains, he was "made of the seed of David, according to the flesh" (Rom. 1:3). As the same Apostle elsewhere says, that he came of the Jews (Rom. 9:5).

Wherefore, our Lord himself, not contented with the name of man, frequently calls himself the Son of man, for he wished to express more clearly that he was a man by true human descent. The Holy Spirit with so much care and plainness, declared a matter which in itself is not abstruse, who could have thought that mortals would have had the effrontery to darken it with their glosses? Many other passages are at hand, were it wished to produce more: for instance, that one of Paul that says, "God sent forth his Son, made of a woman" (Gal. 4:4), and innumerable others, which show that he was subject to hunger, thirst, cold, and the other infirmities of our nature.

But from the many we must chiefly select those which may conduce to build up our minds in true faith, as when it is said, "Both he that sanctifies and they who are sanctified are all of one: for which cause he is not ashamed to call them brethren....Wherefore in all things it behooved him to be made like unto his brethren, that he might be a merciful and faithful high priest" (Heb. 2:11, 17).

TRULY MAN

For though he was crucified through weakness, yet he liveth by the power of God. For we also are weak in him, but we shall live with him by the power of God toward you. —2 Corinthians 13:4

arcion imagines that Christ, instead of a body, assumed a phantom, because it is elsewhere said that he was made in the likeness of man and found in fashion as a man. Thus he altogether overlooks what Paul is then discussing (Phil. 2:7). His object is not to show what kind of body Christ assumed, but that, when he might have justly asserted his divinity, he was pleased to exhibit nothing but the attributes of a mean and despised man. For, in order to exhort us to submission by his example, he shows that when as God he might have displayed to the world the brightness of his glory, he gave up his right and voluntarily emptied himself; that he assumed the form of a servant and, contented with that humble condition, suffered his divinity to be concealed under a veil of flesh. Here, unquestionably, he explains not what Christ was, but in what way he acted. Nay, from the whole context it is easily gatered that it was in the true nature of man that Christ humbled himself. For what is meant by the words, he was "found in

fashion as a man," but that for a time, instead of being resplendent with divine glory, the human form only appeared in a mean and abject condition?

Nor would the words of Peter that he was "put to death in the flesh, but quickened by the Spirits" (1 Pet. 3:18) hold true, unless the Son of God had become weak in the nature of man. This is explained more clearly by Paul, when he declares that "he was crucified through weakness" (2 Cor. 13:4). And hence his exaltation; for it is distinctly said that Christ acquired new glory after he humbled himself. This could fitly apply only to a man endued with a body and a soul. The Apostle does not there speak of the essence of his body as heavenly, but of the spiritual life which derived from Christ quickens us (1 Cor. 15:47). If his body were not of the same nature with ours, there would be no soundness in the argument which Paul pursues with so much earnestness: If Christ is risen, we shall rise also; if we rise not, neither has Christ risen.

BROTHERHOOD

And we know that in all things God works for the good of those who love him, who have been called according to his purpose. For those God foreknew he also predestined to be conformed to the likeness of his Son, that he might be the firstborn among many brothers.
—Romans 8:26–27

t is a frivolous and despicable evasion to say that Christ is called the Son of man because he was promised to men. For it is obvious that, in the Hebrew idiom, the Son of man means a true man, and Christ, doubtless, retained the idiom of his own tongue. Moreover, there cannot be a doubt as to what is to be understood by the sons of Adam. Not to go farther, a passage in the eighth Psalm, which the Apostles apply to Christ, will abundantly suffice: "What is man, that thou art mindful of him? and the son of man, that thou visits him?" (Ps 8:4). Under this figure is expressed the true humanity of Christ. For although he was not immediately descended of an earthly father, yet he originally sprang from Adam. Nor could it otherwise be said in terms of the passage which we have already quoted, "Forasmuch, then, as the children are partakers of flesh and blood, he also himself likewise took part of the same"—these words plainly proving that he was an associate and partner in the same nature with ourselves. In this sense also it is said, that "both he that sanctifies and they who are sanctified are all of one." The context proves that this refers to a community of nature, for it is immediately added, "For which cause he is not ashamed to call them brethren" (Heb. 2:11). Had he said at first that believers are of God, where could there have been any ground for being ashamed of persons possessing such dignity? But when Christ of his boundless grace associates himself with the mean and ignoble, we see why it was said that "he is not ashamed."

It is vain to object that in this way the wicked will be the brethren of Christ; for we know that the children of God are not born of flesh and blood, but of the Spirit through faith. Therefore, flesh alone does not constitute the union of brotherhood. When we say that Christ became man, that he might make us sons of God, the expression does not extend to all classes of persons—the intervention of faith being necessary to our being spiritually infused into the body of Christ.

DAVID'S INTEMPERANCE

O spare me, that I may recover strength, before I go hence, and be no more. —Psalm 39:13

though prayer is the familiar intercourse of believers with God, yet reverence and modesty must be observed: We must not give loose reins to our wishes, nor long for anything farther than God permits; and, moreover, unless the majesty of God should be despised, our minds must be elevated to pure and unblemished reverence. This no man ever performed with due perfection. For, not to speak of the generality of men, how often do David's complaints savor of intemperance? Not that he actually means to complain with God or murmur at his judgments, but failing, through infirmity, he finds no better consolation than to pour his griefs into the bosom of his heavenly Father. Nay, even our stammering is tolerated by God and pardon is granted to our ignorance as often as anything rashly escapes us. Indeed, without this indulgence, we should have no freedom to pray.

But although it was David's intention to submit himself entirely to the will of God, and he prayed with no less patience than fervor, yet irregular emotions appear, nay, sometimes burst forth—emotions not a little at variance with the first law which we laid down. In particular, we may see in a clause of the thirty-ninth Psalm, how this saint was carried away by the intensity of his grief and unable to keep within bounds: "O spare me, that I may recover strength, before I go hence, and be no more" (Ps. 39:13). You would call this the language of a desperate man, who had no other desire than that God should withdraw and leave him to relish in his distresses. Not that his devout mind rushes into such intemperance, or that he wishes to have done with God; he only complains that the divine anger is more than he can bear. During those trials, wishes often escape which are not in accordance with the rule of the Word, and in which the saints do not duly consider what is lawful and expedient. Prayers contaminated by such faults, indeed, deserve to be rejected; yet provided the saints lament, administer self-correction and return to themselves, God pardons.

PARDON IN PRAYER

O LORD God of hosts, how long wilt thou be angry against the prayer of thy people? —Psalm 80:4

he saints have often to struggle with their own coldness, their want and misery not urging them sufficiently to serious prayer. It often happens, also, that their minds wander and are almost lost; hence in this matter also there is need of pardon, lest their prayers (from being languid or mutilated, or interrupted and wandering) should meet with a refusal. A twofold pardon is always to be asked: first, because they are conscious of many faults (the sense of which, however, does not touch them so as to make them feel dissatisfied with themselves as they ought); and, second (insofar as they have been enabled to profit in repentance and the fear of God) they are humbled with just sorrow for their offenses and pray for the remission of punishment by the judge.

Innumerable examples of the same kind occur in the Scriptures, from which it is manifest that the faith of the saints was often mingled with doubts and fears, so that, while believing and hoping, they betrayed some degree of unbelief. But because they do not come so far as were to be wished, that is only an additional reason for their exerting themselves to correct their faults, that they may daily approach nearer to the perfect law of prayer, and at the same time feel into what an abyss of evils those are plunged, who, in the very cures they use, bring new diseases upon themselves. There is no prayer which God would not deservedly disdain, if he did not overlook the blemishes with which all of them are polluted. I do not mention these things that believers may securely pardon themselves in any faults which they commit, but that they may call themselves to strict account, and thereby endeavor to surmount these obstacles.

IN JESUS' NAME

Let us therefore come boldly unto the throne of grace, that we may obtain mercy, and find grace to help in time of need.
—Hebrews 4:16, NIV

Since no man is worthy to come forward in his own name and appear in the presence of God, our heavenly Father (to relieve us at once from fear and shame) has given us his Son, Jesus Christ our Lord, to be our Advocate and Mediator—that under his guidance we may approach securely, confiding that with him for our Intercessor nothing which we ask in his name will be denied to us, as there is nothing which the Father can deny to him (1 Tim. 2:5; 1 John 2:1).

To this it is necessary to refer all that we have previously taught concerning faith; because, as the promise gives us Christ as our Mediator, so, unless our hope of obtaining what we ask is founded on him, it deprives us of the privilege of prayer. For it is impossible to think of the dread majesty of God without being filled with alarm; and hence the sense of our own unworthiness must keep us far away—until Christ interpose and convert a throne of dreadful glory into a throne of grace, as the Apostle teaches that thus we can "come boldly unto the throne of grace, that we may obtain mercy, and find grace to help in time of need" (Heb. 4:16).

And as a rule has been laid down as to prayer, as a promise has been given that those who pray will be heard, so we are specially enjoined to pray in the name of Christ, the promise being that we shall obtain what we ask in his name. "Whatsoever ye shall ask in my name," says our Savior, "that will I do; that the Father may be glorified in the Son.... Hitherto ye have asked nothing in my name; ask, and ye shall receive, that your joy may be full" (John 14:13; 16:24). Hence it is incontrovertibly clear that those who pray to God in any other name than that of Christ contumaciously falsify his orders and regard his will as nothing, while they have no promise that they shall obtain. For, as Paul says, "All the promises of God in him are yea, and in him amen" (2 Cor. 1:20), that is, are confirmed and fulfilled in him.

INTERCESSION

For there is one God and one mediator between God and men, the man Christ Jesus. —1 Timothy 2:5, NIV

ince he himself is the only way and the only access by which we can draw near to God, those who deviate from this way and decline this access have no other remaining; his throne presents nothing but wrath, judgment, and terror. In short, as the Father has consecrated him our guide and head, those who abandon or turn aside from him in any way endeavor, as much as in them lies, to sully and efface the stamp which God has impressed.

Therefore, Christ, is the only Mediator by whose intercession the Father is rendered favorable and gracious (1 Tim. 2:5). For though the saints are still permitted to use intercessions by which they mutually beseech God in behalf of each other's salvation, and of which the Apostle makes mention (Eph. 6:18–19; 1 Tim. 2:1)— yet these depend on that one intercession, so far are they from derogating from it. For as the intercessions which, as members of one body we offer up for each other, spring from the feeling of love, so they have reference to this one head. Being thus also made in the name of Christ, what more do they than declare that no man can derive the least benefit from any prayers without the intercession of Christ?

As there is nothing in the intercession of Christ to prevent the different members of the Church from offering up prayers for each other, so let it be held as a fixed principle that all the intercessions thus used in the Church must have reference to that one intercession. Nay, we must be specially careful to show our gratitude on this very account: that God, pardoning our unworthiness, not only allows each individual to pray for himself but also allows all to intercede mutually for each other. God having given a place in his Church to intercessors who would deserve to be rejected when praying privately on their own account, how presumptuous were it to abuse this kindness by employing it to obscure the honor of Christ?

LIFE AND DEATH

This day I call heaven and earth as witnesses against you that I have set before you life and death, blessings and curses. Now choose life, so that you and your children may live and that you may love the LORD you|God, listen to his voice, and hold fast to him. For the LORD is your life, and he will give you many years in the land he swore to give to your fathers, Abraham, Isaac and Jacob. —Deuteronomy 30:19–20, NIV

In order that a sense of guilt may urge us to seek for pardon, it is of importance to know how our being instructed in the Moral Law renders us more inexcusable. If it is true that a perfect righteousness is set before us in the Law, it follows that the complete observance of it is perfect righteousness in the sight of God—that is, a righteousness by which a man may be deemed and pronounced righteous at the divine tribunal. Wherefore Moses, after promulgating the Law, hesitates not to call heaven and earth to witness that he had set life and death, good and evil, before the people. Nor can it be denied that the reward of eternal salvation, as promised by the Lord, awaits the perfect obedience of the Law (Deut. 30:19).

Again, however, it is of importance to understand in what way we perform that obedience for which we justly entertain the hope of that reward. For of what use is it to see that the reward of eternal life depends on the observance of the Law, unless it moreover appears whether it is in our power in that way to attain eternal life? Herein, then, the weakness of the Law is manifested for, in none of us is that righteousness of the Law manifested, and, therefore, being excluded from the promises of life, we again fall under the curse. I state not only what happens, but what must necessarily happen. The doctrine of the Law transcending our capacity, a man may indeed look from a distance at the promises held forth, but he cannot derive any benefit from them.

Therefore, the only thing remaining for him is to form a better estimate of his own misery from their excellence, while he considers that the hope of salvation is cut off, and he is threatened with certain death.

SCHOOLED BY THE LAW

For what the law was powerless to do in that it was weakened by the sinful nature, God did by sending his own Son in the likeness of sinful man to be a sin offering. And so he condemned sin in sinful man, in order that the righteous requirements of the law might be fully met in us, who do not live according to the sinful nature but according to the Spirit. —Romans 8:3–4, NIV

he office and use of the Moral Law seems to me to consist of exhibiting the righteousness of God—in other words, the righteousness which alone is acceptable to God—it instructs everyone of his own unrighteousness and finally condemns him. This is necessary so man, who is blind and intoxicated with self-love, may be brought at once to know and to confess his weakness and impurity. For until his vanity is made perfectly manifest, he is puffed up with infatuated confidence in his own powers, and never can be brought to feel their feebleness so long as he measures them by a standard of his own choice. However, as soon as he begins to compare them with the requirements of the Law, he has something to tame his presumption. Yet as high his opinion of his own powers may be, he immediately feels that they pant under the heavy load,

then totter and stumble, and finally fall and give way.

But he who is schooled by the Law lays aside the arrogance which formerly blinded him. In like manner must he be cured of pride, the other disease under which we have said that he labors. So long as he is permitted to appeal to his own judgment, he substitutes a hypocritical for a real righteousness and, contented with this, sets up certain factitious observances in opposition to the grace of God. But after he is forced to weigh his conduct in the balance of the Law, renouncing all dependence on this fancied righteousness, he sees that he is at an infinite distance from holiness, and, on the other hand, that he teems with innumerable vices of which he formerly seemed free. The recesses in which the feeling of desire lies hid are so deep and tortuous that they easily elude our view.

TRUE WORSHIP

Observe and hear all these words which I command thee, that it may go well with thee, and with thy children after thee for ever, when thou doest that which is good and right in the sight of the LORD thy God.
—Deuteronomy 12:28

In delivering a perfect rule of righteousness, the Lord has shown that there is nothing more acceptable to him than obedience. But the human mind, in its inhibition, is always inventing different modes of worship as a means of gaining his favor. This irreligious affectation of religion has betrayed itself in every age, and is still doing so—men always longing to devise some method of procuring righteousness without any sanction from the Word of God.

Hence, in those observances which are generally regarded as good works, the precepts of the Law occupy a narrow space, almost the whole being usurped by this endless host of human inventions. But was not this the very license which Moses meant to curb when, after the promulgation of the Law, he thus addressed the people: "Only take heed to thyself, and keep thy soul diligently, lest thou forget the things which thy eyes have seen, and lest they depart from thy heart all the days of thy life" (Deut. 4:8–9)? Foreseeing that the Israelites would not rest after receiving the Law, but would (unless sternly prohibited) give birth to new kinds of righteousness, God declares that the Law comprehended a perfect righteousness. This ought to have been a most powerful restraint, and yet they desisted not from the presumptuous course so strongly prohibited.

We are certainly under the same obligation as they were, for there cannot be a doubt that the claim of absolute perfection which God made for his Law is perpetually in force. Not content with it, however, we labor excessively in fabricating and coining an endless variety of good works, one after another. The best cure for this vice would be a constant and deep-seated conviction that the Law was given from heaven to teach us a perfect righteousness—that the only righteousness so taught is that which the divine will expressly enjoins—and it is vain to attempt by new forms of worship to gain the favor of God, whose true worship consists in obedience alone.

RECONCILIATION

*All this is from God, who reconciled us to himself through Christ and
gave us the ministry of reconciliation: that God was reconciling the
world to himself in Christ, not counting men's sins against them. And
he has committed to us the message of reconciliation.*
—2 Corinthians 5:18–19, NIV

another principal part of our reconciliation with God was that man, who had lost himself by his disobedience, should by way of remedy oppose to it obedience, satisfy the justice of God, and pay the penalty of sin. Therefore, our Lord came forth very man—adopted the person of Adam and assumed his name—that he might in his stead obey the Father, that he might present our flesh as the price of satisfaction to the just judgment of God, and in the same flesh pay the penalty which we had incurred. Finally, since as God only he could not suffer, and as man only could not overcome death, he united the human nature with the divine. He did this so that he might subject the weakness of the one to death as an expiation of sin, and by the power of the other, maintaining a struggle with death, might gain us the victory. Those, therefore, who rob Christ of divinity or humanity either detract from his majesty and glory or obscure his goodness. On the other hand, they are no less injurious to men, undermining and subverting their faith—which, unless it rest on this foundation, cannot stand.

Moreover, the expected Redeemer was that son of Abraham and David whom God had promised in the Law and in the Prophets. Here believers have another advantage. Tracing up his origin in regular series to David and Abraham, they more distinctly recognize him as the Messiah celebrated by so many oracles. But special attention must be paid to what I lately explained: that a common nature is the pledge of our union with the Son of God; that, clothed with our flesh, he warred to death with sin that he might be our triumphant conqueror; and that the flesh which he received of us he offered in sacrifice, in order that by making expiation he might wipe away our guilt and appease the just anger of his Father.

TWO ABSURDITIES

Therefore as by the offence of one judgment came upon all men to condemnation; even so by the righteousness of one the free gift came upon all men unto justification of life. —Romans 5:18, NIV

Corresponding to this is another passage, "The first man is of the earth, earthy: the second man is the Lord from heaven" (1 Cor. 15:47). Accordingly, the same Apostle teaches that Christ was sent "in the likeness of sinful flesh that the righteousness of the law might be fulfilled in us," and distinctly separates him from the common lot, as being true man, and yet without fault and corruption (Rom. 8:3).

It is childish trifling to maintain that if Christ is free from all taint, and was begotten of the seed of Mary by the secret operation of the Spirit, it is not therefore the seed of the woman that is impure, but only that of the man. We do not hold Christ to be free from all taint merely because he was born of a woman unconnected with a man, but because he was sanctified by the Spirit—so that the generation was pure and spotless, such as it would have been before Adam's fall. Let us always bear in mind that wherever Scripture adverts to the purity of Christ, it refers to his true human nature, since it were superfluous to say that God is pure. Moreover, the sanctification of which John speaks in his seventeenth chapter is inapplicable to the divine nature. This does not suggest the idea of a twofold seed in Adam, although no contamination extended to Christ, the generation of man not being in itself vicious or impure, but an accidental circumstance of the fall. Hence, it is not strange that Christ, by whom our integrity was to be restored, was exempted from the common corruption.

Another absurdity which they obtrude upon us—if the Word of God became incarnate, it must have been enclosed in the narrow tenement of an earthly body—is sheer petulance. For although the boundless essence of the Word was united with human nature into one person, we have no idea of any enclosing. The Son of God descended miraculously from heaven, yet without abandoning heaven. He was pleased to be conceived miraculously in the Virgin's womb, to live on the earth, and hang upon the cross, and yet always filled the world as from the beginning.

TWO MAKES ONE

He is the image of the invisible God, the firstborn over all creation.
—Colossians 1:15, NIV

When it is said that the Word was made flesh, we must not understand it as if he were either changed into flesh or confusedly intermingled with flesh, but that he made choice of the Virgin's womb as a temple in which he might dwell. He who was the Son of God became the Son of man—not by confusion of substance but by unity of person. For we maintain that the divinity was so conjoined and united with the humanity that the entire properties of each nature remain entire, and yet the two natures constitute only one Christ.

If, in human affairs, any thing analogous to this great mystery can be found, the most pertinent equivalence seems to be that of man; for man obviously consists of two substances, neither of which is so intermingled with the other as that both do not retain their own properties. For neither is soul body, nor is body soul. Wherefore that is said separately of the soul which cannot in any way apply to the body; and that, on the other hand, of the body which is altogether inapplicable to the soul; and that, again, of the whole man, which cannot be affirmed without absurdity either of the body or of the soul separately. Lastly, the properties of the soul are transferred to the body, and the properties of the body to the soul, and yet these form only one man, and not more than one. Such modes of expression suggest both that there is in man one person formed of two compounds, and that these two different natures constitute one person.

Thus the Scriptures speak of Christ. They sometimes attribute to him qualities which should be referred specially to his humanity, and sometimes qualities applicable peculiarly to his divinity, and sometimes qualities which embrace both natures and do not apply specially to either.

FINAL DELIVERY

Then cometh the end, when he shall have delivered up the kingdom to God, even the Father; when he shall have put down all rule and all authority and power. For he must reign, till he hath put all enemies under his feet. The last enemy that shall be destroyed is death.
—1 Corinthians 15:24–26, NIV

he true substance of Christ is most clearly declared in those passages which comprehend both Christ's natures (of the human and of the divine) at once. Numbers of these exist in the Gospel of John. What we there read—as to his having received power from the Father to forgive sins, as to his quickening whom he will, as to his bestowing righteousness, holiness, and salvation, as to his being appointed judge both of the quick and the dead, as to his being honored even as the Father—are not peculiar either to his Godhead or his humanity, but applicable to both. In the same way he is called the Light of the world, the good Shepherd, the only Door, the true Vine. With such prerogatives the Son of God was invested on his manifestation in the flesh. Though he possessed the same with the Father before the world was created, still it was not in the same manner or respect; neither could they be attributed to one who was a man and nothing more.

In the same sense we ought to understand the saying of Paul that at the end Christ shall deliver up "the kingdom to God, even the Father" (1 Cor. 15:24). The kingdom of God assuredly had no beginning and will have no end. But because he was hid under a humble clothing of flesh, and took upon himself the form of a servant, and humbled himself (Phil. 2:8), and became obedient to the Father and after undergoing this subjection was at length crowned with glory and honor (Heb. 2:7), and exalted to supreme authority that at his name every knee should bow (Phil. 2:10); so at the end he will subject to the Father both the name and the crown of glory and whatever he received of the Father, that God may be all in all (1 Cor. 15:28). For what end were that power and authority given to him, save that the Father might govern us by his hand? In the same sense, also, he, for a time, is said to sit at the right hand of the Father until we enjoy the immediate presence of his Godhead.

UNDERSTANDING

Since you died with Christ to the basic principles of this world, why, as though you still belonged to it, do you submit to its rules?
—Colossians 2:20, NIV

though heretics pretend the name of Christ, the truth is that the foundation is not common to them with the godly, but belongs exclusively to the Church; for if those things which pertain to Christ be diligently considered, it will be found that Christ is with them in name only, not in reality. Thus in the present day, though the Papists have the words "Son of God, Redeemer of the world" sounding in their mouths, yet they deprive him of his virtue and dignity—what Paul says of "not holding the head" is truly applicable to them (Col. 2:19).

Therefore, that faith may find in Christ a solid ground of salvation and so rest in him, we must set out with this principle: The office which he received from the Father consists of three parts. For he was appointed both Prophet, King, and Priest—though little were gained by holding the names unaccompanied by a knowledge of the end and use. We formerly observed that the minds of believers were always impressed with the conviction that the full light of understanding was to be expected only on the advent of the Messiah; though God, by supplying an uninterrupted succession of prophets, never left his people destitute of useful doctrine, such as might suffice for salvation.

Nor was this a mere random presumption which had entered the minds of the Jews. They believed what sure oracles had taught them. But as the common office of the Prophets was to hold the Church in suspense, and at the same time support it until the advent of the Mediator, we read that the faithful (during the dispersion) complained that they were deprived of that ordinary privilege. "We see not our signs: there is no more any prophet, neither is there among us any that know how long" (Ps. 74:9). But when Christ was now not far distant, a period was assigned to Daniel "to seal up the vision and prophecy" (Dan. 9:24). This was not only that the authority of the prediction there spoken of might be established, but that believers might (for a time) patiently submit to the want of the Prophets—the fulfillment and completion of all the prophecies being at hand.

PROTECTED BY CHRIST

Once have I sworn by my holiness that I will not lie unto David. His
seed shall endure for ever, and his throne as the sun before me.
It shall be established for ever as the moon, and as a faithful witness in
heaven. Selah. —Psalm 89:35–37

I come to Christ's Kingly office—of which it were in vain to speak without previously reminding the reader that its nature is spiritual—because it is from thence we learn its efficacy, the benefits it confers, its whole power and eternity (eternity, moreover, which in Daniel an angel attributes to the office of Christ (Dan. 2:44), in Luke an angel justly applies to the salvation of his people (Luke 1:33). But this is also twofold, and must be viewed in two ways. The one pertains to the whole body of the Church, and the other is proper to each member. To the former is to be referred what is said in the Psalms, "Once have I sworn by my holiness, that I will not lie unto David. His seed shall endure forever, and his throne as the sun before me. It shall be established forever, as the moon, and as a faithful witness in heaven" (Ps. 89:35, 37). There can be no doubt that God here promises that he will be, by the hand of his Son, the eternal governor and defender of the Church. In none but Christ will the fulfillment of this prophecy be found; for immediately after Solomon's death the kingdom in great measure lost its dignity and, with ignominy to the family of David, was transferred to a private individual. Afterwards decaying by degrees, it at length came to a sad and dishonorable end.

As often as we hear that Christ is armed with eternal power, let us learn that the perpetuity of the Church is thus effectually secured; that amid the turbulent agitations by which it is constantly harassed, and the grievous and fearful commotions which threaten innumerable disasters, it still remains safe. We see that everything which is earthly, and of the world, is temporary and soon fades away. Therefore, to raise our hope to the heavens, Christ declares that his kingdom is not of this world (John 18:36).

WELL EQUIPPED

For the kingdom of God is not a matter of eating and drinking, but of righteousness, peace and joy in the Holy Spirit. —Romans 14:17, *NIV*

that the strength and utility of the kingdom of Christ cannot be fully perceived without recognizing it as spiritual is sufficiently apparent, even from this: During the whole course of our lives having to war under the cross, our condition here is bitter and wretched. We must know that the happiness which is promised to us in Christ does not consist in external advantages—such as leading a joyful and tranquil life, abounding in wealth, being secure against all injury, and having an affluence of delights, such as the flesh is wont to long for—but properly belongs to the heavenly life.

As in the world the prosperous and desirable condition of a people consists partly in the abundance of temporal good and domestic peace, and partly in the strong protection which gives security against external violence; so Christ also enriches his people with all things necessary to the eternal salvation of their souls and fortifies them with courage to stand unassailable by all the attacks of spiritual foes. When we infer that he reigns more for us than for himself, and that both within us and without us; that being replenished with the gifts of the Spirit, of which we are naturally destitute, we may feel from their first fruits that we are truly united to God for perfect blessedness; and then trusting to the power of the same Spirit, may not doubt that we shall always be victorious against the devil, the world, and everything that can do us harm. Not being earthly or carnal but spiritual, it raises us even to eternal life, so that we can patiently live at present under toil, hunger, cold, contempt, disgrace, and other annoyances.

We can live contented that our King will never abandon us, but will supply our necessities until our warfare is ended, and we are called to triumph. Since then he arms and equips us by his power, adorns us with splendor and magnificence, and enriches us with wealth, we here find most abundant cause of glorying—and also are inspired with boldness—so that we can contend intrepidly with the devil, sin, and death. In fine, clothed with his righteousness, we can bravely surmount all the insults of the world: and as he replenishes us liberally with his gifts, so we can in our turn bring forth fruit unto his glory.

GOVERNING THE KINGDOM

And hath put all things under his feet, and gave him to be the head over all things to the church, Which is his body, the fulness of him that filleth all in all. —Ephesians 1:22–23

ecause believers stand invincible in the strength of their King, and his spiritual riches abound towards them, they are not improperly called Christians. Moreover, from this eternity of which we have spoken there is nothing derogatory in the expression of Paul, "Then cometh the end, when he shall have delivered up the kingdom to God, even the Father" (1 Cor. 15:24). And also, "Then shall the Son also himself be subject unto him that put all things under him, that God may be all in all" (1 Cor. 15:28); for the meaning merely is that in that perfect glory the administration of the kingdom will not be such as it now is. For the Father has given all power to the Son; and by his hand he may govern, cherish, sustain us, keep us under his guardianship, and give assistance to us.

Thus, while we wander far as pilgrims from God, Christ may gradually bring us to full communion with God. And, indeed, his sitting at the right hand of the Father has the same meaning as if he was called the vicegerent of the Father, entrusted with the whole power of government. For God is pleased mediately (so to speak) in his person to rule and defend the Church. Thus also his being seated at the right hand of the Father is explained by Paul, in the Epistle to the Ephesians, to mean that "he is the head over all things to the Church, which is his body" (Eph. 1:20, 22). Thus Paul rightly infers that God will then be the only Head of the Church, because the office of Christ, in defending the Church, shall then have been completed.

For the same reason, Scripture throughout calls him Lord, the Father having appointed him over us for the express purpose of exercising his government through him. He reigns by divine authority, because his reason for assuming the office of Mediator was that, descending from the bosom and incomprehensible glory of the Father, he might draw near to us.

THE PRIEST'S SACRIFICE

Day after day every priest stands and performs his religious duties; again and again he offers the same sacrifices, which can never take away sins. But when this priest had offered for all time one sacrifice for sins, he sat down at the right hand of God. —Hebrews 10:11–12, NIV

ith regard to Christ's Priesthood, we must briefly hold its end and use to be that—as a Mediator, free from all taint—he may by his own holiness secure the favor of God for us. But because a deserved curse obstructs the entrance, and God in his character of Judge is hostile to us, expiation must necessarily intervene—that as a priest employed to appease the wrath of God, he may reinstate us in his favor. Wherefore, in order that Christ might fulfill this office, it was proper for him to appear with a sacrifice. For even under the law of the priesthood it was forbidden to enter the sanctuary without blood, to teach the worshipper that however the priest might interpose to deprecate, God could not be propitiated without the expiation of sin. On this subject the Apostle discourses at length in the Epistle to the Hebrews, from the seventh almost to the end of the tenth chapter.

The sum comes to this: The honor of the priesthood was competent to none but Christ, because, by the sacrifice of his death, he wiped away our guilt and made satisfaction for sin. Of the great importance of this matter, we are reminded by that solemn oath which God uttered, and of which he declared he would not repent, "Thou art a priest forever, after the order of Melchizedek" (Ps. 110:4). For, doubtless, his purpose was to ratify that point on which he knew that our salvation chiefly hinged. For there is no access to God for us or for our prayers until the priest, purging away our defilements, sanctify us and obtain for us that favor of which the impurity of our lives and hearts deprives us. Thus we see that if the benefit and efficacy of Christ's priesthood is to reach us the commencement must be with his death.

CONSECRATED BY CHRIST

As thou hast sent me into the world, even so have I also sent them into the world. And for their sakes I sanctify myself, that they also might be sanctified through the truth. —John 17:18–19

he, by whose aid we obtain favor, must be a perpetual mediator. From this again arises not only confidence in prayer but also the tranquility of pious minds, while they recline in safety on the paternal indulgence of God and feel assured that whatever has been consecrated by the Mediator is pleasing to him. But since God under the Law ordered sacrifices of beasts to be offered to him, there was a different and new arrangement in regard to Christ; that is, that he should be at once victim and priest, because no other fit satisfaction for sin could be found, nor was anyone worthy of the honor of offering an only begotten son to God.

Christ now bears the office of priest, not only that by the eternal law of reconciliation he may render the Father favorable and propitious to us, but also admit us into this most honorable alliance. For we—though in ourselves polluted, in him being priests (Rev. 1:6)—offer ourselves and our all to God and freely enter the heavenly sanctuary, so that the sacrifices of prayer and praise which we present are grateful and of sweet odor before him. To this effect are the words of Christ, "For their sakes I sanctify myself" (John 17:19). For being clothed with his holiness, inasmuch as he has devoted us to the Father with himself (otherwise we were an abomination before him), we please him as if we were pure and clean, nay, even sacred. Hence that unction of the sanctuary of which mention is made in Dan. 9:24; for we must attend to the contrast between this ceremony and the shadowy one which was then in use, as if the angel had said that when the shadows were dispersed, there would be a clear priesthood in the person of Christ.

THE SOURCE OF SALVATION

Neither is there salvation in any other: for there is none other name under heaven given among men, whereby we must be saved.
—*Acts 4:12*

Condemned, dead, and lost in ourselves, we must in him seek righteousness, deliverance, life and salvation, as we are taught by the celebrated words of Peter, "Neither is there salvation in any other: for there is none other name under heaven given among men whereby we must be saved" (Acts 4:12). The name of Jesus was not given him at random, or by accident, or by the will of man, but was brought from heaven by an angel, as the herald of the supreme decree—the reason also being added, "for he shall save his people from their sins" (Matt. 1:21). In these words attention should be paid to what we have elsewhere observed: that the office of Redeemer was assigned him in order that he might be our Savior. Still, however, redemption would be defective if it did not conduct us by an uninterrupted progression to the final goal of safety. Therefore, the moment we turn aside from him in the minutest degree, salvation (which resides entirely in him) gradually disappears so that all who do not rest in him voluntarily deprive themselves of all grace. The observation of Bernard well deserves to be remembered: "The name of Jesus is not only light but food also, yea, oil, without which all the food of the soul is dry; salt, without which as a condiment whatever is set before us is insipid; in fine, honey in the mouth, melody in the ear, joy in the heart, and, at the same time, medicine; every discourse where this name is not heard is absurd."

But here it is necessary diligently to consider in what way we obtain salvation from him, that we may not only be persuaded that he is the author of it, but having embraced whatever is sufficient as a sure foundation of our faith, may abstain from all that might make us waver.

VALUING DELIVERANCE

Christ redeemed us from the curse of the law by becoming a curse for us, for it is written: Cursed is everyone who is hung on a tree. He redeemed us in order that the blessing given to Abraham might come to the Gentiles through Jesus Christ, so that by faith we might receive the promise of the Spirit. —Galatians 3:13–14, NIV

The mode in which the Spirit usually speaks in Scripture is as follows: God was the enemy of men until they were restored to favor by the death of Christ (Rom. 5:10); they were cursed until their iniquity was compensated by the sacrifice of Christ (Gal. 3:10, 13); and they were separated from God until by means of Christ's body they were received into union (Col. 1:21–22). Such modes of expression are accommodated to our capacity that we may the better understand how miserable and calamitous our condition is without Christ.

For were it not said in clear terms that divine wrath and vengeance and eternal death lay upon us, we should be less sensible of our wretchedness without the mercy of God and less disposed to value the blessing of deliverance. Let a person be told, as Scripture teaches, that he was estranged from God by sin, an heir of wrath, exposed to the curse of eternal death, excluded from all hope of salvation, a complete alien from the blessing of God, the slave of Satan, captive under the yoke of sin—in fine, doomed to horrible destruction, and already involved in it—then Christ interposed, took the punishment upon himself and bore what (by the just judgment of God) was impending over sinners, and with his own blood amended the sins which rendered them hateful to God. By this amendment he satisfied and duly propitiated God the Father, by this mediation appeased his anger, on this basis founded peace between God and men, and by this tie secured the divine benevolence toward them. Will not these considerations move that person the more deeply, the more strikingly they represent the greatness of the calamity from which he was delivered?

UNLESS CHRIST UNITES US

For if, when we were God's enemies, we were reconciled to him through the death of his Son, how much more, having been reconciled, shall we be saved through his life! Not only is this so, but we also rejoice in God through our Lord Jesus Christ, through whom we have now received reconciliation. —Romans 5:10–11, NIV

God, who is perfect righteousness, cannot love the iniquity which he sees in all. Therefore, all of us have that within which deserves the hatred of God. Hence, in respect of our corrupt nature and of the depraved conduct following upon it, we are all offensive to God, guilty in his sight, and by nature the children of hell. But as the Lord wills not to destroy in us that which is his own, he still finds something in us which in kindness he can love. For though it is by our own fault that we are sinners, we are still his creatures; though we have brought death upon ourselves, he had created us for life. Thus, mere gratuitous love prompts him to receive us into favor. But if there is a perpetual and irreconcilable repugnance between righteousness and iniquity, so long as we remain sinners we cannot be completely received. Therefore, in order that all ground of offence may be removed and he may completely reconcile us to himself, by means of the compensation set forth in the death of Christ, he abolishes all the evil that is in us—so that we, formerly impure and unclean, now appear in his sight just and holy.

Accordingly, God the Father, by his love, prevents and anticipates our reconciliation in Christ. Nay, it is because he first loves us that he afterwards reconciles us to himself. But because the iniquity (which deserves the indignation of God) remains in us until the death of Christ comes to our aid—and that iniquity is in his sight accursed and condemned—we are not admitted to full and sure communion with God, unless Christ unites us. And, therefore, if we would indulge the hope of having God gracious and favorable to us, we must fix our eyes and minds on Christ alone as to him alone it is owing that our sins, which necessarily provoked the wrath of God, are not imputed to us.

BY CHRIST'S OBEDIENCE

But when the fulness of the time was come, God sent forth his Son, made of a woman, made under the law, To redeem them that were under the law, that we might receive the adoption of sons.
—Galatians 4:4–5

When it is asked how Christ, by abolishing sin, removed the enmity between God and us and purchased a righteousness which made him favorable and kind to us, it may be answered generally that he accomplished this by the whole course of his obedience. This is proved by the testimony of Paul, "As by one man's disobedience many were made sinners, so by the obedience of one shall many be made righteous" (Rom. 5:19). And he elsewhere extends the ground of pardon which exempts from the curse of the Law to the whole life of Christ, "When the fullness of the time was come, God sent forth his Son, made of a woman, made under the law, to redeem them that were under the law" (Gal. 4:4–5). Thus, even at his baptism, he declared that a part of righteousness was fulfilled by his yielding obedience to the command of the Father. In short, from the moment when he assumed the form of a servant, he began to pay the price of deliverance.

Scripture, however, the more certainly to define the mode of salvation, ascribes it peculiarly and specially to the death of Christ. He himself declares that he gave his life a ransom for many (Matt. 20:28). Paul teaches that he died for our sins (Rom. 4:25). John the Baptist exclaimed, "Behold the Lamb of God, which takes away the sin of the world" (John 1:29). In another passage Paul declares, "We are justified freely by his grace, through the redemption that is in Christ Jesus: whom God has set forth to be a propitiation through faith in his blood" (Rom. 3:25). And, "Being justified by his blood, we shall be saved from wrath through him" (Rom. 5:9). Also, "He has made him to be sin for us, who knew no sin; that we might be made the righteousness of God in him" (2 Cor. 5:21).

VOLUNTARY SUBJECTION

But made himself of no reputation, and took upon him the form of a servant, and was made in the likeness of men: And being found in fashion as a man, he humbled himself, and became obedient unto death, even the death of the cross. —Philippians 2:7–8

In the Confession of Faith, called the Apostles' Creed, the transition is admirably made from the birth of Christ to his death and resurrection, in which the completion of a perfect salvation consists. Still, there is no exclusion of the other part of obedience which he performed in life. Thus Paul comprehends, from the beginning even to the end, his having assumed the form of a servant, humbled himself, and become obedient to death, even the death of the cross (Phil. 2:7). And, indeed, the first step in obedience was his voluntary subjection, for the sacrifice would have been unavailing to justification if not offered spontaneously. Hence, our Lord, after testifying, "I lay down my life for the sheep," distinctly adds, "No man takes it from me" (John 10:15, 18). In the same sense, Isaiah says, "Like a sheep before her shearers is dumb, so he opened not his mouth" (Isa. 53:7). The Gospel history relates that he came forth to meet the soldiers; and instead of defending himself in the presence of Pilate, he stood to receive judgment.

This, indeed, he did not without a struggle; for he had assumed our infirmities also, and in this way it was proper for him to prove that he was yielding obedience to his Father. It was no ordinary example of incomparable love towards us to struggle with dire terrors, and amid fearful tortures to cast away all care of himself that he might provide for us. We must bear in mind that Christ could not duly propitiate God without renouncing his own feelings and subjecting himself entirely to his Father's will. To this effect the Apostle appositely quotes a passage from the Psalms, "Lo, I come (in the volume of the book it is written of me) to do thy will, O God" (Heb. 10:5; Ps. 40:7–8). Thus, as trembling consciences find no rest without sacrifice and ablution by which sins are expiated, we are properly directed thither, the source of our life being placed in the death of Christ.

OUR JUST DISTRESS

Behold, I will corrupt your seed, and spread dung upon your faces, even the dung of your solemn feasts; and one shall take you away with it. And ye shall know that I have sent this commandment unto you, that my covenant might be with Levi, saith the LORD of hosts. My covenant was with him of life and peace; and I gave them to him for the fear wherewith he feared me, and was afraid before my name. The law of truth was in his mouth, and iniquity was not found in his lips: he walked with me in peace and equity, and did turn many away from iniquity. —Malachi 2:3–6

That the good are tempted is no wonder, when that state of things in the world is in greater confusion. Even Solomon says, "All things happen alike to the just and to the unjust, to him who offers sacrifices, and to him who does not sacrifice" (Eccl. 9:2), hence the earth is full of impiety and contempt. There is then an occasion for indignation and envy offered to us; but as God designedly tries our faith by such confusions, we must remember that we must exercise patience. It is not at the same time enough for us to submit to God's judgment, except we also consider that we are justly distressed; and that though we may be attentive to what is just and upright, many vices still cleave to us, and that we are sprinkled with many spots, which provoke God's wrath against us. Let us then learn to form a right judgment as to what our life is, and then

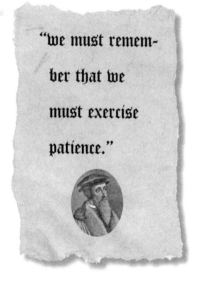

"we must remember that we must exercise patience."

let us bear in mind how many are the reasons why God should sometimes deal roughly with us. Thus all our envying will cease, and our mind will be prepared calmly to obey. In short, these considerations will check whatever perverseness there may be in us, so that neither our wicked thoughts nor our words will be so strong as to rise in rebellion against God.

HEART COMFORT

Therefore, behold, I will allure her, and bring her into the wilderness, and speak comfortably unto her. —Hosea 2:14

to speak to the heart is to bring comfort, to soothe grief by a kind word, to offer kindness, and to hold forth some hope, that he who had previously been worn out with sorrow may breathe freely, gather courage, and entertain hope of a better condition. And this kind of speaking ought to be carefully observed; for God means, that there was now no place for his promises, because the Israelites were so refractory ...The Corinthians, when alienated from Paul, had obstructed, as it were, the passage of his doctrine, that he could not address them in a paternal manner (2 Cor. 6:11-12). So also in this place, the Lord testifies that the floor was closed against his promises; for if he gave to the Israelites the hope of pardon, it would have been slighted; if he had invited them kindly to himself, they would have scornfully refused, yea, spurned the offer with contempt, so great was their ferocity; if he wished to be reconciled to them, they would have despised him, or refused, or proceeded in abusing his

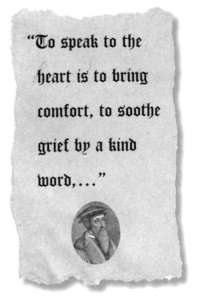

"To speak to the heart is to bring comfort, to soothe grief by a kind word, ..."

kindness as before ... Let us then know, that whenever we are deprived of the sense of God's favour, the way has been closed up through our fault; for God would ever be disposed willingly to show kindness, except our contumacy and hardness stood in the way. But when he sees us so subdued as to be pliable and ready to obey, then he is ready in his turn, to speak to our heart; that is, he is ready to show himself just as he is, full of grace and kindness.

GOD'S GENEROSITY

If any of you lacks wisdom, he should ask God, who gives generously to all without finding fault, and it will be given to him.
—James 1:5, NIV

As our reason and all our feelings are against the thought that we can be happy in the midst of evils, James bids us to ask of the Lord to give us wisdom. For I confine the meaning of "wisdom" here to the subject of the passage, as though James had said: "If this doctrine is higher than what your minds can reach to, ask the Lord to illuminate you by his Spirit; for as this consolation alone is enough to soften all the bitterness of evil—that what is bad to the flesh is good to us— so we must necessarily be overcome with impatience, unless we are sustained by this kind of comfort." Since we see that the Lord does not require from us what is above our strength, but that he is ready to help us (provided we ask), therefore let us learn, whenever he commands anything, to ask from him the power to perform it.

By "all," he means those who ask, for those who seek no remedy for their needs deserve to pine away in them. However, this universal declaration, by which every one of us is invited to ask, without exception, is very important; hence no person ought to deprive herself or himself of so great a privilege.

The word "generously" means a quickness to give. The meaning is, then, that God is so inclined and ready to give that he rejects none and snobbishly puts off no one—God being not like the selfish and grasping, who either sparingly, with a closed hand, give only a little or give but a part of what they could, or argue with themselves a long time over whether to give or not.

The phrase "without finding fault" is added, lest anyone fear to come too often to God. Even the most generous people, when anyone asks too often to be helped, mention their acts of kindness and thus excuse themselves for the future. Hence we are ashamed to weary a mortal person, however open-handed, by asking too often. But James reminds us that there is nothing like this in God, for God is ever ready to add new blessings to former ones, without any end or limitation.

OTHERS' GIFTS

Before destruction the heart of man is haughty, and before honour is humility. —Proverbs 18:12

So blindly do we all rush in the direction of self-love, that every one thinks he has a good reason for exalting himself and despising all others in comparison. If God has bestowed on us something not to be repented of, trusting to it, we immediately become elated, and not only swell, but almost burst with pride... [Scripture] teaches us to remember, that the endowments which God has bestowed upon us are not our own, but His free gifts, and that those who plume themselves upon them betray their ingratitude. "Who maketh thee to differ," saith Paul, "and what hast thou that thou didst not receive it" (1 Cor. 4:7). Then by a diligent examination of our faults let us keep ourselves humble. Thus while nothing will remain to swell our pride, there will be much to subdue it. Again, we are enjoined, whenever we behold the gifts of God in others, so to reverence and respect the gifts, as also to honour those in whom they reside. God having been pleased to bestow honour upon them, it would ill become us to deprive them of it. Then we are told to overlook their faults, not, indeed to encourage by flattering them, but not because of them to

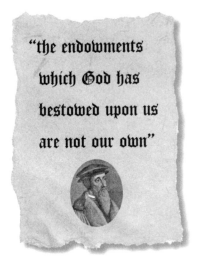

"the endowments which God has bestowed upon us are not our own"

insult those whom we ought to regard with honour and good will. In this way, with regard to all with whom we have intercourse, our behavior will be not only moderate and modest, but courteous and friendly. The only way by which you can ever attain to true meekness, is to have your heart imbued with a humble opinion of yourself and respect for others.

HUMILITY

Pray also for me, that whenever I open my mouth, words may be given me so that I will fearlessly make known the mystery of the gospel, for which I am an ambassador in chains. Pray that I may declare it fearlessly, as I should. —Ephesians 6:19–20, NIV

ray also for me. For himself, in a particular way, he asks the Ephesians to pray. From this we see that there is no one so richly endowed with gifts as not to need this kind of assistance from other Christians, so long as that person remains in this world. Who would ever be more entitled to plead exemption from the need to be prayed for than Paul? Yet he begs the prayers of his siblings, and not hypocritically, but from an earnest desire for their aid. And what does Paul wish that they should ask for him? He asks that words will be given to him. What then? Was he habitually wordless, or did fear restrain him from making an open profession of the Gospel? By no means; but there was reason to fear lest his splendid beginning would not be sustained in his future progress. Besides, his zeal for proclaiming the Gospel was so ardent that he was never satisfied with his exertions. And

indeed, if we consider the weight and importance of the subject, we shall all acknowledge that we are very far from being able to handle it in a proper manner.

Fear hinders us from preaching Christ openly and fearlessly, while the absence of restraint and hiddenness in confessing Christ is demanded from his ministers.... But does not Paul show unbelief when he doubts his own steadfastness, and implores the intercession of others? No.... The only aids on which he relies are those which he knows to be sanctioned by the divine promise.... It is the command of God that believers shall pray for one another. How consoling then must it be to each of us to learn that the care of our salvation is enjoined on all the rest, and to be informed by God that the prayers of others on our behalf are not poured out in vain! Would it be lawful to refuse what the Lord himself has offered?

HIDDEN HYPOCRISY

*If anyone considers himself religious and yet does not keep a tight rein
on his tongue, he deceives himself and his religion is worthless.*
—James 1:26, NIV

James now chastens even those who boasted that they were doers of the Law, a sin under which hypocrites often labor—that is, the looseness of the tongue in detracting others. James has already touched on the duty of restraining the tongue, but for a different end; for he then asked for silence before God so that we might be more fitted to learn. He speaks now of another thing: that the faithful should not employ their tongue in evil speaking.

It is indeed needful that this vice be condemned when the subject [of this section of the book] is the keeping of the Law, for those who have put off the grosser vices are especially subject to this disease. Someone who is neither an adulterer, nor a thief, nor a drunkard, but, on the contrary, seems brilliant with outward shows of sanctity, will set herself or himself off by maligning others—and doing this under the pretense of enthusiasm, but really through the lust of slandering.

The object here, then, was to distinguish between the true worshipers of God and hypocrites, who are so swollen with Pharisaic pride that they seek praise from the faults of others. James says if any one seems to be religious, that is—has a show-off sanctity but in the meantime flatters herself or himself by speaking evil of others—it is hence evident that such a person does not truly serve God. For by saying that her or his religion is vain, James not only suggests that other virtues are blemished by the stain of evil-speaking, but that the conclusion is that the zeal for religion which appears is not sincere.

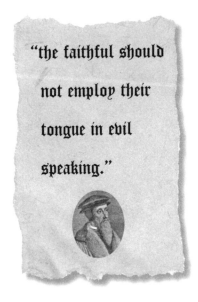

"the faithful should not employ their tongue in evil speaking."

Jesus' Glory

Therefore God exalted him to the highest place and gave him the name
that is above every name, that at the name of Jesus every knee should
bow, in heaven and on earth and under the earth, and every tongue
confess that Jesus Christ is Lord, to the glory of God the Father.
—Philippians 2:9–11, NIV

Paul shows that to be lowered, which the human mind fears, is in the highest degree desirable. There is no one, it is true, who wouldn't acknowledge that it is a reasonable thing that is required of us when we are exhorted to imitate Christ. This consideration, however, stirs us up to imitate him the more cheerfully: when we learn that nothing is better for us than to be conformed to his image. Now, Paul shows by Jesus' example that all are blessed who, along with Christ, voluntarily lower themselves; for from the most abject condition Christ was exalted to the highest elevation. All, therefore, who humble themselves will in similar manner be exalted. Who would now be reluctant to exercise humility, by means of which the glory of the heavenly kingdom is attained?

This passage has given an opportunity to bogus philosophers, or rather they have seized hold of it, to allege that Christ did his deed first for himself, and afterwards for others. Who does not see that this is a suggestion of Satan—that Christ suffered upon the cross so that he might acquire for himself, by the merit of his work, what he did not possess? For it is the plan of the Holy Spirit that we should, in the death of Christ, see and taste and ponder and feel and recognize nothing but God's unmixed goodness, and the love of Christ toward us, which was great and inestimable, and that, regardless of himself, he devoted himself and his life for our sakes. In every instance in which the Scriptures speak of the death of Christ, they assign its advantage and value to us—that by means of it we are redeemed, reconciled to God, restored to righteousness, cleansed from our pollutions, life is purchased for us, and the gate of life opened.

THE RIGHT KIND OF FEAR

At Iconium Paul and Barnabas went as usual into the Jewish syna-
gogue. There they spoke so effectively that a great number of Jews and
Gentiles believed. But the Jews who refused to believe stirred up the
Gentiles and poisoned their minds against the brothers. So Paul and
Barnabas spent considerable time there, speaking boldly for the Lord,
who confirmed the message of his grace by enabling them to do
miraculous signs and wonders.
The people of the city were divided; some sided with the Jews, others
with the apostles. There was a plot afoot among the Gentiles and Jews,
together with their leaders, to mistreat them and stone them. But they
found out about it and fled to the Lycaonian cities of Lystra and Derbe
and to the surrounding country, where they continued to preach the
good news. —Acts 14:1–7, NIV

Notice how far forth the holy champions of Christ did suffer. They did not give up ground when their enemies only set themselves against them. But when the agitation grew hottest, and they were in danger of stoning, though they had many supporters of their doctrine, they go no further but remembering the saying of Christ in which he warns the faithful to patiently possess their souls, they avoid the fury of the enemy. And though they leave, lest they throw themselves headlong into death, yet their constancy in preaching the Gospel sufficiently declares that they feared not danger. For Luke says that they preached the Gospel in other places also. This is the right kind of fear: when the servants of Christ do not run willfully into the hands of their enemies to be murdered by them, and yet they do not abandon their duty, nor does fear hinder them from obeying God when he calls. And so, consequently, they can afford, if need be, to go even through death itself to do their duty.

FUTURE LIFE

The land shall not be sold for ever: for the land is mine; for ye are strangers and sojourners with me. —Leviticus 25:23

Whatever be the kind of tribulation with which we are afflicted, we should always consider the end of it to be, that we may be trained to despise the present, and thereby stimulated to aspire to the future. For since God well knows how strongly we are inclined by nature to a slavish love of this world, in order to prevent us from clinging too strongly to it, he employs the fittest reason for calling us back, and shaking off our lethargy. Every one of us, indeed, would be thought to aspire and aim at heavenly immortality during the whole course of his life. For we would be ashamed in no respect to excel the lower animals; whose condition would not be at all inferior to ours, had we not a hope of immortality beyond the grave. But when you attend to the plans, wishes, and actions of each, you see nothing in them but the earth. Hence our stupidity; our minds being dazzled with the glare of wealth, power, and honours, that they can see no farther . . . We duly profit by the discipline of the cross, when we learn that this life, estimated in itself, is restless, troubled, in numberless ways wretched, and plainly in no respect happy; that what are estimated its blessings are uncertain, fleeting, vain, and vitiated by a great admixture of evil. From this we conclude, that all we have to seek or hope

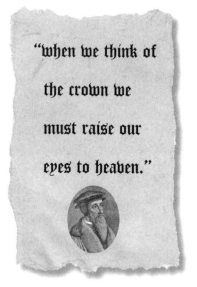

"when we think of the crown we must raise our eyes to heaven."

for here is contest; that when we think of the crown we must raise our eyes to heaven. For we must hold, that our mind never rises seriously to desire and aspire after the future, until it has learned to despise the present life.

LIFE WORTH LESS THAN THE GIVER OF LIFE

However, I consider my life worth nothing to me, if only I may finish the race and complete the task the Lord Jesus has given me—the task of testifying to the gospel of God's grace. —Acts 20:24, NIV

All the godly must be so framed in their minds that, setting all things apart, they make haste to obey God. Life is, indeed, a more excellent gift than that it ought to be neglected: seeing we are created after the image of God, to the end we may think upon that blessed immortality which is laid up for us in heaven, in which the Lord does now by diverse testimonies and tokens show himself to be our Father.

But because [life] is ordained to be, for us, like a race, we must always hasten toward the finish line and overcome all hindrances, lest anything hinder or slow us in our course. For it is a filthy thing for us to be so held down with a blind desire to live that we lose the grounding and cause of life for life itself; this is what Paul is saying. For he does not simply make light of his life, but he disregards the respect of it so that he may finish his race, so that he may fulfill the ministry which he has received of Christ, as if he should say that he does not desire to live unless he may satisfy the calling of God; and that, therefore, it shall be no grief to him to lose his life, so that he may come by death to the goal of the job prescribed to him by God.

For the joy of a good conscience is more deeply and surely laid up than something that could be taken away by any external trouble, or any sorrow of the flesh. It triumphs more joyfully than it can be oppressed.

THE DANGER OF AMBITION

Even from your own number men will arise and distort the truth in order to draw away disciples after them. —Acts 20:30, NIV

The fountain and beginning of this evil is noted, because they will "draw disciples after them." Therefore, ambition is the mother of all heresies. For the sincerity of the Word of God flourishes when the pastors join hand in hand to bring disciples to Christ, because this alone is the sound state of the Church, that he be heard alone. Thus, both the doctrine of salvation must be perverted, and also the safety of the flock must be ignored, where humans be desirous of control. And as this place teaches that almost all corruptions of doctrine flow from the pride of humans, so we learn again in the same place that it cannot otherwise be, but that ambitious people will turn away from right purity and corrupt the Word of God. For seeing that the pure and sincere handling of the Scripture tends to this end, that Christ alone may have control, and that humans can challenge nothing to themselves but shall take so much from the glory of Christ, it follows that those who are addicted to themselves and study to advance their own glory (which can only darken that of Christ) are corrupters of sound doctrine—which doth only darken Christ.

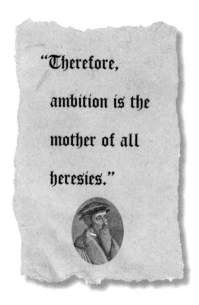

"**Therefore, ambition is the mother of all heresies.**"

HIS OWN

You only have I known of all the families of the earth.
—Amos 3:2a

hrist brings none to the Father, but those given him by the Father, and this donation we know, depends on eternal election; for those whom the Father has destined to life, he delivers to the keeping of his Son, that he may defend them. This is what he says by John, "All that the Father hath given me, will come to me" (John 6:37). That we then submit to God by the obedience of faith, let us learn to ascribe this altogether to his mercy; for otherwise we shall never be led to him by the hand of Christ. Besides, this doctrine supplies us with strong ground of confidence; for who can tremble under the guidance and protections of Christ? Who, while relying on such a keeper and guardian, would not boldly disregard all dangers? And doubtless, when Christ says, "Behold, I and the children," he really fulfills what he elsewhere promises, that he will not suffer any of those to perish whom he has received from the Father (John 10:28).

We must observe lastly, that though the world with mad stubbornness reject the Gospel, yet the sheep ever recognize the voice of their shepherd. Let not therefore the impiety of almost all ranks, ages, and nations, disturb us, provided Christ gathers together his won, who have been committed to his protection. If the reprobate rush headlong to death by their impiety, in this way the plants which God hath not planted are rooted up (Matt. 15:13). Let us at the same time know that his won are known to him, and that the salvation of them all is sealed by him, so that not one of them shall be lost (2 Tim. 2:19). Let us be satisfied with this seal.

OUR HEAVENLY INHERITANCE

Praise be to the God and Father of our Lord Jesus Christ! In his great mercy he has given us new birth into a living hope through the resurrection of Jesus Christ from the dead, and into an inheritance that can never perish, spoil or fade—kept in heaven for you, who through faith are shielded by God's power until the coming of the salvation that is ready to be revealed in the last time.
—1 Peter 1:3–5, NIV

The three words which follow the phrase "into an inheritance" are intended to amplify God's grace. For Peter had this goal [in writing]: to impress our minds thoroughly as to the excellence [of grace].

Every word which follows is important. The inheritance is said to be reserved, or preserved, so that we may know that it is beyond the reach of danger. For, were it not in God's hand, it might be exposed to endless dangers. That he might then free us from fear, he testifies that our salvation is placed in safety beyond the harms which Satan can do. But as the certainty of salvation can bring us but little comfort, unless everyone knows that it belongs to himself, Peter adds "for you." For consciences can calmly rest here, that is, when the Lord cries to them from heaven, "Behold, your salvation is in my hand and is kept for you."

We should notice the connection when Peter says that we are kept shielded while in the world, and at the same time our inheritance is reserved in heaven. Otherwise this thought would immediately creep in: "What good does it do us that our salvation is laid up in heaven, when we are tossed here and there in this world as in a turbulent sea? The Apostle, therefore, anticipates objections of this kind when he shows that though we are in the world exposed to dangers, we are yet kept by faith; and that though we are thus nigh to death, we are yet safe under the guardianship of faith. But as faith itself, through the sickness of the flesh, often trembles and fears, we might be always anxious about future were not the Lord to aid us. As, then, we are begotten by faith, so faith itself receives its stability from God's power. Hence is its security, not only for the present, but also for the future.

EXHORTING ONE ANOTHER

And Jesus answering them began to say, Take heed lest any man deceive you. —Mark 13:5

As by nature we are inclined to evil, we have need of various helps to retain us in the fear of God. Unless our faith be now and then raised up, it will lie prostrate; unless it be warmed, it will be frozen; unless it be roused, it will grow torpid. He would have us then to stimulate one another by mutual exhortations, so that Satan may not creep into our hearts, and by his fallacies draw us away from God. And this is a way of speaking that ought to be especially observed; for we fall not immediately by the first assault into this madness of striving against God; but Satan by degrees accosts us artfully by indirect means, until he holds us ensnared in his delusions. Then indeed being blinded, we break forth into open rebellion.

We must then meet this danger in due time, and it is one that is nigh us all, for nothing is more possible than to be deceived; and from this deception comes at length hardness of heart. We hence see how necessary it is for us to be roused by the incessant goads of exhor- tations. Nor does the Apostle give only a general precept, that all should take heed to them- selves, but he would have them also to be solicitous for the sal- vation of every member, so that they should not suffer any of those who had been once called to perish through their neglect. And he who feels it is his duty so to watch over the salvation of the whole flock as to neglect no one sheep, per- forms in this case the office of a good shepherd.

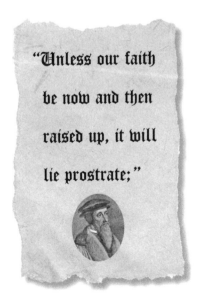

"Unless our faith be now and then raised up, it will lie prostrate;"

TAKING PRIDE IN LOWNESS

The brother in humble circumstances ought to take pride in his high position. But the one who is rich should take pride in his low position, because he will pass away like a wild flower. For the sun rises with scorching heat and withers the plant; its blossom falls and its beauty is destroyed. In the same way, the rich man will fade away even while he goes about his business. —James 1:9–11, NIV

In speaking of "the one who is rich," James has mentioned the particular person in place of the general; for this message pertains to all those who excel in honor, or in dignity, or in any other external thing. James bids them to glory in their lowness or littleness, in order to repress the arrogance of those who are usually inflated with well-being. But he calls it lowness because the kingdom of God that has been shown to us ought to lead us to despise the world, as we know that all the things we previously greatly admired are either nothing or very little things. For Christ, who is not a teacher except of children, checks by his doctrine all the pride of the flesh. Lest, then, the vain joy of the world should captivate the rich, they ought to make themselves ready for glory in the casting down of their fleshly excellence.

Glorying in riches is foolish and preposterous, because they pass away in a moment like a wild flower. The philosophers teach the same thing, but the song is sung to the deaf, until the ears are opened by the Lord to hear the truth concerning the eternity of the celestial kingdom.

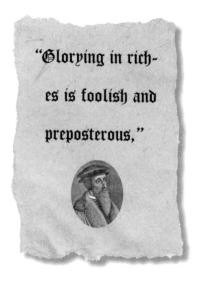

"Glorying in riches is foolish and preposterous,"

PART ONE

THE ARMOR OF GOD

Put on the full armor of God so that you can take your stand against the devil's schemes. For our struggle is not against flesh and blood, but against the rulers, against the authorities, against the powers of this dark world and against the spiritual forces of evil in the heavenly realms. —Ephesians 6:11–12, NIV

God has given us various defensive weapons, so long as we do not indolently refuse what is offered. But we are almost all chargeable with carelessness and hesitation in using the offered grace; just as if a soldier, about to meet the enemy, should take his helmet, and neglect his shield. To correct this security, Paul borrows a comparison from the military art, and bids us put on the whole armor of God. The Lord offers to us arms for repelling every kind of attack. It remains for us to apply them to use, and not leave them hanging on the wall. To quicken our vigilance, he reminds us that we must not only engage in open warfare, but that we have a crafty and insidious enemy to encounter, who frequently lies in ambush; for such is the meaning of the Apostle's phrase "the devil's schemes."

To impress them still more deeply with their danger, he points out the nature of the enemy, which he illustrates by a comparative statement, "Not against flesh and blood." The meaning is that our difficulties are far greater than if we had to fight with humans. Where we resist human strength, sword is opposed to sword, man contends with man, force is met by force, and skill by skill; but here the case is widely different. All amounts to this, that our enemies are such as no human power can withstand. This is no bodily struggle.

Let us remember this when the mean treatment of others provokes us to revenge. Our natural temperament would lead us to direct all our exertions against the wrongdoers themselves; but this foolish desire will be restrained by the consideration that the people who annoy us are nothing more than darts thrown by the hand of Satan. While we are employed in destroying those darts, we lay ourselves open to be wounded on all sides. To wrestle with flesh and blood will not only be useless, but highly pernicious. We must go straight to the enemy, who attacks and wounds us from his concealment.

PART TWO

THE ARMY OF GOD

Therefore put on the full armor of God, so that when the day of evil comes, you may be able to stand your ground, . . . Stand firm then, with the belt of truth buckled around your waist, with the breastplate of righteousness in place, and with your feet fitted with the readiness that comes from the gospel of peace. In addition to all this, take up the shield of faith, with which you can extinguish all the flaming arrows of the evil one. —Ephesians 6:14–16, NIV

Stand firm. Now follows a description of the arms which they are told to wear. Truth, which means sincerity of mind, is compared to a girdle. Now, a girdle was, in ancient times, one of the most important parts of military armor. Our attention is thus directed to the fountain of sincerity; for the purity of the Gospel ought to remove from our minds all craftiness, and from our hearts all hypocrisy. Secondly, he recommends righteousness, and desires that it should be a breastplate for protecting the breast. He enjoins us to be adorned, first, with integrity, and next with a devout and holy life.

When he says, "And your feet fitted," the allusion is to the military greaves. As soldiers covered their legs and feet to protect them against cold and other injuries, so we must be shod with the Gospel, if we would pass unhurt through the world.

It is the Gospel of peace, for it is the message of our reconciliation to God, and nothing else gives peace to the conscience. We are told to lay aside every hindrance, and to be prepared both for journey and for war. By nature we dislike work and lack agility. A rough road and many other obstacles slow our progress, and we are discouraged by the smallest annoyance. On these accounts, Paul holds out the Gospel as the fittest means for undertaking and performing the expedition.

It is not without reason that the most necessary instruments of warfare—a sword and a shield—are compared to faith, and to the Word of God. In the spiritual combat, these two hold the highest rank. By faith we repel all the attacks of the devil, and by the word of God the enemy himself is slain. If we enter the field unarmed, if we lack our sword, how shall we sustain that character?

PART THREE

THE ARMOR OF GOD

Take the helmet of salvation and the sword of the Spirit, which is the word of God. And pray in the Spirit on all occasions with all kinds of prayers and requests. With this in mind, be alert and always keep on praying for all the saints. —Ephesians 6:17–18, NIV

The head is protected by the best helmet when, elevated by hope, we look up towards heaven to that salvation which is promised. It is only therefore by becoming the object of hope that salvation is a helmet.

Having instructed the Ephesians to put on their armor, he now tells them to fight by prayer. This is the true method. To call upon God is the chief exercise of faith and hope; and it is in this way that we obtain from God every blessing. Prayer and supplication are not greatly different from each other, except that supplication is only one branch of prayer.

We are exhorted to persevere in prayer. Every tendency to weariness must be counteracted by a cheerful performance of the duty. With unabated fire we must continue our prayers, even if we do not immediately obtain what we desire. But what is the meaning of "always"? When everything flows on prosperously—when we are easy and cheerful—we seldom feel any strong excitement to prayer; or rather,

we never flee to God, except when we are driven by some kind of distress. Paul therefore desires us to allow no opportunity to pass—on no occasion to neglect prayer, so that praying always is the same thing, with praying both in prosperity and in adversity.

There is not a moment of our life at which the duty of prayer may not be urged by our own needs. But unremitting prayer may likewise be enforced by the consideration that the necessities of our siblings in Christ ought to move our sympathy. If, at any time, we are colder or more indifferent about prayer than we ought to be, let us instantly reflect how many of our fellow Christians are worn out by varied and heavy afflictions—are weighed down by sore perplexity, or are reduced to the lowest distress. If reflections like these do not rouse us from our lethargy, we must have hearts of stone. But are we to pray for believers only? Though the apostle states the claims of the godly, he does not exclude others.

KEEPING QUIET HEARTS

My dear brothers, take note of this: Everyone should be quick to listen, slow to speak and slow to become angry, for man's anger does not bring about the righteous life that God desires. —James 1:19–20, NIV

Having then set before us the goodness of God, James shows how it is becoming in us to be prepared to receive the blessing, which God exhibits towards us. And this doctrine is very useful, for spiritual regeneration is not the work of one moment. Since some remnants of the sinful person ever abide in us, we must necessarily be renewed throughout life until the flesh be abolished; for either our perverseness, or arrogance, or laziness, is a great impediment to God in perfecting in us his work. Thus, since James wants us to be swift to hear, he commends promptness, as though he had said, "When God so freely and kindly presents himself to you, you also ought to make yourselves teachable, lest your slowness should cause him to stop speaking."

But inasmuch as, when we seem to ourselves to be very wise, we do not calmly hear God speaking to us but by our haste interrupt him when he addresses us, the Apostle requires us to be silent, to be slow to speak. And, doubtless, no one can be a true disciple of God, except she or he hears God in silence. James does not require [the quietness demanded by the Greek philosopher Pythagoras], which won't allow inquiry when knowledge is needed. James would simply have us correct and restrain our assertiveness so that we may not, as commonly happens, unseasonably interrupt God, and that as long as he opens his sacred mouth, we may open to him our hearts and our ears and not prevent him to speak.

Wrath also, I think, is condemned in terms of the hearing which God demands to be given to him, as if our making a tumult disturbs and impedes God, for God cannot be heard except when the mind is calm and sedate. Hence, he adds, that as long as wrath rules us there is no place for the righteousness of God. In short, except the heat of angry argument be banished, we shall never give God that calm silence of which James has just spoken.

COMMUNITY

Woe to you who add house to house and join field to field till no space is left and you live alone in the land. —Isaiah 5:8, NIV

Isaiah now reproves insatiable avarice and greed, from which acts of cheating, injustice, and violence are wont to arise. It cannot be condemned as in itself wrong, if someone adds field to field and house to house; but Isaiah looks at the disposition of mind which cannot at all be satisfied when it is once inflamed by the desire of gain. So great is the intensity of covetous people that they desire to possess everything by themselves alone, and reckon everything belonging to others to be something they want which has been taken from them. Hence the beautiful observation of John Chrysostom that "covetous people, if they could, would willingly take the sun from the poor." For they envy their brethren the common elements and would gladly swallow them up—not that they might enjoy them, but because such is the madness to which their greed carries them.

Isaiah therefore accuses covetous and ambitious people of such folly that they would wish to have other people removed from the earth so that they might possess it alone, and consequently they set no limit to their desire of gain. For what madness is it to wish to have those people driven away from the earth whom God has placed in it along with us, and to whom, as well as to ourselves, he has assigned it as their home! Certainly nothing more ruinous could happen to these people than to obtain their wish. Were they alone, they could not plough, or reap, or perform other offices indispensable to their livelihood, or supply themselves with the necessaries of life. For God has linked people so closely together that they need the assistance and labor of each other, and none but a lunatic would disdain other people as hurtful or useless to herself or himself. Ambitious people cannot enjoy their renown but amidst a multitude. How blind are they, therefore, when they wish to drive and chase away others, that they may reign alone!

PRAISING AT ALL TIMES

After they had been severely flogged, they were thrown into prison, and the jailer was commanded to guard them carefully. Upon receiving such orders, he put them in the inner cell and fastened their feet in the stocks. About midnight Paul and Silas were praying and singing hymns to God, and the other prisoners were listening to them.
—Acts 16:23–25, NIV

Even when they lay bound with stocks, Luke writes that in prayer they praised God, from which we see that neither the embarrassment they suffered, nor the wounds which made their flesh sting, nor the stink of the deep dungeon, nor the danger of death, which was hard on their heels, could hinder them from giving thanks to the Lord joyfully and with glad hearts.

We must note this general rule: that we cannot pray the way we should unless we also praise God. For even if the desire to pray arises from the feeling of our deprivation and miseries and therefore is, for the most part, joined with sorrow and worry, yet the faithful must bridle their feelings so that they do not murmur against God. They must do this so that the right form of prayer joins two affections together: worry and sorrow (by reason of the present need which keeps us down) and joyfulness (by reason of the obedience by which we submit ourselves to God, and by reason of the hope which, showing us the safe place near at hand, refreshes us even in the midst of shipwreck). Paul prescribes this form to us: Let your prayers, he says, be made known to God with thanksgiving (Phil. 4:6). But in this history we must notice the circumstances. For though the pain of the wounds was grave, though the prison was troublesome, though the danger was great, seeing that Paul and Silas did not cease to praise God, we gather by this how greatly they were encouraged to bear the cross.

SURE AND STEADFAST

The voice of the LORD is upon the waters: the God of glory thundereth: the LORD is upon many waters. The voice of the LORD is powerful; the voice of the LORD is full of majesty. The voice of the LORD breaketh the cedars; yea, the LORD breaketh the cedars of Lebanon.
—Psalm 29:3–5

a s long as we sojourn in this world, we stand not on firm ground, but are tossed here and there as it were in the midst of the sea, and that indeed very turbulent; for Satan is incessantly stirring up innumerable storms, which would immediately upset and sink our vessel, were we not to cast our anchor fast in the deep. For nowhere a haven appears to our eyes, but wherever we look water alone is in view; yea waves also arise and threaten us; but as the anchor is cast through the waters into a dark and unseen place, and while it lies hid there, keeps the vessel beaten by the waves from being overwhelmed; so must our hope be fixed on the invisible God. There is this difference— the anchor is cast downwards into the sea, for it has the earth as its bottom; but our hope rises upwards and soars aloft, for in the world it finds nothing on which it can stand, not ought it to cleave to created things, but to rest on God alone. As the cable also by which the anchor is suspended joins the vessel with the earth through a long and dark intermediate space, so the truth of God is a bond to connect us with himself, so that no distance of place and no darkness can prevent us from cleaving to him. Thus when united to God, though we must struggle with continual storms, we are yet beyond the peril of shipwreck. Hence he says, that this anchor is sure and steadfast, or safe and firm. It may indeed be that by the violence of the waves the anchor may be plucked off, or the cable be broken, or the beaten ship be torn to pieces. This happens on the sea; but the power of God to sustain us is wholly different, and so also is the strength of hope and the firmness of his Word.

TRADITION

I want men everywhere to lift up holy hands in prayer, without anger or disputing. I also want women to dress modestly, with decency and propriety, not with braided hair or gold or pearls or expensive clothes, but with good deeds, appropriate for women who profess to worship God. A woman should learn in quietness and full submission. I do not permit a woman to teach or to have authority over a man; she must be silent.
—1 Timothy 2:8–12, NIV

I approve only of those human constitutions which are founded on the authority of God and derived from Scripture, and are therefore altogether divine. I say, that it is a human tradition, and that at the same time it is divine. It is of God, inasmuch as it is a part of decency, the care and observance of which is recommended by the Apostle; and it is human, inasmuch as it specifically determines what was indicated as a general principle. From this one example, we may judge what is to be thought of the whole class: that the whole sum of righteousness, and all the parts of divine worship, and everything necessary to salvation, the Lord has faithfully made clear, and clearly unfolded, in his sacred oracles, so that in them he alone is the only master to be heard. But as in external discipline and ceremonies, he has not been pleased to prescribe every particular that we ought to observe (God foresaw that this depended on the nature of the times, and that one form would not suit all ages), in them we must have recourse to the general rules which he has given, employing them to test whatever the needs of the Church may require to be adopted for order and decency. Lastly, as he has not delivered any express command, because things of this nature are not necessary to salvation, and, for the edification of the Church, should be accommodated to the varying circumstances of each age and nation, it will be proper, as the interest of the Church may require, to change and abrogate the old, as well as to introduce new forms. I confess, indeed, that we are not to innovate rashly or incessantly, or for trivial causes. Charity is the best judge of what tends to hurt or to edify: if we allow her to be guide, all things will be safe.

PROTECT THE POOR

Listen, my dear brothers: Has not God chosen those who are poor in the eyes of the world to be rich in faith and to inherit the kingdom he promised those who love him? But you have insulted the poor. Is it not the rich who are exploiting you? Are they not the ones who are dragging you into court? —James 2:5–6, NIV

James proves now by a two-fold argument that they acted preposterously when, for the sake of the rich, they despised the poor. The first part is that it is unbecoming and disgraceful to cast down those whom God exalts, and to treat reproachfully those whom he honors. As God honors the poor, then, everyone who rejects them reverses the order of God. The other argument is taken from common experience: Since the rich are for the most part a vexation to the good and innocent, it is very unreasonable to render them a reward for the wrongs they do, and it is unreasonable that they should be more approved by us than the poor, who help us more than they harm us.

God has chosen those who are poor indeed, not exclusively, but God wished to begin with them—so that he might beat down the pride of the rich. This is also what Paul says: that God has chosen not many noble, not many mighty in the world, but those who are weak, so that he might make ashamed those who are strong. In short, though God pours his grace on the rich as well as the poor, yet God's will is to prefer these to those, that the mighty might learn not to flatter themselves and that the menial and the unknown might give credit to the mercy of God, and that both might be trained up to meekness and humility.

There are, indeed, some of the rich who are just, and meek, and hate all unrighteousness; but few such people are to be found. For as humans commonly exercise their power in doing what is wrong, it hence happens that the more power any one has, the worse he or she is and the more unjust towards her or his neighbors. The more careful, then, ought the rich to be, lest they should contract any of the sickness which everywhere prevails among those of their own rank.

DEALING WITH DESPAIR

Jerusalem hath grievously sinned; therefore she is removed: all that honored her despise her, because they have seen her nakedness: yea, she sigheth, and turneth backward. Her filthiness is in her skirts; she remembereth not her last end; therefore she came down wonderfully: she had no comforter. O LORD, behold my affliction: for the enemy hath magnified himself. —Lamentations 1:8–9

When Jeremiah says that Israel did not consider her future, I understand this to mean that the Jews were so overwhelmed with despair that they did not raise up their thoughts to God's promises. For it is no ordinary source of comfort, and what even common sense dictates to us, to take a deep breath in extreme evils, and extend our thoughts farther, for misery will not always oppress us—some change for the better will happen. As then humans have a tendency thus to sustain themselves in adversities, Jeremiah says that the Jews remembered not their future; that is, they were so demented by their sorrow that they became stupified and kept no hope for the future. In short, by these words, Jeremiah means extreme despair, for the Jews were so stupified that they could not raise their minds to any hope.

Jerusalem succumbed under its miseries, so that it could not turn its thoughts to any hope, nor think of another end, but became stupid in its miseries—as people usually become desperate when they think that there is no deliverance for them.

These things ought to be carefully observed, for Satan at this day uses various means to lead us to despair. In order to distract us from all confidence in the grace of God, he sets before us extreme calamities. And when sorrow lays such hold on our minds that the hope of grace does not shine forth, from that immoderate sorrow arises impatience, which may drive us to madness. Thus we murmur and then shout against God.

Jeremiah now encourages them to pray and suggests words to them, for he speaks as if speaking for all. He exhorts them, according to the obligations of his office, to entertain good hope, and encourages them to pray.

GLORY ONLY FOR GOD

In Lystra there sat a man crippled in his feet, who was lame from birth and had never walked. He listened to Paul as he was speaking. Paul looked directly at him, saw that he had faith to be healed and called out, "Stand up on your feet!" At that, the man jumped up and began to walk. When the crowd saw what Paul had done, they shouted in the Lycaonian language, "The gods have come down to us in human form!" Barnabas they called Zeus, and Paul they called Hermes because he was the chief speaker. The priest of Zeus, whose temple was just outside the city, brought bulls and wreaths to the city gates because he and the crowd wanted to offer sacrifices to them. But when the apostles Barnabas and Paul heard of this, they tore their clothes and rushed out into the crowd, shouting: "Men, why are you doing this? We too are only men, human like you. We are bringing you good news, telling you to turn from these worthless things to the living God, who made heaven and earth and sea and everything in them."
—Acts 14:8–15, NIV

We must take good care that we do not allow honor to be given us which may darken the glory of God, but rather, so soon as any profaning of God's glory appears, let this passion break out of which we have an example in Paul and Barnabas. And though the teachers of the Church especially ought to be full of zeal, there is no one of the godly who shouldn't be sorely displeased when he or she sees the worship of God polluted or given to someone else.

Moreover, no greater injury can be done to holy people than when the honor which is taken from God is given to them, which must happen when any divine thing is ascribed and given them.

OVERCOMING BY FAITH

God is not a man, that he should lie; neither the son of man, that he should repent: hath he said, and shall he not do it? or hath he spoken, and shall he not make it good? —Numbers 23:19

We hear what Christ says, that if we seek to save our lives in this world, we shall lose them for ever. If, therefore, the real love of a future resurrection dwells in our hearts, it will easily lead us to the contempt of death. And doubtless we ought to live only so as to live to God: As soon as we are not permitted to live to God, we ought willingly and not reluctantly to meet death. Moreover, by this verse the Apostle confirms what he had said, that the saints overcome all sufferings by faith; for except their minds had been sustained by the hope of a blessed resurrection, they must have immediately failed.

We may hence also derive a needful encouragement, by which we may fortify ourselves in adversities. For we ought not to refuse the Lord's favour of being connected with so many holy men, whom we know to have been exercised and tried by many sufferings. Here indeed are recorded, not the sufferings of a few individuals, but the common persecutions of the Church, and those not for one or two years, but such as continued sometimes from grandfathers even to their grandchildren. No wonder, then, if it should please God to prove our faith at this day by similar trials; nor ought we to think that we are forsaken by him, who, we know, cared for the holy fathers who suffered the same before us.

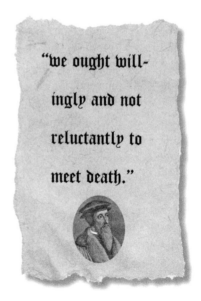

"we ought willingly and not reluctantly to meet death."

ETERNAL LIFE

Now we know that if the earthly tent we live in is destroyed, we have a building from God, an eternal house in heaven, not built by human hands. —2 Corinthians 5:1, NIV

Paul's goal here is to correct in us impatience, dread, and dislike of the cross; contempt for what we consider to be "beneath ourselves"; in two words, "pride" and "weakness," and this can only be accomplished by raising up our minds as high as heaven, through contempt of the world. Now he relies on two arguments. On the one hand, he shows the miserable condition of mankind in this life, and on the other hand, the supreme and perfect blessedness which awaits believers in heaven after death. For what is it that keeps humans so firmly bound in a misplaced attachment to this life, but their deceiving themselves with a false imagination—thinking themselves happy in living here? On the other hand, it is not enough to be aware of the miseries of this life, if we do not at the same time keep in view the felicity and glory of the future life. This is common to good and bad alike—that both desire to live. This, also, is common to both— that when they consider how many and how great miseries they are here exposed to, they often groan, often deplore their condition, and desire a remedy for their evils. As, however, all people naturally view death with horror, unbelievers never willingly quit this life, except when they throw it off in disgust or despair. Believers, on the other hand, depart willingly, because they have a better hope set before them beyond this world.

This knowledge does not spring from the human intellect, but takes its rise from the revelation of the Holy Spirit. Hence it is particular to believers. Even the heathens had some idea of the immortality of the soul, but there was not one of them that had assurance of it.

Besides, it is to be observed that this knowledge is not merely of a general kind, as though believers were merely in a general way persuaded that the children of God will be in a better condition after death, and had no assurance for themselves specifically; for how little help this would give in consoling believers! On the contrary, every one must have a knowledge particular to herself or himself, for this, and this only, can inspire me to meet death with cheerfulness—if I am fully persuaded that I am departing to a better life.

REDEMPTION

The wolf will live with the lamb, the leopard will lie down with the goat, the calf and the lion and the yearling together; and a little child will lead them. —Isaiah 11:6, NIV

Isaiah again returns to describe the character and habits of those who have submitted to Christ. The Prophet's discourse amounts to a promise that there will be a blessed restoration of the world. He describes the order which was at the beginning, before human unbelief produced the unhappy and melancholy change under which we groan. From where comes the cruelty of brutes, which prompts the stronger to seize and tear and devour with dreadful violence the weaker animals? There would certainly have been no discord among the creatures of God, if they had remained in their first and original condition. When they exercise cruelty towards each other, and the weak need to be protected against the strong, it is an evidence of the disorder which has sprung from the sinfulness of man. Christ having come in order to reconcile the world to God by the removal of the curse, it is not without reason that the restoration of a perfect state is credited to him; "Christ will come to drive away everything hurtful out of the world, and to restore to its former beauty the world which lay under the curse." Though Isaiah says that the wild and the tame beasts will live in harmony so that the blessing of God may be clearly and fully manifested, yet he mainly means what I have said: that the people of Christ will have no need to do injury, no fierceness or cruelty. They were formerly like lions or leopards, but will now be like sheep or lambs; for they will have laid aside every cruel and brutish disposition.

What does he mean when he says, "And a little child will lead them?" This means that beasts which formerly were cruel and untameable, will be ready to yield cheerful obedience, so that there will be no need of violence to restrain their fierceness. Yet we must notice the spiritual meaning that all who become Christ's followers will obey Christ, though they may formerly have been savage wild beasts, and will obey him in such a manner that as soon as he lifts his finger, they will follow his footsteps, as it is said that his people shall be willing. Let us, therefore, permit ourselves to be ruled and governed by him, and let us willingly submit to those whom he has appointed over us, though they appear to be like little children.

LOVE SINCERELY

Now that you have purified yourselves by obeying the truth so that you have sincere love for your brothers, love one another deeply, from the heart. For you have been born again, not of perishable seed, but of imperishable, through the living and enduring word of God.
—1 Peter 1:22–23, NIV
The goal of this command is love, which comes from a pure heart and a good conscience and a sincere faith. —1 Timothy 1:5, NIV

Paul briefly reminds us what God especially requires in our life, and the mark to which all our endeavors should be directed. And this is what we ought more carefully to notice, because the world makes its own idea of holiness to consist of the smallest trifles, and almost overlooks this, the chief thing. We see how the [some religious groups] tire themselves out with a thousand invented superstitions: in the meantime, the last thing is that love which God especially commends. This, then, is the reason why Peter calls our attention to it, when speaking of a life rightly formed. He had before spoken of the mortification of the flesh, and of our conformity with the will of God; but he now reminds us of

what God would have us to cultivate through life: mutual love towards one another; for by that we testify also that we love God; and by this evidence God proves who they are who really love him.

He calls it "sincere," as Paul calls faith in 1 Timothy 1:5; for nothing is more difficult than to love our neighbors in sincerity. For the love of ourselves rules in us, which is full of hypocrisy; and besides, every one carefully considers the love which they show to others in terms of their own advantage, and not by the rule of doing good. Peter adds "deeply," for the more lazy we are by nature, the more ought we all to stimulate ourselves to fervor and sincerity, and that not only once, but more and more daily.

EVENTUAL CORRECTION

The righteous man wisely considereth the house of the wicked: but God overthroweth the wicked for their wickedness. —Proverbs 21:12

When the faithful see that it is well with the wicked, they are necessarily tempted to be envious; and this is a very dangerous trial; for present happiness is what all desire. Hence the Spirit of God carefully dwells on this, in many places, as well as in the thirty-seventh Psalm, lest the faithful should envy the prosperity of the ungodly. The same is what Peter speaks of, for he shews that afflictions ought to be calmly borne by the children of God, when they compare the lot of others with their own. But he takes it as granted that God is the judge of the world, and that, therefore, no one can escape his hand with impunity. He hence infers, that a dreadful vengeance will soon overtake those whose condition seems now favorable. The design of what he says, as I have already stated, is to shew that the children of God should not faint under the bitterness of present evils, but that they ought, on the contrary, calmly to bear their afflictions for a short time, as the issue will be salvation, while the ungodly will have to exchange a fading and fleeting prosperity for eternally perdition.

But the argument is from the less to the greater; for if God spares not his own children whom he loves and who obey him, how dreadful will be his severity against enemies and such as are rebellious! There is, then, nothing better than to obey the Gospel, so that God may kindly correct us by his paternal hand for our salvation.

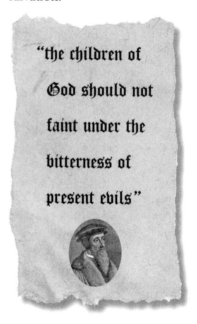

"the children of God should not faint under the bitterness of present evils"

THE PRICE OF REDEMPTION

For you know that it was not with perishable things such as silver or gold that you were redeemed from the empty way of life handed down to you from your forefathers, but with the precious blood of Christ, a lamb without blemish or defect.
—1 Peter 1:18–19, NIV

here is another reason, drawn from the price of our redemption, which we ought always and continually to remember whenever our salvation happens to be spoken of. To anyone who rejects or despises the grace of the Gospel, not only that person's own salvation worthless, but also the blood of Christ is worthless, by which God has manifested its value. But we know how dreadfully sacrilegious it is to regard the blood of the Son of God as something common. There is thus nothing which ought so much to stimulate us to the practice of holiness, as the memory of this price of our redemption.

For the sake of amplifying what he said before, he mentions silver and gold in contrast, so that we may know that the whole world and all things that the human race declares to be precious are nothing to the excellence and value of this price. But he says that they had been redeemed from their vain way of life in order that we might know that the whole life of a human, until that person is converted to Christ, is a ruinous labyrinth of wanderings. Peter also suggests that it is not through our own personal merits that we are restored to the right way, but because it is God's will that the price [of Jesus's blood] offered for our salvation should be effective on our behalf. From this we see that the blood of Christ is not only the pledge of our salvation, but also the cause of our calling.

LIVING FAITH

What good is it, my brothers, if a man claims to have faith but has no deeds? Can such faith save him? Suppose a brother or sister is without clothes and daily food. If one of you says to him, "Go, I wish you well; keep warm and well fed," but does nothing about his physical needs, what good is it? In the same way, faith by itself, if it is not accompanied by action, is dead. —James 2:15–17, NIV

When he asked, "Can such faith save him?" this is the same as though James had said that we do not attain salvation by a frigid and bare knowledge of God, which everyone knows is most true. For salvation comes to us by faith for this reason: because it joins us to God. And this comes in no other way than by being united to the body of Christ, so that, living through his Spirit, we are also governed by him. There is no such thing as this in the dead image of faith. There is then no wonder that James denies that salvation is connected with it.

James then takes an example from what was connected with his subject, for James had been exhorting his audience to do the duties of love. If any one, on the contrary, boasted of being satisfied by faith without works, James compares this shadowy faith to the saying of someone who bids a famished person to be filled without supplying her or him with the food of which she or he is destitute. As, then, someone who sends away a poor person with words and offers no help mocks that person, so do those who devise for themselves faith without works, and without any of the duties of religion, trifle with God.

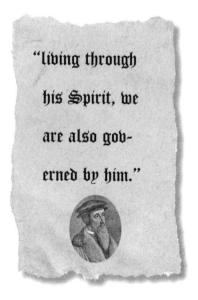

"living through his Spirit, we are also governed by him."

KEEPING PLEASURE UNDER CONTROL

Woe to those who rise early in the morning to run after their drinks, who stay up late at night till they are inflamed with wine. They have harps and lyres at their banquets, tambourines and flutes and wine, but they have no regard for the deeds of the LORD, no respect for the work of his hands. —Isaiah 5:11–12, NIV

saiah adds the instruments of pleasures by which people addicted to excess provoke their appetite. Now, Isaiah does not blame music— for it is a skill which ought not to be despised—but he describes a nation swimming in every kind of luxury and too much disposed to indulge in pleasures.

When Isaiah says, "They have no regard for the deeds of the LORD," it is as if he had said, "They are as faithful in their luxurious indulgence, and as much devoted to it, as if this had been the purpose for which they were born and reared; and they do not consider why the LORD supplies them with what is necessary." Humans were not born to eat and drink and wallow in luxury, but to obey God, to worship him devoutly, to acknowledge his goodness, and to endeavor to do what is pleasing in his sight. But when they give themselves up to luxury, when they dance, and sing, and have no other object in view than to spend their life in the highest mirth, they are worse than beasts. For they do not consider for what end God created them, in what manner he governs this world by his providence, and to what end all the actions of our life ought to be directed. It is enough to know that all who are obsessed with pleasure are here subjected by the Prophet to the reproach that they have voluntarily become like brute beasts, when they do not direct their minds to God, who is the author of life.

HUMBLE IN THE SIGHT OF GOD

Behold every one that is proud, and abase him. Look on every one that is proud, and bring him low; and tread down the wicked in their place.
—Job 40:11b–12

t is a most grievous threatening, when he says, that all who seek to elevate themselves, shall have God as their enemy, who will lay them low. But, on the contrary, he says of the humble, that God will be propitious and favourable to them. We are to imagine that God has two hands; the one, which like a hammer beats down and breaks in pieces those who raise up themselves; and the other which raises up the humble who willingly let down themselves, and is like a firm prop to sustain them. Were we really convinced of this, and had it deeply fixed in our minds, who of us would dare by pride to urge war with God? But the hope of impunity now makes us fearlessly to raise up our horn to heaven. Let, then, this declaration of Peter be as a celestial thunderbolt to make men humble.

But he calls those humble, who being emptied of every confidence in their own power, wisdom, and righteousness, seeks every good from God alone. Since there is no coming to God except in this way, who, having lost his own glory, ought not willingly to humble himself.

> "he says of the humble, that God will be propitious and favourable to them."

334

JESUS' SELF-EMPTYING

Your attitude should be the same as that of Christ Jesus: who, being in very nature God, did not consider equality with God something to be grasped, but made himself nothing, taking the very nature of a servant, being made in human likeness. And being found in appearance as a man, he humbled himself and became obedient to death—even death on a cross! —Philippians 2:5–8, NIV

Christ's humility consisted in his abasing himself from the highest point of glory to the lowest shame; our humility consists in refraining from exalting ourselves by a false pride. Jesus gave up his right; all that is required of us is that we do not assume for ourselves more than we ought. Hence he sets out with this: Inasmuch as Jesus was in the form of God, Paul does not reckon it an unlawful thing for Jesus to show himself in that form, yet Jesus emptied himself. Since, then, the Son of God descended from so great a height, how unreasonable that we, who are nothing, should be lifted up with pride!

There would have been no wrong done even if Jesus had shown himself to be equal with God. For when Paul says Jesus "did not consider," it is as though Paul had said, "Jesus knew, indeed, that this was lawful and right for him," that we might know that his degradation was voluntary, not necessary.

Even this was great humility—that from being Lord he became a servant. But Paul says that Jesus went farther than this, because, while he was not only immortal but also the Lord of life and death, he nevertheless became obedient to his Father, even so far as to endure death. This was extreme abasement, especially when we take into view the kind of death [Jesus suffered], which Paul immediately mentions in order to enhance it. For by dying in this manner, Jesus was not only covered with shame in the sight of humans, but was also accursed in the sight of God. It is assuredly such a pattern of humility as ought to absorb the attention of all mankind—so far is it from being possible to unfold it in words in a manner suitable to its dignity.

THE USE OF FASTING

Paul and Barnabas appointed elders for them in each church and, with prayer and fasting, committed them to the Lord, in whom they had put their trust. —Acts 14:23, NIV

they had a double goal and reason for their prayer. The first was that God would direct them with the spirit of wisdom and discretion to choose the best and most appropriate men, for they knew that they were not furnished with great enough wisdom to be sure they were not deceived. Neither did they put so much trust in their hard work as not to realize that the principal point was the blessing of God. And if this rule is to be observed in all circumstances whenever the government of the Church is in hand, which depends wholly on God's will and pleasure, we must make sure that we attempt nothing unless we have God for our guide and governor. And the second goal of their prayer was that God would furnish those chosen pastors with the necessary gifts. They fast, likewise, so that it will help to stir up the fervency of their prayers, for we know how great our coldness is otherwise. Not because it is always necessary that we pray fasting, seeing that God invites even those who are full to give thanks, but when we are urged by any necessity to pray more fervently than we are used to, this is a very profitable aid. And it is profitable for us to notice this use, and other uses of fasting—seeing that it is worth nothing itself, neither is it of any importance with God, except inasmuch as it is applied to another goal.

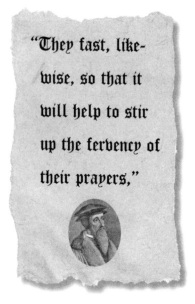

"They fast, likewise, so that it will help to stir up the fervency of their prayers,"

BUSINESS REPLY MAIL
FIRST-CLASS MAIL   PERMIT NO. 91   DAYTON, OH

POSTAGE WILL BE PAID BY ADDRESSEE

CATECHIST

PO BOX 49726
DAYTON, OH 45449-9913

CATECHIST

Yes! Start my one-year (7 issues) subscription to CATECHIST magazine for only $24.95. Each issue will be packed with activities, prayer services, crafts, Gospel reflections, and much more to make teaching easier and my classes more exciting!

☐ **Please bill me.**   ☐ **Payment enclosed.**

Name _____

Email Address _____ @ _____

Title   ☐ Catechist   ☐ DRE/CRE   ☐ Teacher   ☐ Other ____

Parish/School _____

Address _____

City/State/Zip _____

Fax Number _____ Phone Number _____

GUARANTEE: If CATECHIST doesn't live up to my expectations, I can cancel my subscription and receive a full refund on all unmailed issues left in my subscription.

All orders are payable in US dollars. Outside US, add $5.00 per subscription. Canadian orders add GST. Offer expires 10/31/06. Need multiple subscriptions? Call 1.800.558.2292, ext. 1128 and ask about our bulk prices.

CODE: B620
CODE: B630

THE FIRE OF GOD

The appearance of the living creatures was like burning coals of fire or like torches. Fire moved back and forth among the creatures; it was bright, and lightning flashed out of it.
—Ezekiel 1:13, NIV

Something divine ought to shine forth in this vision, because God set forth the face of a man and of an ox, of an eagle and of a lion, and in this he lowers himself to the stupidity of the people and also to the Prophet, because, as we are humans, our minds cannot penetrate beyond the sky. And from this we see how kindly, how tolerantly God deals with us. For, as on his part, he sees how small is our understanding, so he comes down to us

The Prophet now expresses the form of the fire more clearly: that the coals were like lamps. For lamps send out their brightness to a distance, and seem to scatter their rays in every direction, like the sun when it shines through the serene air. On the whole, the Prophet means, that the fire was not dark but full of sparks, and shows that rays were diffused like lighted lamps. Afterwards, he says that they walked between the living creatures. The Prophet sees, as it were, a fiery form moving among the living creatures themselves. Thus God wished to show the power and life of his own spirit in all actions, that we should not measure it in our manner, according to the depravity which is innate with us.

Afterwards he says that the fire was bright, and that lightning came from it. The Prophet means something very special here, as if he had said that the fire is not like that arising from lighted wood, but that it was resplendent, from which we may readily understand that God here sets before us his visible glory: and for the same reason Ezekiel says that lightning came from the fire. But we know that lightning cannot be seen without fear, for in a moment the air seems inflamed, just as if God would in some way or other absorb the world: hence the appearance of lightning is always terrible to us. Therefore when God wishes to become familiarly known to us, he strips us of all pride and all security: lastly, humility is the beginning of true intelligence. Now we understand why lightning issued from the fire: he afterwards confirms this.

AVOIDING JUDGING OTHERS

We all stumble in many ways. If anyone is never at fault in what he says, he is a perfect man, able to keep his whole body in check. When we put bits into the mouths of horses to make them obey us, we can turn the whole animal. Or take ships as an example. Although they are so large and are driven by strong winds, they are steered by a very small rudder wherever the pilot wants to go. Likewise the tongue is a small part of the body, but it makes great boasts. Consider what a great forest is set on fire by a small spark. —James 3:2–5, NIV

After having said that there is no one who does not sin in many things, he now shows that the disease of evil-speaking is more odious than other sins. For by saying that someone who doesn't offend in speech is perfect, James suggests that the restraining of the tongue is a great virtue, one of the chief virtues. Hence those persons act most perversely who curiously examine every fault, even the least, and yet so grossly indulge themselves.

James then indirectly touches on the hypocrisy of censors, because in examining themselves they omit the chief thing, and that was of great importance: their evil-speaking. For those who reprove others pretend a passion for perfect holiness, but they ought to have begun with the tongue if they wished to be perfect. As they make no attempt at bridling the tongue, but, on the contrary, bite and tear others, they exhibit only a fictitious holiness. It is hence evident that they are the most reprehensible of all, because they neglect a primary virtue.

By two comparisons James proves that a large part of true perfection is in the tongue, and that it exercises dominion, as he has just said, over the whole life. He compares the tongue—first to a bridle, and then to a helm of a ship. Though a horse is a ferocious animal, yet it is turned about at the will of its rider because it is bridled; no less can the tongue serve to govern man. So also with regard to the helm of a ship, which guides a large vessel and overrides the impulsiveness of winds. Though the tongue is a small member of the body, yet it does much toward regulating a person's life.

THE RIGHT WAY TO ARGUE FOR FAITH

A group of Epicurean and Stoic philosophers began to dispute with him. Some of them asked, "What is this babbler trying to say?" Others remarked, "He seems to be advocating foreign gods." They said this because Paul was preaching the good news about Jesus and the resurrection. Then they took him and brought him to a meeting of the Areopagus, where they said to him, "May we know what this new teaching is that you are presenting? You are bringing some strange ideas to our ears, and we want to know what they mean." (All the Athenians and the foreigners who lived there spent their time doing nothing but talking about and listening to the latest ideas.)
—Acts 17:18–21, NIV

Luke adds now that Paul began to combat with the philosophers. Paul himself had commanded godly teachers to be furnished with spiritual weapons, with which they may valiantly defend the truth if any enemies set themselves against it (Titus 1:9). For it is not always our choice whom we must deal with, but the Lord often allows stubborn and argumentative persons to arise to exercise us, that by their denials the truth may more plainly appear. Yet the end shall show that Paul did not dispute sophistically, neither was he carried away into any unprofitable and wasteful argumentation, but he lived by that modesty which he himself commands in other places. And thus must we do, so that by refuting vain and bad arguments meekly and modestly, we may utter that which is sound and true; and we must always avoid this danger, that ambition or desire to show off our cleverness do not wrap us in superfluous and pointless contests of wit.

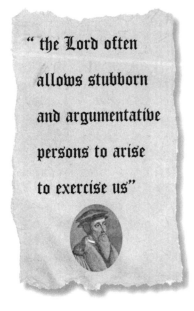

" the Lord often allows stubborn and argumentative persons to arise to exercise us"

FEAR AND TREMBLING

Therefore, my dear friends, as you have always obeyed—not only in my presence, but now much more in my absence—continue to work out your salvation with fear and trembling, for it is God who works in you to will and to act according to his good purpose.
—Philippians 2:12–13, NIV

Paul concludes the whole of the exhortation with a general statement: that they should humble themselves under the Lord's hand, for that will very readily ensure that, laying aside all arrogance, they will be gentle and indulgent to each other. This is the only befitting way in which the human mind may learn gentleness, when someone who, having viewed himself or herself apart, pleased in his or her hiding-places, comes to examine herself or himself as compared with God.

Paul would have the Philippians testify and approve their obedience by being submissive and humble. Now the source of humility is this: acknowledging how miserable we are, and how devoid of all good. Paul calls them to do so in his statement, "with fear and trambling." For where comes pride, but from the assurance produced by blind confidence when we please ourselves and are more puffed up with confidence in our own virtue, than we are prepared to rest upon the grace of God? In contrast with this vice is the fear to which he exhorts [the Philippians].

Now it seems as if the grace of God [were] a sweet occasion for rest; for if God works in us, why should we not indulge ourselves at our ease? There is nothing that ought to train us more to modesty and fear, than our being taught that it is by the grace of God alone that we stand, and will instantly fall down if he even in the slightest degree withdraw his hand. Confidence in ourselves produces carelessness and arrogance. We know from experience that all who confide in their own strength grow insolent through presumption and, at the same time, devoid of worries, resign themselves to sleep. The remedy for both evils is when, distrusting ourselves, we depend entirely on God alone.

CARRYING BURDENS

Carry each other's burdens, and in this way you will fulfill the law of Christ. If anyone thinks he is something when he is nothing, he deceives himself. —Galatians 2:2–3, NIV

The weaknesses or sins, under which we groan, are called burdens. This is singularly appropriate in an exhortation to kind behavior, for nature dictates to us that those who bend under a burden ought to be relieved. Paul tells us to bear the burdens. We must not indulge or overlook the sins by which our brethren are pressed down, but relieve them—which can only be done by mild and friendly correction.

The word "law," when applied here to Christ, serves the place of an argument. There is an implied contrast between the law of Christ and the law of Moses. "If you desire to keep a law, Christ gives you a law which you are bound to prefer to all others, and that is to cherish kindness towards each other. Whoever lacks this has nothing." On the other hand, Paul tells us that when everyone compassionately assists her or his neighbor the law of Christ is fulfilled; by which he suggests that every thing which does not proceed from love is superfluous. But as no one performs in every respect what Paul requires, we are still at a distance from perfection. The person who comes the nearest to it compared to others, is yet far distant compared to God.

Paul's meaning in verse three is clear. The phrase "when he is nothing" appears at first view to mean: "if any person, who is in reality nothing, claims to be something," as there are many people of no real worth who are elated by a foolish admiration of themselves. But the meaning is more general: "Since all people are nothing, anyone who wishes to appear something and persuades himself that he is somebody, deceives himself." First, then, Paul declares that we have nothing of our own of which we have a right to boast, but lack everything good, so that all our glorying is mere vanity. Secondly, Paul infers that those who claim something as their own deceive themselves. Now, since nothing arouses our indignation more than that others should lie to us, it seems the highest folly that we should willingly lie to ourselves. This consideration will render us much more candid with others.

THE LORD'S TABLE

While they were eating, Jesus took bread, gave thanks and broke it, and gave it to his disciples, saying, "Take and eat; this is my body." Then he took the cup, gave thanks and offered it to them, saying, "Drink from it, all of you. This is my blood of the new covenant, which is poured out for many for the forgiveness of sins." —Matthew 26:26–28, NIV

after God has received us into his family, it is not that he may regard us in the light of servants, but of children, performing the role of a kind and anxious parent, and providing for our well-being during the whole course of our lives. And, not contented with this, he has been pleased by a pledge to assure us of his continued generosity. To this end, he has given another sacrament to his Church by the hand of his only-begotten Son: a spiritual feast, at which Christ testifies that he himself is living bread on which our souls feed, for a true and blessed immortality. The signs are bread and wine, which represent the invisible food which we receive from the body and blood of Christ. For as God, regenerating us in baptism, ingrafts us into the fellowship of his Church, and makes us his by adoption, so we have said that he performs the office of a kind parent, in continually supplying the food by which he may sustain and preserve us in the life to which he has begotten us by his Word. Moreover, Christ is the only food of our soul, and, therefore, our heavenly Father invites us to him, that, refreshed by communion with him, we may ever and anon gather new vigor until we reach the heavenly immortality. But as this mystery of the secret union of Christ with believers is incomprehensible by nature, he exhibits its figure and image in visible signs adapted to our capacity. He makes it as certain to us as if it were seen by the eye; the familiarity of the similitude giving it access to even the dullest minds, and showing that souls are fed by Christ just as the bodily life is sustained by bread and wine. We now, therefore, understand the end which this mystical benediction has in view: to assure us that the body of Christ was once sacrificed for us, so that we may now eat it, and, eating, feel within ourselves the power of that one sacrifice—that his blood was once shed for us so as to be our perpetual drink.

342

BE HOLY

*The LORD said to Moses, "Speak to the entire assembly of Israel and
say to them: `Be holy because I, the LORD your God, am holy.'"
—Leviticus 19:1–2, NIV*

The Scripture system of which we speak aims chiefly at two goals. The first is, that the love of righteousness, to which we are by no means naturally inclined, may be instilled and implanted into our minds. The latter is, to prescribe a rule which will prevent us while in the pursuit of righteousness from going astray. It has numerous admirable methods of recommending righteousness. With what better foundation can it begin than by reminding us that we must be holy, because God is holy? For when we were scattered abroad like lost sheep, wandering through the labyrinth of this world, he brought us back again to his own fold. When mention is made of our union with God, let us remember that holiness must be the bond; not that we came into communion with him by the merit of holiness— we ought rather first to cleave to him, in order that, pervaded with his holiness, we may follow wherever he calls—but because it greatly concerns his glory not to have any fellowship with wickedness and impurity. Thus he tells us that this is the end of our calling, the goal to which we ought ever to have respect if we would answer the call of God. For what good is it that we were rescued from the iniquity and pollution of the world into which we were plunged, if we allow ourselves, during our whole lives, to wallow in them?

> "When mention is made of our union with God, let us remember that holiness must be the bond;"

WORLDLY THINGS

What I mean, brothers, is that the time is short. From now on those who have wives should live as if they had none; those who mourn, as if they did not; those who are happy, as if they were not; those who buy something, as if it were not theirs to keep; those who use the things of the world, as if not engrossed in them. For this world in its present form is passing away. —1 Corinthians 7:29–31, NIV

by these basics we are at the same time well instructed by Scripture in the proper use of earthly blessings, a subject which, in forming a scheme of life, should not be neglected. For if we are to live, we must use the necessary supports of life; nor can we even shun those things which seem more useful for delight than necessity. We must therefore observe a balance, that we may use them with a pure conscience, whether for necessity or for pleasure. This the Lord prescribes by his Word, when he tells us that to his people the present life is a kind of pilgrimage by which they hasten to the heavenly kingdom. If we are only to pass through the earth, there can be no doubt that we are to use its blessings only in so far as they assist our progress, rather than retard it. But as this is a slippery place, and there is great danger of falling on either side, let us fix our feet where we can stand safely. There have been some good and holy people who, when they saw intemperance and luxury perpetually carried to excess wherever they were not strictly curbed, and were desirous to correct such a pernicious evil, imagined that there was no other way than to allow humans to use earthly goods only in so far as they were necessary: a counsel pious indeed, but unnecessarily austere. Many also in the present day, seeking a pretext for carnal intemperance in the use of external things, so that they could at the same time pave the way for licentiousness, take for granted that this liberty is not to be restrained by any modification, but left to everyone's conscience to use them as far as that person thinks lawful. I indeed confess that here consciences neither can nor ought to be bound by fixed and definite laws; but that Scripture having laid down general rules for the legitimate uses we should keep within the limits which they prescribe.

KEEPING AN OPEN MIND

Some men came down from Judea to Antioch and were teaching the brothers: "Unless you are circumcised, according to the custom taught by Moses, you cannot be saved." This brought Paul and Barnabas into sharp dispute and debate with them. So Paul and Barnabas were appointed, along with some other believers, to go up to Jerusalem to see the apostles and elders about this question. The church sent them on their way, and as they traveled through Phoenicia and Samaria, they told how the Gentiles had been converted. This news made all the brothers very glad. When they came to Jerusalem, they were welcomed by the church and the apostles and elders, to whom they reported every-thing God had done through them. Then some of the believers who belonged to the party of the Pharisees stood up and said, "The Gentiles must be circumcised and required to obey the law of Moses." The apos-tles and elders met to consider this question. —Acts 15:1–6, NIV

he cloak and [rank] of the men who came down from Judea was very forceful in deceiving even good people then. Jerusalem was honored not without cause among all churches, for the Gospel had been diverted, as it were, by pipes and conduits from that fountain. They had seen that circumcision and other cere-monies of the Law were ob-served at Jerusalem, and wher-ever they end up, they can put up with nothing which does not conform to this, as if the example of one church bound all the rest of the churches with a certain law.

Therefore, we must beware first of this plague, that some people do not prescribe a law to others based on their own manner, so that the example of one church doesn't become a prejudice of a common rule. Also, we must use another cau-tion: that the [importance of certain people] does not hin-der or darken the examination of an issue or problem. Therefore, there is one only remedy: to come to search out the matter with sound judg-ments.

CHRIST'S HUMANNESS

For there is one God and one mediator between God and men, the man Christ Jesus, who gave himself as a ransom for all men—the testimony given in its proper time. —1 Timothy 2:5–6, NIV

When he declares that Christ is a man, Paul does not deny that the Mediator is God, but, intending to point out the bond of our union with God, Paul mentions the human nature rather than the divine. This ought to be carefully observed. From the beginning, humans, by creating this or that mediator for themselves, departed farther from God; and the reason was that, being prejudiced in favor of the wrong idea that God was at a great distance from them, they did not know where to turn. Paul remedies this evil when he represents God as present with us; for he has descended even to us, so that we do not need to seek him above the clouds. And, indeed, if it were deeply impressed on the hearts of all that the Son of God holds out to us the hand of a brother, and that we are united to him by the fellowship of our nature, in order that, out of our low condition, he may raise us to heaven, who would not choose to keep by this straight road, instead of wandering in uncertain and stormy paths! Accordingly, whenever we ought to pray to God, if we remember that exalted and unapproachable majesty let us, at the same time, remember "the man Christ," who gently invites us and takes us, as it were, by the hand, in order that the Father, who had been the object of terror and alarm, may be reconciled by him and made friendly to us. This is the only key to open for us the gate of the heavenly kingdom, so that we may appear in the presence of God with confidence.

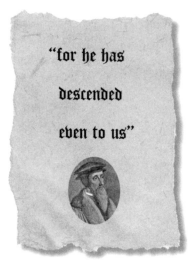

"for he has descended even to us"

THE WORKINGS OF FAITH

After much discussion, Peter got up and addressed them: "Brothers, you know that some time ago God made a choice among you that the Gentiles might hear from my lips the message of the gospel and believe. God, who knows the heart, showed that he accepted them by giving the Holy Spirit to them, just as he did to us. He made no distinction between us and them, for he purified their hearts by faith. Now then, why do you try to test God by putting on the necks of the disciples a yoke that neither we nor our fathers have been able to bear? No! We believe it is through the grace of our Lord Jesus that we are saved, just as they are." —Acts 15:7–9, NIV

Surely it is the job of faith to bring unto us that which is proper to Christ, and to make it ours by free participation—so that there is a mutual relationship between faith and the grace of Christ. For faith does not itself make us clean as if it were a virtue or quality poured into our souls, but because it receives that cleanness which is offered in Christ. We must also note the phrase, that God "purified the hearts"; by this phrase Luke both makes God the author of faith, and he teaches also that cleanness is God's gift. To make short, he signifies to us the thing that is given to humans by the grace of God is what they cannot give to themselves. But since we said that faith takes that thing from Christ which it transfers into us, we must now see how the grace of Christ makes us clean so that we may please God. And there is a double manner of purging: because Christ offers and presents us clean and just in the sight of his Father, by putting away our sins daily, which he has once purged by his blood; secondly, because, by killing the lusts of the flesh by his Spirit, he reforms us unto holiness of life.

THE MIND EXISTS TO SEEK GOD

Paul then stood up in the meeting of the Areopagus and said: "Men of Athens! I see that in every way you are very religious. For as I walked around and looked carefully at your objects of worship, I even found an altar with this inscription: TO AN UNKNOWN GOD. Now what you worship as something unknown I am going to proclaim to you. The God who made the world and everything in it is the Lord of heaven and earth and does not live in temples built by hands. And he is not served by human hands, as if he needed anything, because he himself gives all men life and breath and everything else. From one man he made every nation of men, that they should inhabit the whole earth; and he determined the times set for them and the exact places where they should live. God did this so that men would seek him and perhaps reach out for him and find him, though he is not far from each one of us."
—Acts 17:22–27, NIV

The last sentence has two parts: that it is humanity's duty to seek God, and that God himself comes forth to meet us, and shows himself by such visible signs that we can have no excuse for our ignorance. Therefore, let us remember that those people wickedly abuse this life and that they are unworthy to dwell upon earth who do not apply their studies to seek God. And, surely, nothing is more absurd than that humans should be ignorant of their Author, who are given the ability to understand principally for this use. And we must especially note the goodness of God, in that he does so closely insinuate himself that even the blind may grope after him. Wherever humans cast their eyes, upward or downward, they must necessarily light upon lively and also infinite images of God's power, wisdom, and goodness. For God has not darkly shadowed his glory in the creation of the world, but he has everywhere engraved such manifest marks that even blind people may know them by groping. From this we gather that humans are not only blind but dumb as stones when, being helped by such excellent testimonies, they profit nothing.

JOY AND SORROW

In this you greatly rejoice, though now for a little while you may have had to suffer grief in all kinds of trials. —1 Peter 1:6, NIV

It seems somewhat inconsistent when he says that the faithful, who exulted with joy, were at the same time sorrowful, for these are contrary feelings. But the faithful know by experience how these things can exist together, much better than can be expressed in words. However, to explain the matter in a few words, we may say that the faithful are not logs of wood, nor have they so emptied themselves of human feelings, that they are not hurt by sorrow, scared by danger, and smitten by poverty as an evil, and by persecutions as hard and difficult to be borne. Hence they experience sorrow from trouble, but it is so mitigated by faith that they cease not at the same time to rejoice. Thus sorrow does not prevent their joy but, on the contrary, gives place to it. Again, though joy overcomes sorrow, yet it does not put an end to it, for it does not empty us of humanity. And hence it appears what true patience is: Its beginning and, as it were, its root is the knowledge of God's blessings, especially of that free adoption with which he has favored us—for all who raise their minds to it find it an easy thing calmly to bear all evils. For whence is it that our minds are pressed down with grief, except that we have no participation in spiritual things? But all they who regard their troubles as necessary trials for their salvation not only rise above them, but also turn them to an occasion of joy.

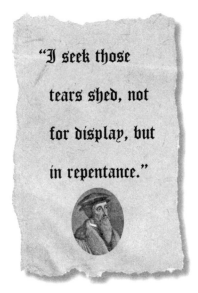

"I seek those tears shed, not for display, but in repentance."

THE CHURCH

You said, "I have made a covenant with my chosen one, I have sworn to David my servant, I will establish your line forever and make your throne firm through all generations." Selah. —Psalm 98:3–4, NIV

It is necessary to consider what the holiness is in which [the Church] excels, lest by refusing to acknowledge any church, save one that is completely perfect, we leave no Church at all. The Lord is daily smoothing its wrinkles, and wiping away its spots. Hence, it follows that its holiness is not yet perfect. Such, then, is the holiness of the Church: It makes daily progress, but is not yet perfect; it daily advances, but as yet has not reached the goal. Let us not understand [the Bible] in such as way as to think no blemish remains in the members of the Church— but only that with their whole hearts they aspire after holiness and perfect purity—and hence that purity which they have not yet fully attained is, by the kindness of God, attributed to them. And though the indications of such a kind of holiness existing among men are too rare, we must understand that at no period since the world began has the Lord been without his Church, nor ever shall be till the final consummation of all things. Let us learn, from her single title of Mother, how useful, nay, how necessary the knowledge of the Church is, since there is no other means of entering into life unless she conceive us in the womb and give us birth, unless she nourish us at her breasts, and, in short, keep us under her charge and government until, divested of mortal flesh, we become like the angels. For our weakness does not permit us to leave the school until we have spent our whole lives as scholars.

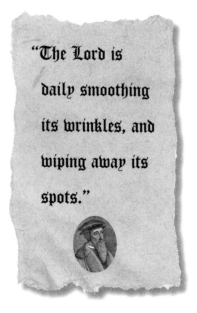

"The Lord is daily smoothing its wrinkles, and wiping away its spots."

INTEGRITY

Be perfect, therefore, as your heavenly Father is perfect.
—Matthew 5:48, NIV

I do not insist that the life of the Christian shall breathe nothing but the perfect Gospel, though this is to be desired, and ought to be attempted. I insist not so strictly on evangelical perfection, as to refuse to acknowledge as a Christian anyone who has not attained it. In this way everyone would be excluded from the Church, since there is no one who is not far removed from this perfection, while many, who have made but little progress, would be undeservedly rejected. What then? Let us set this before our eye as the end at which we ought to aim, constantly: For you cannot divide the matter with God, undertaking part of what his Word enjoins, and omitting part at your own pleasure. For, in the first place, God uniformly recommends integrity as the principal part of his worship, meaning by integrity real singleness of mind, devoid of gloss and fiction, and to this is opposed a double mind; as if it had been said that the spiritual commencement of a good life is when the internal affections are sincerely devoted to God, in the cultivation of holiness and justice. But seeing that, in this earthly prison of the body, no one is supplied with enough strength to hasten in his course perfectly, while most are so oppressed with weakness that hesitating, and halting, and even crawling on the ground, they make little progress, let every one of us go as far as his or her humble ability allows, and finish the journey once begun. No one will travel so badly as not daily to make some degree of progress. Let us not despair because of the small measure of success. However little the success may correspond with our wish, our labor is not lost when today is better than yesterday, provided with true singleness of mind we keep our aim, and aspire to the goal, not speaking flattering things to ourselves, nor indulging our vices, but making it our constant endeavor to become better, until we attain to goodness itself. If during the whole course of our life we seek and follow, we shall at length attain it, when relieved from the infirmity of flesh we are admitted to full fellowship with God.

ENJOYMENT

He makes grass grow for the cattle, and plants for man to cultivate—
bringing forth food from the earth: wine that gladdens the heart of
man, oil to make his face shine, and bread that sustains his heart.
—*Psalm 104:14–15, NIV*

Let this be our principle: that we do not err in the use of the gifts of Providence when we put them to the end for which their author made and destined them, since he created them for our good and not for our destruction. No one will keep the true path better than someone who shall have this end carefully in view. Now then, if we consider for what end God created food, we shall find that God gave thought not only for our necessity, but also for our enjoyment and delight. Thus, in clothing, the goal was, in addition to necessity, beauty and honor; and in herbs, fruits, and trees, besides their various uses, gracefulness of appearance and sweetness of smell. Were it not so, the Prophet would not enumerate among the mercies of God "wine that gladdens the heart of man, oil to make his face shine" The Scriptures would not everywhere mention, in commending God's benevolence, that he had given such things to humans. The natural qualities of things themselves demonstrate to what end, and how far, they may be lawfully enjoyed. Has the Lord adorned flowers with all the beauty which spontaneously presents itself to the eye, and the sweet odor which delights the sense of smell, and shall it be unlawful for us to enjoy that beauty and this odor? What? Has he not so distinguished colors as to make some more agreeable than others? Has he not given qualities to gold and silver, ivory and marble, thereby rendering them precious above other metals or stones? In short, has he not given many things a value without having any necessary use?

FLEEING GOD?

But Jonah ran away from the LORD and headed for Tarshish. He went down to Joppa, where he found a ship bound for that port. After paying the fare, he went aboard and sailed for Tarshish to flee from the LORD.
—Jonah 1:3, NIV

Now, as to Jonah's flight, we must bear in mind what I have before said—that all who do not willingly obey his commandments run away from the presence of God; not that they can depart farther from him, but they seek, as far as they can, to confine God within narrow limits, and to excuse themselves from being subject to his power. No one indeed openly admits to this; yet the fact itself shows that no one withdraws himself from obedience to God's commands without seeking to diminish and, as it were, to take from God his power, so that he may no longer rule. For all those, then, who do not willingly subject themselves to God, it is the same as though they would turn their backs on him and reject his authority so that they may no more be under his power and dominion.

Grant, Almighty God, that, as when we were alienated from every hope of salvation you did not send a Jonah to us, but have given your Son to be our teacher, to clearly show us the way of salvation, and not only to call us to repentance by threats and fear, but also kindly to allure us to the hope of eternal life, and to be a pledge of your parental love—O grant that we may not reject so remarkable a favor offered to us, but obey you willingly and from the heart; and though the requirements you put before us in your Gospel may seem hard, and though the bearing of the cross is bitter to our flesh, yet may we never shun obeying you, but present ourselves to you as a sacrifice; and having overcome all the hindrances of this world, may we thus continue in the course of our holy calling, until we are at length gathered into your celestial kingdom under the guidance of Christ your Son, our Lord. Amen.

GOD'S CARE CONTINUES

All the sailors were afraid and each cried out to his own god. And they threw the cargo into the sea to lighten the ship. But Jonah had gone below deck, where he lay down and fell into a deep sleep.
—Jonah 1:5, NIV

Jonah no doubt retreated before the storm arose. As soon then as they sailed from the harbor, Jonah withdrew to some hidden corner that he might sleep there. But this was inexcusable insensitivity on his part, since he knew that he was a fugitive from the presence of God: he ought to have been agitated by unceasing terrors. But it often happens that when any one has looked for hiding places, he brings on himself a stupor almost like that of a beast; he thinks of nothing, he cares for nothing, he is anxious for nothing. Such was the insensitivity which possessed the soul of Jonah when he went down to some hidden place in the ship, that he might there indulge himself in sleep. Since it thus happened to the holy Prophet, who among us shouldn't fear for himself or herself? For what prevented ruin from wholly swallowing up Jonah, except for the mercy of God, who pitied his servant and watched for his safety even while he was asleep?

We hence see that the Lord often cares for his people when they care not for themselves, and that he watches while they are asleep. But this ought not to nourish our self-indulgence; for we are all already more indulgent to ourselves than we ought to be: but, on the contrary, this example of Jonah, whom we see to have been so near destruction, ought to excite and urge us so that when any of us has gone astray from her or his calling, that person will not lie secure in that state, but, on the contrary, run back immediately to God. And if God is not able to draw us back to himself without some violent means, let us at least follow in this way the example of Jonah.

TRUE REPENTANCE

The sea was getting rougher and rougher. So they asked him, "What should we do to you to make the sea calm down for us?" "Pick me up and throw me into the sea," he replied, "and it will become calm. I know that it is my fault that this great storm has come upon you."
—Jonah 1:11–12, NIV

nd now we may learn from these words a most useful instruction: Jonah does not argue with God, nor angrily complain that God punished him too severely, but willingly bears his charged guilt and his punishment. How could he confess the true God, whose great anger he was then experiencing? But Jonah, we see, was so defeated that he did not fail to ascribe God his due honor. So the same thing is repeated in this place: "Behold," he says, "I know that this great tempest has happened on my account." Someone who takes all the blame is certainly not someone who murmurs against God. It is then a true confession of repentance when we acknowledge God, and willingly admit before others that God is just, even though, according to the judgment of our flesh, God may deal violently with us. When however we give to him the praise due to his justice, we then really show our repentance, for unless God's wrath brings us down to this humble state of mind we shall be always full of bitterness.

Grant, Almighty God, that as you urge us daily to repentance and each of us is also stung with the consciousness of our own sins—O grant that we may not grow stupid in our vices, nor deceive ourselves with empty flattery, but that each of us may on the contrary carefully examine her or his own life and then with one mouth and heart confess that we are all guilty not only of light offenses, but of offenses deserving eternal death, and that no other relief remains for us but your infinite mercy; and that we may seek to become partakers of that grace which has been once offered to us by your Son, and is daily offered to us by his Gospel, so that, relying on him as our Mediator, we will not cease to have hope even in the midst of thousand deaths, until we are gathered into that blessed life which has been gotten for us by the blood of your only Son. Amen.

REMEMBERING OUR SINS

At one time we too were foolish, disobedient, deceived and enslaved by all kinds of passions and pleasures. We lived in malice and envy, being hated and hating one another. —Titus 3:3, NIV

nothing is better adapted to conquer our pride and, at the same time, to moderate our strictness [with others], than when it is shown that everything that we hold against others may fall back on our own head. For someone forgives easily who needs to ask for pardon in return. And indeed, ignorance of our own faults is the only thing that makes us unwilling to forgive others. Those who have a true zeal for God are, indeed, harsh to those who sin; but because they begin with themselves, their severity is always mixed with compassion. In order that believers, therefore, will not arrogantly and cruelly mock others who are still held in ignorance and blindness, Paul brings back to their remembrance what sort of persons they formerly were; as if he had said, "If such fierce treatment is done to those on whom God has not yet bestowed the light of the Gospel, at one time you might have been just so harshly treated with equally good reason. Undoubtedly you would not wish that any person should be so cruel to you; therefore exercise now the same moderation towards others."

Those who have now been enlightened by the Lord, being humbled by the memory of their former foolishness, should not exalt themselves proudly over others, or treat others with greater harshness and severity than that which they think ought to have been shown to themselves, back when they were what those others now are. The second is that they should consider, based on what has taken place in themselves, that those who today are strangers may tomorrow be received into the Church, and, having been led to change their sinful practices, may become partakers of the gifts of God, of which they are now destitute. The grace of God, which they now enjoy, is a proof that others may be brought to salvation.

THE WORST OF SINNERS

Here is a trustworthy saying that deserves full acceptance: Christ Jesus came into the world to save sinners—of whom I am the worst.
—1 Timothy 1:15, NIV

Paul shows that it was good for the Church that he had been the kind of person he was, before he was called to the apostleship; because Christ, by giving him as a pledge, invited all sinners to the certain hope of obtaining pardon. For when he, who had been a fierce and savage beast, was changed into a pastor, Christ gave a remarkable display of his grace, from which all might be led to believe firmly that the gates of salvation are shut against no sinner, however heinous and inflamed her or his sins might have been.

Paul wrote, "Christ Jesus came into the world to save sinners." Let this preface be to our ears like the sound of a trumpet, proclaiming the praises of the grace of Christ, in order that we may believe it with a stronger faith. Let it be to us as a seal, to impress on our hearts a firm belief in the forgiveness of sins, which otherwise finds entrance into the hearts of people only with difficulty.

The word "sinners" is emphatic; for those who acknowledge that it is the job of Christ to save have difficulty in admitting the thought that such a salvation belongs to "sinners." Our mind is always ready to look at our worthiness; and as soon as our unworthiness is seen, our confidence sinks. Accordingly, the more any one is oppressed by personal sins, let that person the more courageously go to Christ, relying on this doctrine, that Christ came to bring salvation not to the righteous, but to "sinners."

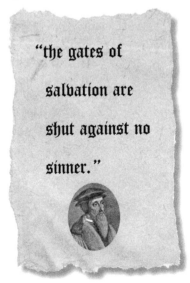

"the gates of salvation are shut against no sinner."

RESPECT YOUR CALLING

Make it your ambition to lead a quiet life, to mind your own business and to work with your hands, just as we told you, so that your daily life may win the respect of outsiders and so that you will not be dependent on anybody. —1 Thessalonians 4:11–12, NIV

The last thing to be observed is that the Lord asks every one of us, in all the actions of life, to have respect to our own calling. He knows the boiling restlessness of the human mind, the unreliable way it is moved here and there, its eagerness to hold opposites at one time in its grasp, its ambition. Therefore, lest all things should be thrown into confusion by our folly and rashness, he has assigned distinct duties to each in the different modes of life. It is enough to know that in every thing the call of the Lord is the foundation and beginning of right action. Someone who does not act with reference to it will never, in the discharge of duty, keep the right path. That person will sometimes be able, perhaps, to give the appearance of something good, but whatever it may be in the sight of humans, it will be rejected before the throne of God; and besides, there will be no harmony between the different parts of such a person's life.

Hence, someone only who directs his life to this end will have a life that is properly framed; because, free from the impulse of rashness, that person will not attempt more than her or his calling justifies, knowing that it is unlawful to overleap the prescribed bounds. Someone who is obscure will not be afraid to cultivate a private life, so as not to desert the post at which God has placed her or him. Again, in all our cares, toils, annoyances, and other burdens, it will be no small satisfaction to know that all these are under the authority of God. Every one in his particular mode of life will, without overmuch complaining, suffer its inconveniences, cares, uneasiness, and anxiety, persuaded that God has laid on the burden. This, too, will afford admirable consolation, that in following your proper calling, no work will be so mean and sordid as not to have a splendor and value in the eye of God.

GOD'S OMNIPRESENCE

The center of the fire looked like glowing metal, and in the fire was
what looked like four living creatures. In appearance their form was
that of a man, but each of them had four faces and four wings.
—Ezekiel 1:4b–6, NIV

With regard to their number, I do not doubt that God wished to teach us that his influence is diffused through all regions of the world; for we know the world to be divided into four parts. Since, therefore, God works by angels, and uses them as ministers of his power, then when angels are brought forward, there the providence of God is obvious, and his power in the government of the world. This, then, is the reason why not only two cherubim, but four, were placed before the Prophet's eyes: because God's providence ought to be evident in earthly things, for the people then imagined that God was confined to heaven; hence the Prophet teaches not only that he reigns in heaven, but that he rules over earthly affairs. And for this reason, and with this purpose, he extends his power over the four quarters of the globe. Why, then, has each animal four heads? I answer, that by this, angelic virtue is shown to be in all the animals. God by his angels works not only in humans and other animals, but throughout creation; and because inanimate things have no motion in themselves, and because God wished to instruct an unthinking and dull people, he sets before them the image of all things under that of animals. Among living creatures, then, humanity holds the first place, because it was made in the image of God. Now, as it is equally clear that no creature moves by itself, but that all movements are by the secret instinct of God, therefore each cherub has four heads, as if it were said that angels administer God's kingdom not in one part of the world only, but everywhere; and next, that all creatures are so moved as if they were joined together with angels themselves. The Prophet then describes each as having four heads, because if we can trust our eyes when observing the way God governs the world, angelic virtue will appear in every movement of it: it is, in fact, just as if angels had the heads of all animals: that is, within themselves, openly and conspicuously, are all elements and all parts of the world.

TRUE REPENTANCE

To him give all the prophets witness, that through his name whosoever believeth in him shall receive remission of sins. —Acts 10:43

It is of great moment to be fully persuaded, that when we have sinned, there is a reconciliation with God ready and prepared for us: We shall otherwise carry always a hell within us. Few, indeed, consider how miserable and wretched is a doubting conscience; but the truth is, that hell reigns where there is no peace with God. The more, then, it becomes us to receive with the whole heart this promise which offers free pardon to all who confess their sins. Moreover, this is founded even on the justice of God, because God who promises is true and just. For they who think that he is called just, because he justifies us freely, reason, as I think, with too much refinement, because justice or righteousness here depends on fidelity, and both are annexed to the promise. For God might have been just, were he to deal with us with all the rigour of justice; but as he has bound himself to us by his Word, he would not have himself deemed just except he forgives.

But this confession, as it is made to God, must be in sincerity; and the heart cannot speak to God without newness of life: it then includes true repentance. God, indeed, forgives freely, but in such a way, that the facility of mercy does not become an enticement to sin.

> "it becomes us to receive... this promise which offers free pardon to all who confess their sins."

PRAYING THE RIGHT WAY

For they cried to God in the battle, and he was intreated of them; because they put their trust in him. —1 Chronicles 5:20b

hough God has promised to do whatsoever his people may ask, yet he does not allow them an unbridled liberty to ask whatever may come to their minds; but he has at the same time prescribed to them a law according to which they are to pray. And doubtless nothing is better for us than this restriction; for if it was allowed to everyone of us to ask what he pleased, and if God were to indulge us in our wishes, it would be to provide very badly for us. For what may be expedient we know not; nay, we boil over with corrupt and hurtful desires. But God supplies a twofold remedy, lest we should pray otherwise that according to what his own will has prescribed; for he teaches us by his Word what he would have us to ask, and he has also set over us his Spirit as our guide and rules, to restrain our feelings, so as not to suffer them to wander beyond due bounds. For what or how to pray, we know not, says Paul, but the Spirit helpeth our infirmity, and excites in us unutterable groans (Rom. 8:26). We ought also to ask the mouth of the Lord to direct and guide our prayers; for God in his promises has fixed for us, as it has been said, the right way of praying.

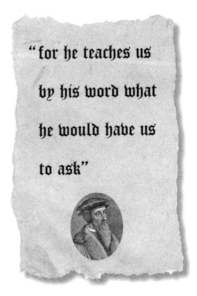

"for he teaches us by his word what he would have us to ask"

COUNT IT ALL JOY

*I have commanded my sanctified ones, I have also called my mighty
ones for mine anger, even them that rejoice in my highness.*
—Isaiah 13:3

We must doubtless take temptations or trials as including all adverse things; and they are so called, because they are the tests of our obedience to God. He bids the faithful, while exercised with these, to rejoice; and that not only when they fall into one temptation, but into many, not only of one kind, but of various kinds. And doubtless, since they serve to mortify our flesh, as the vices of the flesh continually shoot up in us, so they must necessarily be often repeated. Besides, as we labour under diseases, so it is no wonder that different remedies are applied to remove them.

The Lord then afflicts us in various ways, because ambition, avarice, envy, gluttony, intemperance, excessive love of the world, and the innumerable lusts in which we abound, cannot be cured by the same medicine.

When he bids us to count it all joy, it is the same as though he had said, that temptations ought to be so deemed as gain, as to be regarded as occasions of joy. He means, in short, that there is nothing in afflictions which ought to disturb our joy. And thus, he no only commands us to bear adversities calmly, and with an even mind, but shews that there is a reason why the faithful should rejoice when pressed down by them.

It is, indeed, certain, that all the sense of our nature are so formed, that every trial produces in us grief and sorrow; and no one of us can so far divest himself of his nature as not to grieve and be sorrowful whenever he feels any evil. But this does not prevent the children of God to rise, by the guidance of the Spirit, above the sorrow of the flesh. Hence it is, that in the midst of trouble they cease not to rejoice.

Troubles and Adversities

And the LORD said, I have surely seen the affliction of my people which are in Egypt, and have heard their cry by reason of their taskmasters; for I know their sorrows. —Exodus 3:7

The life of men is indeed indiscriminately subject to troubles and adversities; but James did not bring forward any kind of men for examples, for it would have availed nothing to perish with the multitude; but he chose the Prophets, a fellowship with whom is blessed. Nothing so breaks us down and disheartens us as the feeling of misery; it is therefore a real consolation to know that those things commonly deemed evils are aids and helps to our salvation. This is, indeed, what is far from being understood by the flesh; yet the faithful ought to be convinced of this, that they are happy when by various troubles they are proved by the Lord. To convince us of this, James reminds us to consider the end or design of the afflictions endured by the prophets; for as in our own evils we are without judgment, being influenced by grief, sorrow, or some other immoderate feelings as we see nothing under a foggy sky and in the midst of storms, and being tossed here and there as it were by a tempest, it is therefore necessary for us to cast our eyes to another quarter, where the sky is in a manner serene and bright. When the afflictions of the saints are related to us, there is no one who will allow that they were miserable, but, on the contrary, that they were happy.

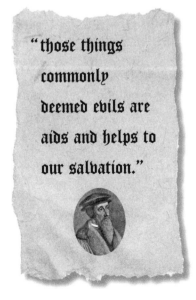

"those things commonly deemed evils are aids and helps to our salvation."

DELIVERY FROM TEMPTATION

He shall abide before God for ever: O prepare mercy and truth, which may preserve him. —Psalm 61:7

hat first offends the weak is, that when the faithful anxiously seek aid, they are not immediately helped by God; but on the contrary he suffers them sometimes as it were to pine away through daily weariness and languor; and secondly, when the wicked grow wanton with impunity, and God in the meantime is silent, as though he connived at their evil deeds. This double offense Peter now removes; for he testifies that the Lord knows when it is expedient to deliver the godly from temptation. By these words he reminds us that this office ought to be left to him, and that therefore we ought to endure temptations, and not to faint, when at any time he defers his vengeance against the ungodly.

This consolation is very necessary for us, for this thought is apt to creep in, "If the Lord would have his won to be safe, why does he not gather them all into some corner of the earth, that they may mutually stimulate one another to holiness? Why does he mingle them with the wicked by whom they may be defiled?" But when God claims to himself the office of helping and protecting his won, that they may not fail in the contest, we gather courage to fight more strenuously.

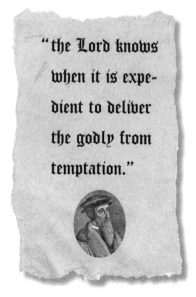

"the Lord knows when it is expedient to deliver the godly from temptation."

HIDING PLACE

Then the mariners were afraid, and cried every man unto his god, and cast forth the wares that were in the ship into the sea, to lighten it of them. But Jonah was gone down into the sides of the ship; and he lay, and was fast asleep. So the shipmaster came to him, and said unto him, What meanest thou, O sleeper? arise, call upon thy God, if so be that God will think upon us, that we perish not. And they said every one to his fellow, Come, and let us cast lots, that we may know for whose cause this evil is upon us. So they cast lots, and the lot fell upon Jonah. Then said they unto him, Tell us, we pray thee, for whose cause this evil is upon us; What is thine occupation? and whence comest thou? what is thy country? and of what people art thou? And he said unto them, I am an Hebrew; and I fear the LORD, the God of heaven, which hath made the sea and the dry land. Then were the men exceedingly afraid, and said unto him, Why hast thou done this? For the men knew that he fled from the presence of the LORD, because he had told them. —Jonah 1:5–10

It often so happens, that when any one has sought hiding-places, he brings on himself a stupor almost brutal; he thinks of nothing, he cares for nothing, he is anxious for nothing. Such then was the insensibility which possessed the soul of Jonah, when he went down to some recess in the ship, that he might there indulge himself in sleep. Since it thus happened to the holy Prophet, who of us ought not to fear for himself? Let us hence learn to remind ourselves often of God's tribunal; and when our minds are seized with torpor, let us learn to stimulate and examine ourselves, lest God's judgment overwhelm us while asleep. For what prevented ruin from wholly swallowing up Jonah, except the mercy of God, who pitied his servant, and watched for his safety even while he was asleep? We hence see that the Lord often cares for his people when they care not for themselves, and that he watches while they are asleep: but this ought not to serve to nourish our self-indulgence; for every one of us is already more indulgent to himself that he ought to be: but, on the contrary, this example of Jonah, whom we see to have been so near destruction, ought to excite and urge us, that when any of us has gone astray from his calling he may not lie secure in that state, but, on the contrary, run back immediately to God.

SCRIPTURE
INDEX

GENESIS–PSALM 25

PSALMS 29–PROVERBS

ECCLESIASTES–MALACHI

Matthew–John 3

JOHN 4–20

ACTS–ROMANS 8

ROMANS 9–GALATIANS

EPHESIANS–II TIMOTHY

TITUS–REVELATION